Climate Change as So

Climate change is not just a scientific fact, nor is it merely a social and political problem. It is also a set of stories and characters that amount to a social drama. This drama, as much as hard scientific or political realities, shapes perception of the issues. Philip Smith and Nicolas Howe use the perspective of Aristotelian cultural sociology to explore this meaningful and visible surface of climate change in the public sphere. Whereas most research aims to explain barriers to awareness, here the authors switch the agenda to look at the moments when global warming actually gets attention. Chapters consider struggles over apocalyptic scenarios, explain the success of Al Gore and *An Inconvenient Truth*, unpack the deeper social meanings of the climate conference and Climategate, critique controversial advertising campaigns and climate art, and question the much touted transformative potential of natural disasters such as Superstorm Sandy.

Philip Smith is Professor of Sociology and codirector of the Yale Center for Cultural Sociology. His work explores the meaningful nature of social life as it plays out in a communicative public sphere. He is the author of *Why War?* (2005) and *Punishment and Culture* (2008) and coauthor of *Incivility: The Rude Stranger in Everyday Life* (Cambridge University Press, 2010), as well as a dozen other books and edited collections.

Nicolas Howe is Assistant Professor of Environmental Studies at Williams College, where he is also affiliated with the American Studies Program and the Department of Anthropology and Sociology. He studies the cultural and religious dimensions of American environmental politics from the perspective of human geography. He is the recipient of fellowships from the Charles Warren Center for Studies in American History at Harvard University, the Charlotte W. Newcombe Foundation, and the National Science Foundation.

Climate Change as Social Drama

Global Warming in the Public Sphere

PHILIP SMITH

Yale University

NICOLAS HOWE

Williams College

CAMBRIDGE UNIVERSITY PRESS

CAMBRIDGE
UNIVERSITY PRESS

32 Avenue of the Americas, New York, NY 10013-2473, USA

Cambridge University Press is part of the University of Cambridge.

It furthers the University's mission by disseminating knowledge in the pursuit of education, learning, and research at the highest international levels of excellence.

www.cambridge.org
Information on this title: www.cambridge.org/9781107503052

© Philip Smith and Nicolas Howe 2015

First published 2015

Printed in Great Britain by Clays Ltd, St Ives plc

A catalog record for this publication is available from the British Library.

Library of Congress Cataloging in Publication Data
Smith, Philip (Philip Daniel), 1964–
Climate change as social drama : global warming in the public sphere / Philip Smith,
Yale University, Nicolas Howe, Williams College.
pages cm
Includes bibliographical references and index.
ISBN 978-1-107-10355-9 (hardback)
1. Climatic changes – Social aspects. 2. Climatic changes – Political aspects.
3. Global warming – Public opinion. I. Title.
QC903.S589 2015
363.738'74–dc23 2014046189

ISBN 978-1-107-10355-9 Hardback
ISBN 978-1-107-50305-2 Paperback

Contents

Acknowledgments

This book was written between 2008 and 2014 with the institutional and cultural support offered by Yale University, Williams College, and The Charles Warren Center for Studies in American History at Harvard University in the United States, as well as the Kulturwissenschaftliches Kolleg, Konstanz University, Germany. A complete first draft of the book was read with great care by Jeffrey Alexander, Annika Arnold, and Lyn Spillman. Their constructive readings led the manuscript in a new direction. Many of the ideas in this book were debated (and improved) by members of the "Cultures of Climate Change" seminar at Williams College. Chapter 5, on climate change art, had the benefit of a vigorous discussion at the workshop for the Yale Center for Cultural Sociology in fall 2011. Chapter 3 first appeared in 2012 in *The Oxford Handbook of Cultural Sociology*. It has been revised for this publication. We thank Oxford University Press for permission to reproduce that material. To ensure the integrity of this book as a unified work, all other chapters are previously unpublished. On the production side we thank Sonika Rai, Holly Monteith, Elizabeth Janetschek, and Robert Dreesen of Cambridge University Press; also the four anonymous reviewers of our manuscript for their time and advice.

Introduction

The Problem of Climate Change

Scientists agree that anthropogenic climate change is real and that it is a very serious threat on multiple levels for the entire planet (IPCC 2014). Economic, social, political, and biological systems are all said to be in trouble. Moreover, the window of opportunity for dealing with the problem is limited. At the same time, the public around the globe is mostly apathetic. Even in countries like Norway, where high levels of environmental concern and political involvement are the norm, climate change often seems more like "background noise" than a problem demanding radical collective action (Norgaard 2011). Contrary to what one might think, a similar situation pertains in the United States. Here, despite an effective right-wing campaign to discredit climate science (Oreskes and Conway 2010), surveys today show that a majority of people believe that climate change is happening and needs to be addressed, including, now, a majority of Republicans (Maibach et al. 2013). Yet many of these same surveys indicate that most Americans are unwilling to make meaningful sacrifices to deal with the problem. There appears to be insufficient support for social mobilization of the kind that will make a real difference (for a dissenting view, see Krosnick and MacInnis 2013). True enough, political and bureaucratic elites can mandate the kinds of policies advocated by climate science, with its long-term, evidence-based views. Yet there will be problems with compliance and implementation when public buy-in is weak. In democratic contexts, electoral sanctions can follow if cultural horizons for responding to climate change are not aligned with public policies (Lorenzoni and Pidgeon 2006).

What exactly is the problem? It is not simply that there is a substantial corps of climate change deniers confusing the public with nefarious tactics, nor is it that the carbon industries have easily bought off political leaders. The issue is more subtle. Whereas the science community sees itself as almost completely unified, the public is more likely to perceive dissent and scientific uncertainty, with many still doubtful about whether climate change is caused by specifically human activity.[1] The public is also rather likely to believe that climate change will not greatly impact upon themselves personally. People see it as a problem for other generations or distant parts of the globe. Whereas the scientific and environmental communities speak of the urgency of the issue and the need to implement radical solutions, the general public is more likely to believe or hope that a painless technological fix will eventually come along. Finally, even though climate change is increasingly said to be a "serious problem," it somehow gets pushed to the bottom of the heap when respondents are asked to prioritize a number of "serious problems" in rank order. Education, health care, jobs, and so forth are generally picked out as the leading priorities facing each nation at any given point in time (e.g., Downing and Ballantyne 2007; Lorenzoni and Pidgeon 2006).

The frustration of the science community is palpable. It has worked patiently for years, often in difficult circumstances, to assemble evidence (Weart 2008). A cross-national, cross-disciplinary field of brilliant minds has emerged that is characterized by unparalleled levels of cooperation. By and large the message from this coalition has remained disciplined and consistent, too. With the Intergovernmental Panel on Climate Change (IPCC), they have built a transparent and exhaustive review process. As the historian of climate science Paul Edwards (2010, 439) puts it, "this is the best knowledge we are going to get." The scientists have done their part. It is a success story. Yet, at the end of the day, neither facts nor experts seem to matter that much when it comes to shaping popular perceptions and motivations, especially in countries like the United States, where climate politics is still sharply divided.

Explaining this gap has become a social science cottage industry. Anthony Giddens (2009, 2) has even given it a name: Giddens's paradox. This states, "since the dangers posed by global warming aren't tangible, immediate or visible in the course of day-to-day life, however awesome

---

[1] For the most detailed and revealing surveys of American public opinion, see the *Global Warming's Six Americas* series put out by the Yale Project on Climate Change Communication and the George Mason University Center for Climate Change Communication (Leiserowitz et al. 2013). For cross-national overviews of public opinion on climate change, see Brechin (2010) and Brechin and Bhandari (2011).

they appear, many will sit on their hands and do nothing of a concrete nature about them. Yet waiting until they become visible and acute before being stirred to serious action will, by definition, be too late." Researchers working with this basic assumption typically isolate several factors that make climate change a tough sell and that dampen the impact of scientific consensus (see Ungar 2000; Wuthnow 2010). These are as follows:

1. As noted in the preceding Giddens quotation, climate change looks to be a chronic rather than an acute condition. It suffers relative to immediate threats, such as the SARS virus, because life never appears to be in clear and present danger. This keeps it on the back burner. The typical analogy here is giving up smoking. What harm will another cigarette do?

2. People tend to discount future discomfort against current pleasure. An increase of a few degrees in temperature or of a couple of feet in sea levels a few decades from now will be a problem only for the "future me," not for "now me." It will cause less pain to "future me" than any action today would cause to "now me."

3. Efforts to identify catastrophic and immediate impacts by pointing to flooding, hurricanes, tornadoes, wars, and so forth seem contrived, as the causal pathways to such specifics from a generic process are indirect or multivariate. Besides, these things all existed before climate change and will exist forever.

4. Dealing with climate change the way that environmental activists wish would dramatically alter all aspects of lifestyle and impose costs right across the social system. The habituated barriers to buy-in are considerable. Denial or disassociation becomes the more attractive psychological option.

5. Scientific nostrums are seemingly contradicted by personal embodied experience on a daily or seasonal basis. The weather changes from day to day. Every time we have snowfall, it seems as if global warming is a myth.

6. Climate change is an ongoing background issue. It must struggle to become newsworthy or attention grabbing because there is no interruption to a pattern. We report an eclipse of the moon, not the fact that it came out last night as usual.

7. The problem is complex in its causality, widespread in its impacts, and not amenable to any easy conversion into compelling cultural forms that transmit danger and urgency to ordinary people.

8. Deeply entrenched values and norms that are reinforced by personal networks are a source of bias. These prevent people from accepting scientific data on climate change, from seeing the real threat, and from being able to change their attitudes and actions.
9. Free rider problems dog efforts at collective action over climate change. The rational strategy is to continue to pollute while others cut their emissions.

Such analyses look persuasive initially. Yet they become less convincing if one thinks counterfactually of a world in which climate change *was* taken seriously as an urgent problem. In that parallel universe, would not many of the same factors be edited, redescribed, and then invoked post hoc a couple of decades later as reasons for success? Most notably, the spatial, temporal, causal, and consequential ubiquity of climate change allowed it to be "seen everywhere" and so never escape our attention (arguments 1, 3, and 6). Furthermore, this complex, large-scale, and octopus-like quality maximized opportunities for the conversion of the danger into compelling cultural forms (argument 7). Multiple amelioration strategies were available, allowing everyone to buy in and gain a sense of participation in addressing the problem (argument 4). As a nagging problem, it was like a toothache that could not be ignored (argument 1). Discourses sentimentalizing childhood and urging stewardship led to action on behalf of future generations. Just as individuals take account of the distant future all the time with things like their pension plans or prepaid funerals, and states plan ahead when they issue thirty-year bonds or dedicate national parks in perpetuity, so did agents also plan ahead for climate change (argument 2). Binding international treaties were easy to develop, as humans are capable of reflexivity and generosity when it comes to the tragedy of the commons. Earlier precedents in fields like nuclear nonproliferation, whaling, and chlorofluorocarbon production bans made it easy to see how to set up such agreements (argument 9). The reality of climate change was confirmed by bodily experience every time there was "unusual" weather (argument 5). (With its record-shattering heat waves, droughts, and wildfires, 2012 sealed the deal.) As for those values and norms and their associated "culture wars" subtext (argument 8), these crumbled amazingly quickly, just as they had with other seemingly visceral and intractable responses to racial segregation in the 1960s or to homosexuality and gay marriage more recently. Just as having a gay child was shown to change the attitudes of hardened Republican politicians, the personal networks that were supposed to hold climate irrationality in place turned out to be the pathways through which progressive attitudes were propagated.

Climate change also had the benefit of being complex and hard to understand, with diffuse causal connections and long-term payoffs (argument 7), like many other cultural forms that have done well in human history. The major world religions, for example, have proven to be very effective at propagating themselves. These, too, are complex, abstract systems that are unverifiable and often contradict experience (e.g., the problem of suffering), offer salvation only after death, and require far-reaching and often sacrificial changes to lifestyle that extend as far as martyrdom. Marxism–communism as a social movement likewise inverted common sense in its problem diagnosis, required deep identity transformations, and offered a payoff for generations in a long distant future. Neoliberal economics has swept the world. Yet this is an idea whose core model famously involves a hand that is as invisible as carbon dioxide. Markets are caught up in complex chains of causation; the payoff to painful economic restructuring is often distant. None of this stopped people from believing in the power of markets, putting shares in their pension plans, or closing down entire industries. What is more, we are accustomed to thinking of nature as responsive to our moral failings. Is it any surprise that when we looked at the modern history of ideas about climatic change, we saw periods of intense anxiety about the disastrous effects of human activity (Behringer 2010; Boia 2005; Fleming 1998; Grove 1995)? Although humans have never faced a problem quite like contemporary global warming (Chakrabarty 2009; McNeill 2008), they *have* changed their societies to prepare for future worlds.

So what is to be done? Most work by social scientists looks backward. It offers a diagnosis of the reasons for failure. By relentlessly indicating the magnitude of the task we face, then itemizing barriers to climate awareness and action, it arguably contributes to the mood of fatalism it purports merely to analyze. It normalizes the status quo rather than trying to open doors. Such a perspective contrasts sharply with that of activists who are incessantly looking for pragmatic ways to break down fatalism, for options to change the game rather than parse its rules. We try to occupy a middle ground. Ours is a scholarly analysis, not an engaged one. Yet we look forward and with hope. Where we diagnose failure, we do so with reference to surmountable contingencies in representation and performance, not the wiring of the brain or the objective features of climate change itself. Like activists, we also turn to culture for answers. More and more scholars are doing the same to explain climate politics, and we cheer this trend.[2] But we also break quite sharply from many of these scholars, and in some important ways. For the most part, as we see in Chapter 2, they use culture to identify deeply rooted and divergent values, epistemologies, and structures of feeling that prevent action. Our focus is more strongly on contingency and on the possibilities that climate change could or should be able to open up for multiple and flexible cultural plays. With some theory and considerable analysis of positive and negative examples, this book explores how such discussions are configured, what gets attention, what is going wrong, and even what might work. At the end of the book, we have no sales manual for climate change activism, but there will have been some lessons learned.

Our principal claim will be that climate change within the public sphere takes the form of a social drama. We expand on this insight in Chapter 2. In the interim, it is sufficient to say that much of what the average citizen follows is an unfolding set of stories with characters and plots. These arrive episodically, sometimes as a portentous saga, sometimes as melodrama, and at other times as soap opera. Paying attention to this drama, exploring its various incarnations, and figuring out just how to study it form the core purpose of our book. This is a different perspective to the usual social scientific investigation of cultural bias, risk perception, or the public understanding of science, but it is not fundamentally incompatible with them. We believe that the theory of social drama brings cultural analysis closer to the actual properties of globally circulating texts and images, which until now have been most creatively studied by researchers in the humanities. In keeping with this interdisciplinary project, we turn away from the so-called leading edge of sociological theory and show that the Greek philosopher Aristotle offers many of the "new" theoretical resources we need to explore this rich world of representation and performance. We mine his thought in a new way by synthesizing his two major texts, the *Poetics* and *Rhetoric*, and connecting him to more contemporary cultural theory. The *Poetics* offers insights into cultural structures and their emotional impacts. The *Rhetoric* exposes the conditions for successful performance when making claims to an audience. Together they provide remarkable leverage when it comes to unpacking dramatic effects in public events.

---

[2] Prominent examples include Beck (2009, 2010), Boykoff (2011), Crate and Nuttall (2009), Demeritt (2001), Doyle (2011), Hulme (2009), Jasanoff (2010, 2011), Kahan et al. (2011), Malone (2009), Norgaard (2011), Rayner and Thompson (1998), Strauss and Orlove (2003), and Urry (2011).

In arguing that climate change is a social drama, we need to be clear at the outset that we are not using the term *social drama* in a pejorative sense. We are not suggesting that it is a panic or even a "moral panic" replete with disproportional responses and false beliefs that will disappear like a flash in the pan. Nor are we saying that activists are overly emotional. Nor are we saying that fiction is more powerful at the end of the day than scientific facts. In Australia and Britain, the phrase "no dramas" is sometimes used interchangeably with "no worries" to suggest that things are under control. The implication is that drama is bad and that, if we can get rid of the dramatic, we can all calm down and get back on track. However, we are not saying that climate change should only be considered or represented in cool, clinical, rational ways and that culture is a barrier to clear understanding – that a "no worries, no dramas" path is one that our society should take. Our argument is quite different. We argue that, like it or not, climate change takes on a certain set of properties once it moves from nature and science and into the public sphere. We see the concept of social drama as capturing much of this. Our intent in this book is to map, explain, and think through what this means.

Hence the empirical chapters that follow scout the social drama over a number of domains where it has moved toward the foreground in public life. Each domain also allows us to highlight in various proportions the centrality of diverse Aristotelian constructs, although we also make use of literatures elsewhere in the humanities and social sciences to make our analytic points. Chapter 3 looks at the role of genre, that is to say, the patterned and predictable qualities of narrative forms. We show how climate change has been represented in various ways over the years and demonstrate that generic representation ties to risk perception. This keys in turn to themes like urgency and permissible sacrifice. Our discussion highlights widespread genre confusion as an enduring problem for activists. Chapter 4 provides a telling and accessible illustration of the continuing relevance of an Aristotelian analysis of *ethos*, or character, as a force in public life. We focus here on Al Gore's rhetorical triumph in the film *An Inconvenient Truth* and, in particular, on the ways in which the movie establishes him as a person of virtue. Chapter 5 looks at another creative activity aimed at improving climate change awareness: climate change art. The analysis confirms Aristotle's hints about the limits of spectacle as a communicative mechanism. The chapter documents the failure of such art to achieve much impact and allocates considerable responsibility to a disorganized art world that is unable to establish *ethos* and convert visual stimuli into meaningful discursive action.

In Chapter 6, we move from the creative industries to the realm of the newsworthy. The chapter begins with an exploration of outrage at bungled climate change advertising campaigns and moves on to consider the leaks of e-mails known as Climategate. Pivotal to our analysis here is the intersection of *ethos* with *pathos*, or audience sympathy. These news stories damaged climate activism by making audience identification with both activists and scientific protagonists unattractive. Chapter 7 continues the study of newsworthy public events by investigating the representation of climate conferences. We suggest that conferences are about more than just treaties and horse-trading; they are also a visible symbol of global solidarity or discord and so might be considered to be acts of theatre. A comparative study of gatherings at Copenhagen, Durban, and Cancun enables us to isolate the qualities of an effective collective performance by participants. We also pay attention to the rhetorical power of individual truth-tellers. Our final empirical chapter, Chapter 8, looks at the role of place, locality, and event and so switches attention from the players to the stage or setting on which the drama unfolds. The spotlight here is on meaningful landscape and on place myths as constitutive dramatic elements. Through analyses of the genocide in Darfur and of Superstorm Sandy in New York, we suggest that place can be thought of as an agent that has particular narrative effects. Although our book is for the most part an anatomy of missed opportunities, our concluding chapter offers some hopeful moments. Following Aristotle, we discuss the positive role of shared emotional engagement in public events. We highlight our positive examples and flag the Aristotelian targets for which activists should be aiming as they seek to engage with *ethos*, *pathos*, and genre.

Approach and Methodology: Justification and Explanation

Before we proceed to these in-depth discussions, we should pause to outline the wider intellectual perspective that underpins this book. Many of our readers will be familiar with the norms of interpretive social science and may wish to skip the next few pages. Those with backgrounds in cultural studies and the environmental humanities, for example, will have an intuitive or theoretical understanding of our approach. Yet given the interdisciplinary reach of climate change as a field, we expect some readers to be from positivist backgrounds in environmental science or those social sciences making use of formal and experimental methods such as social psychology. Such scholars and activists may well be unfamiliar with our root paradigm. A brief orientation can help.

Emerging from the cultural turn in the social sciences more widely, the field of cultural sociology (for a recent collection, see Alexander, Jacobs, and Smith 2012) starts with the premise that meanings shape social outcomes. In this sense, cultural sociology can be thought of as a variant on long-standing philosophical claims about the social construction of reality (famously, Thomas and Thomas 1928). The point is not that reality is "all in the mind" and has no objective basis but rather to recognize that humans, individually and collectively, act on the basis of the meanings through which they interpret and define what is real. Such meanings do not exist in isolation from other factors (power, resources, social ties, etc.), but they do exert a significant independent and "causal" influence that needs to be studied. For example, culture structures shape behaviors and attitudes, offer frameworks and action paths, and offer legitimacy for policy. These meanings are not personal and private but rather public and visible. This public culture circulates through society and takes the form of grammars, codes, narratives, symbols, and icons. Individuals try to shape the prevailing set of meanings through cultural performances, although their capacity to do so is often limited by human failings and by the unintended consequences of action. The analyst's job is to reconstruct the influential systems of public interpretation and understanding that emerge from this process.

This is no easy task. The meanings at play have to be isolated and distilled from their visible traces in the speech acts, mass media reports, images, and Internet chatter that make up the world of public culture and communication. The method involved is one of hermeneutic reconstruction, in which deep reading permits the analyst to get to the nub of a complex world of circulating texts and symbols. It is not claimed that all possible meanings are identified in this book but rather that dominant or prevalent patterns within particular contexts are located and described. Importantly, establishing the truth or falsity of public knowledge relative to the agreed-upon scientific facts is not a primary task of analysis. Unlike much research on "communicating climate change," we are not centrally concerned with measuring the public understanding of climate change and holding this up to a scientific benchmark. False beliefs are worth studying not because they are false but because they are beliefs. Regardless of their accuracy, representations matter, be they partial, flawed, distorted, or stylized, because people believe them to be true, feel in certain ways in response to them, and act accordingly. As Thomas and Thomas argued long ago, social constructions of reality are not the same as reality itself, but they are real in their consequences.

Cultural sociology typically relies on the case study method rather than on formal sampling and coding (see, e.g., the chapters in Alexander, Jacobs, and Smith 2012), with its seductive belief that complex meanings can be easily captured with tallies and tick-boxes. As Richard Biernacki (2012) has shown, efforts to make interpretation more "scientific" through quantification and coding actually make it less so, in large part because they render the work of translation and selection invisible through rhetorical and ritualistic deference to positivist norms. It is a kind of sleight of hand. The result is thin interpretation. As pegs of diverse contour are hammered into square holes, complex systems of meaning are reduced to implausibly simple formulations that do not, in fact, accurately capture their spirit. For this reason, generally the presentation of a case in our qualitative work is accompanied by multiple items of qualitative "data" (those pegs, if you will, but this time treated with respect) that illustrate the play of meanings in that case. This method allows readers to see how we as authors came to conclusions and also to get a "feel" for the issues. This texture-rich approach is akin to the method of exposition that Clifford Geertz dubbed "thick description," although we would argue that "deep interpretation" or "thick interpretation" are more accurate terms. With certain variations it is also the method used by Michel Foucault, Roland Barthes, Stuart Hall, Claude Lévi-Strauss, and other giants of cultural analysis (although we by no means compare ourselves to these luminaries). In contrast to abstract theoretical pronouncements, plausibility can be reviewed as readers match the evidence presented to its reconstruction by ourselves. If they are not satisfied, they are entitled to return to our primary sources (or even find their own with a little time on the Internet looking at our case studies) and attempt a falsification, a more refined analysis, or an alternative interpretation (for three examples of this, see Biernacki 2012, or see Smith 2008 for a data-based reinterpretation of some of Foucault's major exhibits). In effect, this method is a variation on the hermeneutic tools of the humanities where scholars present evidence for the accuracy of their interpretation of a book or painting, writer or artist.

Importantly, for the cultural sociologist, interpretation is shaped not only by the data but also by cultural theory. This gives the analyst clues as to the nature of cultural structures and offers resources for interpretation that move us beyond the limits of commonsense summary. For example, narrative theory tells us that much shared meaning in public life takes the form of stories. That same theory alerts us to the importance of characters, plot, and emotional moods and the relationships between these.

Exploring the impacts of any particular story (say, Climategate) may well involve drawing on these resources to explain how particular impacts might eventuate (in the case of Climategate, on trust for and solidarity with scientists).

Of course, complaints about arbitrary case studies and the selective presentation of confirmatory data haunt all qualitative work in the social sciences, including that of truly influential scholars. We take our task too seriously to load the dice. Methodologically, our case studies were selected according to several criteria that can better be dubbed thoughtful than "rigorous" or "systematic":

- Most can be generally greed upon as unusually important or influential and hence worthy of study. In this book, *An Inconvenient Truth* would be such an example. So would the Copenhagen Climate Conference, Climategate, Cape Farewell, and Superstorm Sandy. Each was the most significant example of its type in the public sphere: the failed conference, the science scandal, the artistic enterprise, and the natural event.
- Some examples we discuss are less well known but result from our immersion in the field. Rather than setting tight sampling and research design parameters that might limit inquiry, we endorse the ethnographer Mitchell Dunier's (2000) injunction to "follow the thing" to arrive at a full understanding (a phrase and method also deployed by leading figures such as Arjun Appadurai, James Clifford, and James Scott). During long hours of research we were often led away from where we started to new places that illustrated the range and depth of the phenomenon in question in new ways. For example, our research on climate change and place started with the obvious example of Darfur. Reading around our topic and looking at how "climate change" and "place" were considered beyond the world of politics, we discovered less visible discussions on the Great Lakes of the United States or Cornwall in the United Kingdom. These offered new insights into how this relationship might be configured, especially how it potentially impacted a more subtle sense of place rather than contexts of genocide and war.
- Other cases were selected because they illustrated particularly well a prevalent cultural pattern we had identified or provided a second data point for an argument. For example, our research into climate change art suggested this generally did not result in productive discourse on science, technology, and human values. This failure was well captured

in the disorganized Internet threads associated with the Deviant Art contest and the *Rethink* art exhibition. These were arguably not the single most important events of their kind but they were useful didactically. Furthermore, they offered confidence that the unproductive pattern we had identified in public responses to the world-renowned artist Antony Gormley was not an outlier emerging from his celebrity status.

- We were particularly interested in material from 2005 onward. We do not see ourselves engaging in a systematic study of climate change's social history nor as documenting the most significant public events in that history; rather, we want to understand current forms of representation and performance. Given changing audience knowledge, technological advances, and so forth, paying attention to recent events would seem to optimize case study relevance.

- At the microlevel of raw data, we generally select and display quotations and other forms of visible culture that indicate or capture a prevailing mode of discourse or public response. In this book, commentary from newspaper editorials and journalists on an event (e.g., the Copenhagen conference), Internet postings and threads (e.g., on the 10/10 advertising campaign), critical reviews (e.g., of climate art), and so forth, are deployed in such a way. We also make use of remarks by opinion leaders and opinion-leading media. Such individuals and institutions are empirically important not only in setting agendas; they also serve as bookmarks with which to map a range of opinions in the wider discursive fields of the public sphere (see Jacobs and Townsley 2011). For this reason, readers will see we also make heavy use of certain "quality" newspapers and media outlets (such as the *New York Times*, the *London Times*, the *Guardian*, the *Daily Telegraph*, the *Economist*, and the British Broadcasting Corporation or BBC) and their websites to evaluate opinion and reception. Aside from leading the pack in the somewhat hierarchical and parasitic world of news journalism, and hence determining what is deemed newsworthy and setting the talking points for opinion columns in the minor leagues, many of these have the communicative advantage of being of known political valence by our readers. The *Guardian*, for example, represents the liberal Left and believes in the reality of climate change. It is a favored newspaper of teachers, students, and activists. The *Daily Telegraph*'s readers are older, conservative, and skeptical. The BBC tries hard to be neutral but is generally thought to have a slight liberal bias. The *Economist* pitches itself as having a politics-free and evidence-based approach. Its prescriptions are often for market solutions. Familiarity with these sources will assist readers in understanding (and, we hope, critiquing) our book as they interpret and evaluate quotations and comments. Some will be disappointed that we were not more inclusive of fringe sources (e.g., climate-skeptic blogs; activist newsletters) and also that we did not make more of international and regional sources of opinion. We would point out in our defense that we do in fact draw on environmentalist media, global sources, and so forth, at many places in our book. However, the truth is that pragmatic issues relating to scope, page limitations, shared audience knowledge, and the need to give priority to building theory rather than exhaustive documentation of diverse geographic effects drew us to the global information clearinghouse of the English language core. This offers a conceptual lingua franca of sorts at a worldwide level. We certainly believe that future studies on discourse and representation, making use of sources from Indonesia, Brazil, and Sudan, for example, will be extremely important, and we encourage other scholars to take up the baton in dedicated studies that can do proper justice to local cultural and political complexities. We simply cannot do this in the context of our present text.

- Finally, we make use of microlevel exhibits that captured a particular view extremely well, often through effective reasoning or the pithy use of language. Often we sifted through our files of commentary and opinion looking for a statement that would nail a particular issue or allow us best to illustrate the nub of a theoretical point. In this case the quality of the discourse and its fit with our agendas determined which items are displayed in this book. The actual universe of material we read was, of course, far wider. Skillful practitioners whose use of language gets to the heart of the matter tend to be oversampled for this reason. So do editorials. Such examples are not "typical" of discourse, but they are the "best," much as Shakespeare would be dominant in a survey of Elizabethan drama. At times, however, we do turn to the vox pop of Internet threads to try to assay a range of nonelite discourses. For example, in the contexts of climate art and the 10/10 advertising campaign, the measured prose of experts with its attendant reasoned justifications did not truly capture the indignation, irrelevance, and irony that characterized many responses to such initiatives.

The result of all this activity has been in our book the reconstruction of systems of meaning using theory and the presentation of a layered range of illustrative materials showing these in action. The former steps back from everyday experience to give perspective; the latter anchors analysis in familiar forms of visible evidence. We follow this method as we believe that the truth or falsity of our work is a matter of importance. So is transparency. Our aim in this book has not been to offer virtuoso interpretations that only academic audiences can understand (a point of contrast with much work in the cultural studies tradition, for example) but to provide an accurate and accessible account of how climate change plays out in the public sphere. En passant, we have also offered some analysis of the effectiveness of particular strategies and performances – although this has not been our central goal. Furthermore, we have sought to develop new theoretical tools for this and related tasks confronting cultural sociology. We hope we have been successful at one or more of these tasks. We also hope for our failure and that our shortcomings will provoke efforts at dialogue, falsification, and challenge. Making sense of the meanings of climate change should be a collective endeavor. Our approach is only one among the many that are on the table.

Climate Change as Social Drama

Gus Speth is often called the "Dean of the environmental movement."[1] In a recent manifesto published in *Orion Magazine* (2012), this consummate technocrat makes a startling admission:

Regarding the language we use and the messages we seek to convey, I can see clearly now that we environmentalists have been too wonkish and too focused on technical fixes. We have not developed well the capacity to speak in a language that goes straight to the American heart, resonates with both core moral values and common aspirations, and projects a positive and compelling vision. Throughout my forty-odd years in the environmental community, public discourse on environment has been dominated by lawyers, scientists, and economists – people like me. Now we need to hear a lot more from the preachers, the poets, the psychologists, and the philosophers. And our message must be one that is founded on hope and honest possibility.

Speth is not alone in moving from the "hard" world of policy to the "soft" world of culture. In both academic and popular environmental debate, there has been a clear cultural turn of late. Talk of "iconography" and "ideology" abounds; "myths," "frames," and "symbols" are common currency. Today it has become something of a cliché, even in scientific circles, to describe climate change as first and foremost a "cultural problem."

So culture shapes the perception and politics of climate change. But *just how*? This is not so clear. Scholars and critics offer a number of

---

[1] Among other distinctions, Speth was cofounder of the Natural Resources Defense Council and founder of the World Resources Institute; he has also served as administrator of the United Nations Development Programme, chair of the UN Development Group, dean of the Yale Forestry School, and chairman of the U.S. Council on Environmental Quality in the Carter administration.

competing answers. In this chapter, we try to cut through the confusion by presenting a theory of climate change as social drama. Our approach is deceptively simple. Most theories look to root causes rather than surface effects. Some blame controversy and inaction on conflicting worldviews, value systems, and cosmologies of nature. Others blame the ideological influence of "carbon class power" (Urry 2011), with its deep impacts on commonsense expectations about lifestyle and ethical behavior. These theories are valuable, but they tend to underestimate the pragmatic flexibility and historical dynamism of cultural structures. They underrate the power of performance in the public sphere. They offer little by way of grounds for hope. By contrast, we believe that speech acts make a difference. This is why we look to neither the sociomental nor the structural-economic "root causes" of climate controversy but to that controversy itself. We turn to the surface, visible, public realm of deliberative rhetoric and agonistic ritual – to news stories, protests and performances, charismatic individuals and conferences, advertisements and artworks. If, as we argue, climate change is a story that "everyone knows," just *how* does everyone know it? What form does that knowledge take, and how might it be connected to the "core moral values" and "common aspirations" that Speth attributes to our democratic culture?

Narrative theory provides an essential starting point for our journey.[2] Put simply, climate change exists in a complex field of stories defined by multiple, competing genres. Its discursive environment is deeply layered. It is not simply a discourse about nature, energy production, policy, or scientific facts. It is also at a second level about people and institutions: scientists, activists, politicians, corporations, nation-states. These actors are also spectators and critics, engaging in a yet another, third order of

---

[2] Ecocritics have produced the most insightful work on the narrativization of environmental risk (Buell 2001; Heise 2008; Houser 2014; Nixon 2011). As Ursula Heise (2008, 138) explains, "narrative genres.... provide important cultural tools for organizing information about risks into intelligible and meaningful stories. But to the extent that such genre templates have a cultural power that can make them override alternative stories that fit less well into existing cultural narratives, they can also shape, filter, and rearrange such information in ways that are not always politically or ecologically benign. Narrative analysis should therefore play an important role in examining the ways risk perceptions are generated by and manifest themselves through various forms of representation, from documentaries and journalism to fiction and poetry." Pointing to Lawrence Buell's analysis of "toxic discourse," a risk genre pioneered by Rachel Carson in *Silent Spring* and apotheosized in Don Delillo's novel *White Noise*, Heise notes how such genres "filter and shape information about risk so as to postulate certain causal sequences" (139) – Eden destroyed by hidden pollution, awakening consciousness of contamination, a battle of weak versus strong to restore ecological and human health.

reflexive narration in which the representation of climate change itself is analyzed, dissected, and subject to storytelling. How well is the story being told? they ask. Which story is gaining traction with the public? What will be the next strategy to make people care? Are people *truly* scared yet? It is not only activists and academics who ask themselves these questions. They are also common coin in wider venues for public communicative exchange such as mass media editorials and opinion items. We might think of this debate about meanings, their qualities and fate, as exemplifying the cultural reflexivity of the public sphere. It gives climate change something of the quality of a soap opera, sporting contest, or mythical saga. Who is winning? Who is making the smartest moves? It is a form of deadly serious spectacle aimed at persuasion. This is why narrative is not enough. We also need a theory of performance.

The concept of social drama was famously introduced by the anthropologist Victor Turner (1968, 1974) and used to explain periods of social turmoil in traditional African societies. According to Turner, an initial normative breach or crisis would be followed by a period of instability, tension, uncertainty, and creativity that he called liminality. This in turn would give way either to reunification and the emergence of a renewed political order or to the recognition of an irreparable schism between contending parties. Turner wanted to emphasize that this was not simply a recurring pattern of objective politics. Rather, it was a template of stylized gestures and ritualistic moments, an "experiential matrix" from which all genres of social performance are derived (Turner 1980, 158). Breach was enacted, crisis was enacted, redress was enacted, reconciliation was enacted. Through these enactments, politics was made and social bonds ultimately strengthened or broken.

According to Turner, such cultural performances were not mechanistic in any functionalist way but rather highly reflexive. They were "active agencies of change, representing the eye by which culture sees itself and the drawing board on which creative actors sketch out what they believe to be more apt or interesting 'designs for living'" (Turner 1988, 24). This dimension of "performative reflexivity" Turner defined as "a condition in which a sociocultural group, or its most perceptive members acting representatively, turn, bend or reflect back upon themselves, upon the relations, actions, symbols, meanings, codes, roles, statuses, social structures, ethical and legal rules, and other sociocultural components which make up their public 'selves'" (24). Thus social drama became a way of "scrutinizing the quotidian world – seeing it as tragedy, comedy, melodrama, etc." (27). Whereas advanced levels of ritual accomplishment permitted traditional societies to resolve crisis with performative competence, in complex societies, the process can be derailed in any number of ways. If redressive action repeatedly fails, for example, societies can become mired in bitter conflict and permanent crisis (Turner 1990, 9) – a situation that might well describe climate change. In extreme situations, revolution ensues.

Although somewhat marred by a teleology suggesting an inevitable progress through the designated quasi-ritual phases, Turner's ideas have in fact been productively applied to contingent politics in industrial societies. Scholars like Robin Wagner-Pacifici (1986) and Ronald N. Jacobs (2000) have demonstrated that terrorist activities, racial crises, and judicial inquiries can be fruitfully investigated as dramatic interludes where protagonists perform to concerned publics. These show that a breach has taken place and dramatize resolution. Complex patterns of narration are pivotal to this process. These describe characters, plots, and situations and shape outcomes by opening and closing doors of subjective and objective possibility for agents. When combined with postcritical theories of the mass media and of public-sphere deliberation, a powerful tool emerges for understanding "how societies think" as collectivities through shared and visible public communication as well as via second-order reflexivity about that communication. We expand on the possibilities of such an approach for the climate change field later in this chapter. First we must turn to prevailing visions and explain how they fall short of capturing this colorful play of stories and performances.

Climate Communication and Cultural Bias

With a problem as "wicked" as climate change, it is tempting to see culture in a fatalistic light. Pace Speth, when we consider the incredible inertia of carbon-intensive lifeways – factory farming, air travel, air-conditioned strip malls – culture looks more like an impassable barrier than a useful tool.[3] We speak here in particular of the dominant research tradition that identifies deep "cultural bias" as a block on collective action. When tethered to a raft of sociopsychological mechanisms, this bias is said to prevent belief in anthropogenic climate change, stall collective mobilization, and reinforce the economic status quo. Despite good-faith attempts to imagine alternative possibilities, culture is largely understood in social-psychological terms as a handicap to full rationality. Many researchers

---

[3] On climate change as a wicked problem, see Hulme (2009, 334–337).

end up echoing the entirely understandable but ultimately reductive complaint, *If only people could take off their cultural blinders, they would see how much trouble we are in and get their act together*. There are exceptions, of course, but their voices are marginalized in most social scientific circles.

There are three main problems with this line of reasoning as it currently manifests. First, as numerous scholars have argued (in a literature effectively synthesized by Hulme 2009), "the trouble" itself is a product of cultural interpretation, not simply a physical fact waiting to be discovered. Second, it assumes that culture is mostly epiphenomenal, a by-product of deeper psychological, social, or political-economic processes. Third, it erroneously conceptualizes culture as integrated value commitments or "ways of life" that serve to guard tightly coupled modes of social organization rather than as a flexible domain of play, contingency, strategy, gesture, and interpretation.

In their influential volume *Creating a Climate for Change*, climate change communication experts Susanne Moser and Lisa Dilling (2007, 5–8) illustrate the sociopsychological facet of this general approach, adding "solution skepticism" and "threats to values" to various physical and psychological millstones – perceived remoteness of impacts, time lags, imperfect markets, the tragedy of the commons, and so forth (we counterfactually questioned this kind of argument in the prior chapter). According to Moser and Dilling, "the inherent natural characteristics and deep societal roots of climate change stack the deck against the issue being recognized as an urgent and actionable problem" (8). Researchers in this realist vein tend to treat culture, not as a public realm of communication, but rather as a set of distorting normative lenses. Their hope is that we can polish and grind until people see things clearly – or, as Moser (2010, 36) puts it, to "find clearer, simpler metaphors, imagery, and mental models as well as compelling framing to lay the foundation for more appropriate cognitive processing." Although we share their faith in the power of metaphor and imagery, we have a very different model of culture in mind, one in which cultural codes do much more than mediate between mind and physical reality. Nor do we see inappropriate cognitive processing as the major cultural problem.

Similar arguments can be found in work that critiques the impacts of the neoliberal political economy. Here culture has become a form of ideological power, a set of symbolic tools for guarding the interests of Big Oil and Cold War–era technoscience (Jacques 2009; Jacques et al. 2008; McCright and Dunlap 2000, 2003, 2010, 2011; Oreskes and

Conway 2010). According to sociologists Riley Dunlap and Aaron Mc-Cright, global warming has been projected as a "nonproblem" by a loosely organized but well-funded network of conservative ideologues fighting to preserve the industrial status quo. These "merchants of doubt," as the historian Naomi Oreskes and journalist Eric Conway (2010) call them, use a variety of representational strategies to inject misunderstanding and skepticism into public debate, obfuscate scientific research, and intimidate experts. Meanwhile media outlets have given these pseudo-experts more or less free rein to pollute public debate (Dispensa and Brulle 2003). Although researchers working in this genre have made important contributions by revealing the social organization of antienvironmentalism and exposing the immense power wielded by a relatively small group of plutocrats, they have very little to say about how these reactionary forces have made their stories stick nor about why their audiences have been so receptive to them in the first place. One wonders if money and strategy are enough to explain the lockdown and confusion. Consider, for example, that millions of public relations dollars can do little to protect Big Oil from becoming a populist punching bag whenever there is a major spill or that millions of climate change believers are doing next to nothing to address the problem. In other words, this perspective has had surprisingly little to say about the cultural content or cultural form of environmental attitudes or the conditions under which money can make meanings sticky. Strictly put, the central achievement of analysis has been to unmask efforts at the strategic use of culture to shore up social power – a worthy task, but one that can only take us so far. Even in more hermeneutically nuanced research on climate politics and communication influenced by cultural studies, culture is largely imagined as a kind of dominant ideology or generalized domain of Foucauldian-Gramscian "cultural politics" (see, e.g., Boykoff 2011; Luke 2011). Meaning and knowledge are vehicles for the exercise of power. Like many in the field of cultural sociology, we reject this implicit hierarchy and see meaning at the very heart of power itself.

Against both hard-nosed materialism and more theoretically sensitive cultural studies, a third camp, populated largely by scientific researchers in the field of risk perception, has also been pushing for more serious consideration of culture as cultural bias. Inspired by structuralist anthropology, some in this field have developed a systematic, transposable template for cultural analysis that they call *cultural cognition*. As the name suggests, this is an explicit attempt to make cultural theory psychologically testable and so in fact marks a positivist turn away from deep hermeneutics toward a schematic, cognitive approach to meaning. Cultural cognition is based on a simple premise. As Yale law professor Dan Kahan (2010, 296), one of its leading exponents, explains, "People endorse whichever position reinforces their connection to others with whom they share important commitments." In debates over environmental risks such as climate change, cultural cognition practitioners argue that information is not the problem. Nor even are the seemingly hardwired cognitive biases we mentioned earlier, such as lack of concern for probabilistic time-distant dangers or disregard for future generations. What matters are group values. More than race, class, political ideology, gender, income, education level, personality type, or anything else, it is these values that matter. In the United States, they often can be thought of as trumping information along "culture war" lines. In the case of climate change, for example, the kind of man who (to invoke a stereotype) loves NASCAR and collects guns may well find it impossible to adopt an environmentalist position. New scientific evidence will be neutralized and dismissed. Climate skepticism will be embraced because this stance will enable in-group ties with other so-called NASCAR dads to be reaffirmed.

Cultural cognition represents the merger of two longtime rivals in the world of risk analysis: the psychometric paradigm of social psychologists such as Paul Slovic and the systematic, neo-Durkheimian, anthropological Cultural Theory of Mary Douglas and her colleagues (the capital letters are commonly used – a practice we find vaguely imperialistic, given the variety of cultural theories available today). Practitioners have pitched cultural cognition as a scientifically legitimate, antifunctionalist evolution of the Douglas paradigm (Kahan 2012a). By identifying specific, measurable psychological mechanisms that connect abstract cultural structures to concrete social networks and risk perceptions, they aim to show how levels of concern and political conflict are profoundly social. Other specialists in the psychology of climate change communication have taken Cultural Theory in similar deterministic directions. In an influential study, Anthony Leiserowitz (2006), director of the Yale Project on Climate Change Communication, showed how grid-group position (levels of social integration and hierarchy in an individual's immediate community) conditions affective responses to images of dangerous climate change, and how these affective responses are a more powerful predictor of individual risk perception than levels of scientific knowledge. In other words, it is how people *feel* about climate change that matters most, and how they feel is a function of what they *value*, this coming in turn from their concrete social location and social networks.

At first glance, there is much to recommend this turn toward emotion, trust, and moral solidarity. Sociology moves to the foreground through attention to community and identity. Yet this camp, too, paints a somewhat misleading and reductive picture of culture. For one thing, they bleed much of the hermeneutic complexity and historical richness out of cultural practice, turning what is already one of anthropology's more mechanistic cultural theories into a meaning-creation machine: culture is the operating system that converts group social structure into individual belief. Much like the middle-period Durkheim on whom Mary Douglas relied, this is a theory in need of a Geertzian and Turnerian intervention, one that can highlight play, gesture, ambiguity, and performance. Steering clear of the historical and anthropological literature on trust, credibility, and public reason in scientific controversies, it offers no account of what it means to believe in scientific evidence in the first place, no account of the narration of technoscience in modern society, nor any strong sense of where ideas about environmental danger come from (see Jasanoff 2012 for an up-to-date synthesis of this neglected literature). Second, and even more problematic, it has virtually nothing to say about the cultural process of democratic civil society, a problem inherited from Douglas and her disciples with their somewhat silo-like understanding of coexisting but noncommunicating cultural systems. The cultural cognition approach claims to overcome the crabs-in-a-bucket social vision of rational choice theory and Hobbesian materialism by leaving room for cultural convergence around democratic solutions for "overdetermined" social problems. It contends that divergent value systems can indeed overlap (Kahan 2012b). Yet it fails to see that this overlapping takes place in a public sphere that displays its own layered cultural logic and allows for the dialogue, reflexivity, and critique that might construct or hold back rather than simply host overlappingness.

Risk, Trust, and Cultural Performance

All of this work rests on a key assumption: "In the world's industrial nations, 'risk' has become *the* organising concept that gives meaning and direction to environmental regulation," and thus to environmental politics (Jasanoff 2012, 133). As we have already seen, Mary Douglas did more than anyone to forge the consensus that "risk" and "risk cosmologies" are where the action is. Yet her work is frequently caricatured, and some of its most profound insights have been largely forgotten, even by her followers. In a series of essays on risk and cultural bias written through the 1970s and culminating in her controversial collaboration with the political scientist Aaron Wildavsky, *Risk and Culture* (1983), Douglas identified a limited pool of cosmologies applicable to all known societies that make subjects more or less open to beliefs about environmental instability. Denying neither the empirical reality of environmental hazards nor the rationality of environmental fears, Douglas and Wildavsky very usefully showed that debates about risk are often debates about the moral order of society. What they call "pollution beliefs" trace causal chains from the impure actions of polluted individuals and groups to their disastrous consequences; they divide "the moral from the immoral and so sustain the vision of the good society" (37). Although scientific knowledge and statistical thinking modulate these beliefs, they do not change their essential cultural logic. By decoding the symbolic movements from transgression to blame and retribution that structure these beliefs, the modern risk analyst discovers that "impurities in the physical world or chemical carcinogens in the body are directly traced to immoral forms of economic and political power" (47). Thus, with American environmentalists very much in mind, they write, "No doubt the water in fourteenth century Europe was a persistent health hazard, but a cultural theory of perception would point out that it became a public preoccupation only when it seemed plausible to accuse Jews of poisoning the wells" (7). Needless to say, this relativistic argument initially incensed environmentalists who wished to endorse the objective, scientifically validated nature of their position. Yet it has since been adapted as a touchstone for environmentalist advocacy, including by Douglas (1994) herself.

Since Douglas and Wildavsky's seminal statement, a number of researchers working at the border of anthropology and public policy have usefully refined and codified Cultural Theory, using it to examine a broad range of risk debates, including climate change. As the anthropologists Steve Rayner and Michael Thompson (1998, 266) explain in a definitive overview of this approach, "competing ideas about nature and about equity inform climate change policy debates at all levels from the family hearth to the international negotiation of the Framework Convention on Climate Change (FCCC)." They describe Cultural Theory as an attempt to "map" the "moral landscape" of climate change, and they make the crucial observation that climate change "provides an arena for debating a wide variety of social, economic, and political issues that society finds difficult to address directly" (335). In other words, climate change is not just about climate change. Moreover, it is not just about experts overcoming the network-based cultural biases of the lay public.

Myths of nature are at work on all sides, competing to occupy the moral center of society. What matters is not knowledge and delusion but trust, blame, and consent.

We agree. With this subtext, Douglas, Wildavsky, and a few of their interpreters opened the door to a truly *cultural* sociology of risk. Yet it was slammed shut again by the weight of their more visible and dominant neopositivist sociology of socially structured risk perception. The project also suffered from latent pulls toward morphological reductionism. Egalitarian small-scale societies, cults, and sects, Douglas said, were characterized by intense sensitivity to pollutions and visions of nature as inherently unstable. This was their "cultural bias" – one akin to a witchcraft cosmology. Hierarchical and large-scale societies, by contrast, tended to be more complacent and to have another bias. They believed that administrative, market, and technical solutions could be found to most problems. Her model is elegant for its explanation of the "in here–out there" duality through which societies situate themselves in an environment, but it is dogged by a problem of fit. Put simply, we often find cosmologies in the wrong places. Cosmological views seem to be far more flexible and contingent than her vision of entrenched "cultural bias" might admit. Contemporary societies appear to be repeatedly plagued by premodern doubts and anxieties, when really they should not be. During the 1970s and 1980s, for example, conventional middle-class suburbanites came to share the pollution-sensitive ecological views of what Douglas claims were ecological "cults" that emerged in the 1960s. To account for this, Douglas and her colleagues have had to abandon their systematic model and resort to ad hoc secondary elaborations on theory. Marketing by organizations like the Sierra Club and noted events like the nuclear accident at Three Mile Island are pulled like rabbits from a hat to explain the export of the ecological worldview. From our social drama perspective, a better approach might have been to interrogate more systematically the way the Three Mile Island crisis was narrated and to think about the capacity of these circulating, social context–free narrative forms and dramatic gestures to reach over and across, perhaps even transform, competing rationalities. Contingent cultural alignments and performances make some dangers more pertinent than others, opinions shift due to talk, images stick, minds change. This is how social drama works in a public sphere.

After Douglas, the most influential and theoretically elaborated attempt to connect culture and risk came from the German sociologist Ulrich Beck. Although an extremely fertile source of ideas about postindustrial environmental consciousness, Beck's theory suffers from inattention to contingency and an objectivist-structuralist explanation of risk awareness. Writing in the late 1980s, he argued that we now live in the era of "risk society," this offering an entirely new set of challenges for social administration. Rather than solving problems of uncertainty, modernity has itself produced various new potential dangers, mostly in the form of industrial pollution, chemicals, and radiation. These have contributed in part to a growing culture of social critique with attendant social movements that Beck, with Anthony Giddens and Scott Lash (1994), called *reflexive modernization*. Crucially, Beck isolated many features of these ecological threats. They are resistant to everyday perception. They are often invisible and unknowable without the assistance of science, technology, and statistics. To come to terms with them or to begin to understand them requires faith in scientific expertise. Furthermore, the threats are incalculable in their magnitude and diffuse in their impacts – so at the end of the day, even those scientists can't help us much in figuring out what is going on. Nor is there escape from them by virtue of privilege, as the externalities of modernity will boomerang back onto the affluent. According to Beck, social life is increasingly organized around the control or management of these invisible dangers from which we might never be able to hide.

Beck's thesis is brilliant as a reading of a cultural pattern of anxieties. Yet it is also flawed by a tendency toward objectivism. For Beck the risks are real, their properties endemic to their nature, our anxiety a largely appropriate response to danger (Alexander and Smith 1996). Taking a step back, we might read Beck himself as an exhibit; his treatment of dangers and risks as an exemplar of a particular cosmology. In the sense raised by Douglas, he provided a case of an extended treatise written from a sectlike point of view. His eloquently crafted writing on proliferating, unknown, and invisible dangers, in fact, mirrors that of Douglas's witchcraft cosmologies. A more hermeneutic approach might have allowed Beck to see representations of danger as uncoupled from objective risk properties, the gap between "reality" and "representation" helping to explain variations in concern and its timing. More important still, a social drama approach might treat his best-selling and influential work yet more reflexively as an effective performance through which risk awareness was itself talked into being. Beck might be understood as having captured and articulated a zeitgeist and, in so doing, shaping and generating opinion and activism, at least among the German green Left.

To be fair, Beck seems in his final years to have grown increasingly conscious of the objectivist tendencies in his early work and to advocate for exactly the sort of theoretical shift we said was needed in the previous few sentences. Along with many thinkers in the so-called postenvironmentalist mold, he came to warn against the "seductive naïve catastrophic realism" (Beck 2010, 258) of mainstream environmentalism, going so far as to call the very idea of the environment "politically suicidal" (263). He became, as it were, more reflexive about reflexive modernization. Indeed, in his later writing, much of which focuses on climate change, he was explicitly concerned with what he calls the "staging" of risk. His key question now is how risks become "real" in the minds of diverse actors and institutions, and his answer, "reduced to a formula, is: global risk is the *staging of the reality* [*Realitätsinzeneirung*] of global risk" (Beck 2009, 10).

This turn toward the performative would seem to be exactly what we need. Yet although Beck expanded brilliantly on the phenomenology of global risk, at the end of the day, he merely flirted with the concept of performance. Staging, it turns out, is more theatrical metaphor than analytic necessity. Consequently, Beck underestimated both the theoretical challenges and semantic complexity of cultural performance. Questions of character, plot, and narrative genre are raised but then quickly dropped. He writes, for example,

Far from aggravating a general sense of meaninglessness in the modern world, global ecological threats give rise to a horizon of meaning dominated by avoidance, resistance and assistance, a moral climate that intensifies with the scale of the perceived danger and in which the roles of hero and villain acquire a new political significance. The perception of the world within the coordinates of environmental and industrial self-endangerment combine morality, religion, fundamentalism, desperation, tragedy and tragicomedy – always connected with their opposites: salvation, assistance and liberation – into a universal drama. In this worldwide tragicomedy, business is free to assume the role of the villain of the piece or to slip into the role of the hero and rescuer. (Beck 2009, 99)

Beck intuits something profoundly important but did not sustain his analysis in the way we hope to in this book. For example, he described the Stern Report as a work of "stage management" (101) and speaks of the "top-down staging" of climate change by scientists, politicians, and social movements (72). He also toys with a comparison of religious proselytizing and climate staging, claiming, "as with any religion, in the case of the global climate risk there are also heretics, agnostics, mystics, unbelievers, the ignorant and also radical secularists" (72).

Here, as in his earlier work, Beck offers a metacommentary or gloss but failed to engage in the deep empirical work that would illustrate his views or put them to the test. Simon Cottle's (1998) analysis from long ago still rings true. He remarked of Beck's breakthrough work *Risk Society* that, although not "blind to the intimate relationship between the media and surrounding culture," his "statements on cultural resonance of the environment remain underdeveloped" (15, 17). A turn to middle range and case study scholarship on the representation and reception of environmental and other risks, Cottle argued, might have allowed Beck to resolve some of the instabilities within his own theoretical edifice: the relative weight of risk reality and risk representation, the relationship of scientific uncertainty to social reflexivity, and so forth. The same holds today. We are left with provocative speculations that fly too high to provide answers. For example, Beck (2010, 255) asks, "The hardcore sociological question is: Where is the support for ecological changes supposed to come from, the support which in many cases would undermine their lifestyles, their consumption habits, their social status and life conditions in what are already truly very uncertain times? Or, to put it in sociological terms: How can a kind of cosmopolitan solidarity across boundaries become real, a greening of societies, which is a prerequisite for the necessarily transnational politics of climate change?"

Yet without a proper theory of performance and representation, without the sort of detailed case study research we provide in this book, Beck could not actually answer his own questions. His metatheoretical speculations about "staging" are consistent with the commonsense knowledge of the ecological community but left a yawning gap between semantics and pragmatics.

We think Beck's utopian streak led him to vastly underestimate the difficulty of winning the genre war or generating the performative resignification of climate change that he so strongly desires. Along with sociologists such as John Urry and Bruno Latour, he seems to assume that new structures of meaning will naturally emerge from new modes of social organization, just as the reflexive modernity of risk society would give rise to the progressive politics of the people Beck once dubbed "freedom's children." In this sense, his final nod toward "staging" can be read, perhaps too generously, as a halfhearted apology to the late-Durkheimian tradition, an acknowledgment that the material processes of reflexive modernization cannot *on their own* change how society makes sense of its situation. For such cultural change, we need systems of collective representation, background symbols, and foreground scripts (Alexander 2004). Yet Beck, like many other late-career converts to culture, such as Charles Tilly, was too deeply saturated in Weberian and Marxist traditions to accept the full demands of cultural autonomy, even if elements of his vocabulary hint at a deep conversion. Paradoxically, this resulted for him in an anguished materialist idealism, a utopian faith in the spontaneous emergence of new forms of cosmopolitan consciousness from sociotechnological innovation (for dystopian variations on the same theme, see Urry 2011). He seemingly believed that environmental politics will begin anew with an inverted set of cultural systems. Yet we cannot simply choose to "love our monsters," as Latour (2012) has said of ecocidal technologies. As the cultural sociology of movements has repeatedly demonstrated, people cannot innovate their way out of conflict by pulling a rabbit from a hat. As we show repeatedly in this book, they try to *work* their way out using the symbolic systems at hand.

This fact has not been lost on everyone. A growing body of ethnographic research has shown how the interpretation of climate change is inevitably shaped by local experience, collective memory, and cultural identity (Crate 2011; Strauss and Orlove 2003). In the first such study of a rich industrial democracy (Norway), the American sociologist Kari Marie Norgaard (2011) seeks to explain how nonresponse to global warming is produced through the cultural practices of everyday life. Relying on Anne Swidler's (1986) influential theory of culture as "tool kit" and Eviatar Zerubavel's (2007) work on the social construction of denial, Norgaard shows how Norwegians use norms of conversation, emotion, and attention to manage their fear of irrevocable climatic change. More than just embodied interactional routines, these norms are further rooted in legitimating background narratives of national identity. In their national mythology, Norwegians are "close to nature, egalitarian, simple, and humble" (140) – a small, ecologically virtuous country deeply devoted to cosmopolitan democracy. By ritualistically invoking these myths, they are able to deflect attention from the economic and ecological reality of Norwegian life, which – notwithstanding the extensive use of hydroelectric power – makes a disproportionate contribution to global warming through oil production and export. They do this, moreover, by maligning "Amerika," Norway's supposed environmental antithesis. In what amounts to a metanarrative about the Global North's failure to deal with climate change, Norwegians say, "We aren't so bad; at least we aren't like *them*" (165). Yet by treating these narratives as "emotion management strategies" and privileging the psychosocial dynamics of everyday life, Norgaard gets us only partway toward a cultural pragmatics of climate change. She considers the deep symbolic background of public-sphere environmental conflict and narration almost as an afterthought, a way of setting the stage for the real cultural action, which takes place in the realm of embodied, routine practice. "Tool kits" are only part of the equation. We also need instruction manuals and stories about how and when to use them.

Toward a Theory of Social Drama

We have reached the end of our literature review; so where do things stand? Climate activism has called for a cultural turn with an eye to creative solutions. Yet existing scholarly approaches lock people into static meaning systems. They are imprisoned by their psychological biases, by their social networks, by their social location, by misinformation from nefarious organizations, and even by everyday life. What is explained is mostly why people – like toddlers having a tantrum or smiling at a slavering bear – are irrational, are stubborn, won't change, and can't understand those with different views or how much danger they are in. Notwithstanding scattered and incomplete moments in Beck and Douglas, and despite recognition among the top activist intellectuals and even scientists that myth and performance need to be enlisted, the cultural turn within academia has ended up theorizing the limits of culture, not its possibilities, in a truly positive and dogged way. It has explored the parameters around culture that constrain it, not its inner logic and outer texture. In this book we propose something different. We dig into culture as a structure of meanings. We think more closely about contingency and performance. We look not for hidden roots of belief but at the blindingly obvious ways that culture plays out in the visible activity of the public sphere as it represents and discusses climate change. We see culture as both a bridge and a roadblock, this depending on context, choice, and the skill of practitioners. To do all this, we must next return to and then extensively rework the concept of social drama that we introduced a few pages ago. This will take some time.

In conventional sociological applications the social drama has been understood as an unexpected, exceptional event of somewhat limited duration that compels continuous attention. Typically it will disrupt everyday routines and broadcast schedules, be a topic of conversation, and generate strong emotions. It will be the kind of moment described as a turning point, or as shaping a national destiny, or as a crisis involving schism and the need for unity. Often violence is involved at the point of breach. This seems to disrupt the social order, challenge a society's self-understanding, or threaten the sense of ontological security that tells us tomorrow will be much like today. Representative examples from the literature include riots, hostage situations, terrorist acts, assassinations, and natural disasters. Wagner-Pacifici (1986), for example, looks at the kidnapping of Italian prime minister Aldo Moro and the anxieties this produced about Italian political stability and state authority. Jacobs (2000) explores the fallout of the Rodney King beating and the Los Angeles riots for reform in city hall and the police department; beneath all this was a deep concern about racial equality, race tension, and racism in America. Ron Eyerman (2008) examines the multiple meanings imputed to the assassination of the controversial Dutch filmmaker Theo Van Gogh. Christine Walley (2004) investigates the contentious formation of a national park in coastal Tanzania. Following the classical social drama pattern, Simon Cottle (2012) shows that the South Asian Tsunami of 2004 generated initial expressions of collective grief – a narrative eventuated of disruption, then the reconstitution of the social.

Fair enough; but what we want to suggest here is that such an intense and event-focused application of Turner's theory is too restrictive. Dramas can be very short or very long in duration. They can be intense or diffuse. A milestone in our opinion was Cottle's (2004, 2008) analysis of the aftermath of the racist murder of Stephen Lawrence in London in 1993. He shows a social drama *extending* episodically for more than ten years and sustained by periodic social activism, judicial inquiries, and court trials. It also *diffused*. No longer just about the death of Lawrence the expanding set of stories and signifiers drew into its orbit discussions about policing, the mass media, social justice, the definition of racism, and the possibility of multiculturalism. Although there is a risk to precision and a danger of banality when any theoretical concept is stretched beyond its original formulation, the payoff can also be a freeing up of repressed analytic potential. For this reason we wager that the concept of social drama should be taken even beyond Cottle's marker.

We suggest that, through their lives, people navigate and witness extremely diffuse dramas in episodic, half-aware ways. In the sense elaborated by Clifford Geertz, the cultural life of a society consists of multiple overlapping dramatic webs. These are the myths, narratives, and spectacles that any competent member of that society will to some extent understand. As Eleanor Townsley (2001, 99) puts it, they are "what everyone knows": a commonsense, shorthand selection and condensation from complexity. By becoming "what everyone knows," social dramas are meaning-clusters that have broken out of narrow sphere-specific domains of communication and association such as science, religion, or administration to become part of the common currency of exchange in a wider civil sphere or popular culture. Sometimes these narratives pass through generations. As such they offer a resource for interpreting new events and evaluating actors, inserting them into a plot and giving them a dramatic quality. Of course, the fact that a social drama is "what everyone knows" does not necessarily imply that there is agreement about the meaning, morality, or impact of events and actions any more than the fact that "everyone knows" a great novel or film or political celebrity will lead them to agree on particular points of interpretation. Nor does it mean in a pedantic and literal sense that every single member of a population has the same interest and knowledge of every issue of every field. It is easy enough to point to exceptions, such as children or the seriously mentally ill. Rather, the point is that there is a widely shared recognition among the averagely intelligent, moderately literate, news-following population of an issue as important, public, and "dramatic," and of the players in the drama as belonging to that issue. There is likely to be a common agreement on certain moments as somehow pivotal to the unfolding of the drama and as central to the effort of interpretation. And there is an awareness, however dim, that these moments express something like the spirit of the age.

We might take the civil rights movement (Alexander 2006) as a case in point. Here is a social drama that has persisted for decades and that is profoundly embedded in the American lexicon of competent citizenship. It starts with the corrupting breach of the transatlantic slave trade and moves toward redemption. Particular events, such as the *Dred Scott* decision, the iconic marches and protests in the Deep South in places like Selma and Birmingham, the speeches of Dr. Martin Luther King Jr., and the presidential election of Barack Obama, stand out as dramatic highlights. These offer nodes for symbolic and interpretative activity, but they cannot really be understood merely as isolated happenings. Rather, they are connected to each other by the deeper, longer, persistent, morally persuasive drama of civil rights of which most citizens have some awareness. They provide data points for reflecting on that social drama in turn, operating as signals and hinges for thinking and debating racial inclusion and exclusion. Likewise, the incident at Three Mile Island should properly be considered a key plot point in the extended, multi-issue, multisite social drama that is the long running contest over nuclear power in the United States (Erikson 1994; Gamson and Modigliani 1989; Walker 2004). The entire Clinton presidency can be thought of in this way, too. As Jason Mast (2012) shows, high-visibility individual events, such as Clinton's denial of sex with Monica Lewinsky or his emotive vow to seek retribution on the Oklahoma City bombing terrorists, are not really self-contained social dramas at all. Rather, they are dramatic episodes in a wider story of Clinton's rise and fall. Whether or not we like Bill Clinton, whether or not we think of him as a crook or a savior, we share recognition of this bigger story. Dramas frequently connect to others in turn as interpreters seek their ultimate meaning. So interest in Clinton is linked to that relating to the ultimate significance and consequences of the social upheavals of the 1960s (Smith 2012; Townsley 2001); or of America as a zone of "culture wars"; or of those relating to gender politics. It is no accident that Clinton's critics, such as Pat Buchanan, often spoke of his "Woodstock values." A single epithet like this can activate a complex semiotic sequence – and it makes sense precisely because it taps silently and efficiently into the broader narrative that "everybody knows." But note that although millions of citizens within the United States might share a deep or intuitive sense of these events as long-standing dramas and be able to insert particular news items into them, they still disagree on their implications. Most think that the civil rights movement was a great thing, but some feel it produced overreach in areas like affirmative action, welfare, and school bussing. President Clinton, of course, remains much admired and much reviled. Nuclear power might save us from climate change or provide a supplemental environmental catastrophe, as it did at Fukushima, Japan.

The understanding that social dramas entail collective memory and semiotic switching can be easily extended to natural risks. Cottle (2012) convincingly shows that these are subject to ritualized, mediatized narration, but he also tends to focus on each as an isolated dramatic episode. We feel there is more to it than this. Disasters are always compared to each other. They can also cluster and combine to form dense mythologies extending forward through time. West and Smith (1997), for example, show that drought discourses in Australia have remained constant for more than one hundred years and have a formulaic quality. People claim each one is the worst ever; assert that idle city dwellers have no understanding of tough rural realities; cry out that solidarity is needed; and so forth. This is a ritualized response. More interesting is the fact that droughts are woven into the fabric of the national imagination, as is the realization that they are recurrent. They confirm self-understandings of Australia as a land of pioneer struggle, or of marginality and rugged manliness. Put another way, each individual drought provides fuel for the renewal of myth and is interpreted, in part, in terms of the ongoing, serial narration of the nation. It is one episode connected to many others in the slow-burning social drama that entails conquest of nature, the decline of the bush, and the precarious quality of life in the Antipodes. This tale is not simply told in everyday life in the manner of Norgaard's Norwegian informants. Rather, West and Smith show it circulates and is reproduced in the civil discourse of the Australian public sphere – in letters to the editor, in editorials, in public gatherings, in cartoons and political speeches.

If social dramas are shared and are all around us, some questions follow: What exactly do we find in them? What should the analyst be looking for? Here the Turnerian tradition seems strangely wanting in theoretical resources. His theory captures a sense of turmoil, possibility, and shared emotion. Yet it is also curiously similar to crowd psychology theory when contrasted to his other, more semiotic work. Turner's social drama theory is surprisingly devoid of useful tools and analytic strategies for unpacking the grammars of culture.

Other than Turner, the two most relevant efforts to theorize social life as a dramatic activity have come from Erving Goffman (1959) and Jeffrey Alexander (2004). Grounded in microsociology, Goffman suggests that everyday life consists of shallow and instrumental performances where individuals present idealized or preferred versions of themselves or play to their expected social roles (for more critique, see the end of this chapter). Alexander, for his part, emerges from the cultural sociology perspective and is far more attentive to public-sphere dynamics, moral choices, and symbolic environments of action. He suggests that effective performance is a central part of social life and that agents attempt to fuse themselves with circulating myths. Politics, for Alexander, consists of performances and counterperformances in which individual and collective actors attempt to embody the sacred and discredit their opponents. He has persuasively applied this perspective to the civil rights movement, the events of 9/11, the election of Barack Obama, and the Arab Spring in Egypt. Although Alexander's theory takes us much of the way toward an understanding of contemporary public performance, our belief is that a return to the origin of dramatic and performative theory might offer new tools and so move us further away from familiar ways of seeing. The Aristotelian tradition helps sociology address a core challenge: connecting cultural pragmatics to a structural understanding of culture.

Like Alexander, Geertz, and Goffman, we find a crucial directional clue in the work of Kenneth Burke, the literary theorist and rhetorician. In his social theory of "dramatism," Burke (1945, 1950) suggested that language and symbolic systems were important not only in literature but also in everyday life. He argued that they shaped perceptions (the "terministic screen") and generated a sense of emotional connection or solidarity (what he termed "identification") and hence influenced policies and outcomes. In formulating this brilliant and (then) original stance, Burke drew heavily on Aristotle and wrote as a philosopher of language influenced by pragmatism. So in what follows, we turn also to this source. Our next task is to ask how this ancient Greek thinker might be reconciled with the contemporary cultural–sociological approach to social drama – one that looks to public narrative and to the civil sphere and that is informed by the legacies of structuralism, mid-range social theory, and empirical sociological research over a range of domains.

The fundamentals of staged drama were identified in Aristotle's *Poetics* some thousands of years ago, but his systematic cultural models have only rarely been used in sustained ways in sociological analysis (for exceptions, see Baker 2014; Jacobs 2000; Smith 2005). Aristotle's great achievement was to demonstrate that every (staged) drama must contain certain predictable relationships, themes, and elements.[4] These are universal.

- There are actors who are protagonists, antagonists, and witnesses. Usually these are individual humans ("the objects of imitation are men in action" [II, 1]). However, they can also be groups or something more abstract, such as the city-state.
- These actors have motivations to act. These propel the drama forward. So can acts of chance and divine intervention. In comic genres, the agents are somehow "less than us," whereas in tragic ones, they seem to be "greater than us."
- The drama takes place in a location and at a specific time with a specific set of circumstances at hand. This offers a stage for events that marks it out as distinctive, offering color but also often constraining opportunities for action. For example, a character on an island might not be able to leave without a boat.
- There is a plot or "story" that moves forward through time ("by plot I here mean the arrangement of the incidents" [VI, 6]). Events are not reversible. In the course of this plot, the fortune, luck, influence, prestige, and power of characters will rise or fall. Indeed the chief source of interest in a drama is often the turning point at which this happens.

---

[4] There are many English translations of the *Poetics*. We rely on the venerable translation by Samuel Henry Butcher ([1902] 1998), which is freely available online.

- Plots fall out in genres, these being marked by emotional registers, action motivations, and character trajectories. Aristotle spoke especially of comedy and tragedy. Comedic genres tend to be optimistic and to culminate in pro-social outcomes. The tragic genre suggests that life is deeply serious. It hints that human actors are powerless or misguided and that events are driven by a cruel fate that they cannot control. Tragic narratives tend to end in social fragmentation.
- Not all points in a drama are equally important. Aristotle suggested we pay special attention to pivotal moments where intense change happens. He developed two concepts to capture this. *Peripeteia* involves a turning point or reversal of fortunes. This is the moment in which the status quo for a character is overturned. For example, the protagonist might become poor instead of rich or sick instead of healthy. *Anagnorisis* often accompanies *peripeteia*. The term refers to moments of recognition where the protagonist learns something new about herself, about her character or her relationship to others in a play.
- There is an audience. Actors play to this audience. In the classical Aristotelian formulation the audience becomes intensely involved in the drama through an emotional rather than an intellectual or rational connection. By mobilizing the emotions of pity and terror, the drama can help the audience attain what he termed *catharsis* and emotional balance.
- There are onlooking experts, critics, and analysts, such as Aristotle himself. These figures make public evaluations and offer second-order interpretations that can be influential. Aristotle, for example, was an advocate of the playwright Sophocles.

We will find the same elements in a social drama. Clearly a social drama as deployed by contemporary sociology[5] is not the same as an item of classical Greek theatre. There we had defined events (a play) that had

---

[5] For recent theoretical elaborations on the theme of social drama, see the contributions by Alexander, Alexander and Mast, Mast, and Reed in Alexander, Giesen, and Mast (2006). See also Alexander (2011), Cottle (2004), and McFarland (2004). The most influential statement in sociology is still Wagner-Pacifici (1986). In cultural anthropology, Turner's ideas have largely fallen by the wayside, although they still exert a strong influence in performance studies (see, e.g., Schechner 2003). For the most comprehensive and detailed overview of Turner's contribution to performance theory across a range of fields, see St. John (2008). The concept of social drama has essentially no currency in environmental studies. For an important exception, see Christine Walley's (2004) excellent ethnography of the Mafia Island marine park in Tanzania, which treats environmental conflict as a form of social drama.

scripted outcomes. There were clear boundaries between players, audience, and critics. The entire event took place within an evening in a setting marked off from ordinary social life: the theatre. People collaborate in the enterprise as performers and audiences. With a social drama, things are different. Crucially, the drama is part of social life, not partitioned from it and requiring any suspension of disbelief. The social drama may be ongoing and without current resolution. It will involve improvisation and conflict. There might be deliberate efforts to "be dramatic" and gain public sympathy and attention or to "avoid drama" and get down to business. We might find a complex layering of genres, with romantic and solidaristic actions narrated for some contexts (a new solar array for an indigenous community) at the same time as a tragic one in other (yet another failed climate conference, despite the best of intentions). Audiences might participate intensively, but they might also have a range of involvement. Some will be highly engaged by the issues, some voyeuristic, others bemused. The conditions of spectatorship are also distinctive. No longer copresent with performers, audiences are distant witnesses to events relayed to them by the mass media. As with reading the movie reviews or the gossip pages, representations and critiques of performances and actions – a distant speech, a German advertising campaign, a fraught all-night conference session on another continent – may well be a more important source of cultural influence than direct personal observation. Further narrative processes related to politics, the media, and intellectual entrepreneurship will frame some events as relevant to a drama and others as outside of it. Nevertheless, the most basic point of commonality holds: *the world of public affairs is very much one that is constructed by players, narrated by observers, and read by audiences in a dramatic mode* (Mast 2006, 2012). What is more, people intuitively know this. From deep socialization they have a familiarity with the culture structures of the dramatic form, applying these in the effort to make sense of the world. The structures identified by Aristotle as lying at the core of Greek drama also shape the way we read events and identify and narrate a social drama. Ideas about events as tragic and comedic, ideas about heroes and villains, ideas about chance and fate, the ever-present possibility for *pertipeteia* and *anagnorisis*, run through our culture. These elementary forms simplify reality and exert persuasive force as they shape both interpretation and cultural production at various social levels.

What does this all mean for climate change? As we have intimated, this is not simply a natural process, nor just a matter of scientific communication and (faulty) risk perception, but also an ongoing, interpreted saga. Scientists and environmentalists often bemoan the fact that citizens do not understand the facts of climate science, the range of policy options, and the problems of collective action. But in truth, society already understands climate change – and in a profoundly consequential way. It is the drama of a contested claim. Like the political trope of "the Sixties" explored by Townsley, the environmental trope of climate change compresses and organizes a messy, complex range of meanings into a definite space and time. Regardless of the extent to which any particular member of the public believes in or even particularly cares about anthropogenic climate change, pretty much everyone will know that it is a competition between two camps for interpretative and political power. It may be largely "background noise" for many (Norgaard 2011), but even they know that there are problems of collective action; that there are treaties that might be formed or fall apart; that there is a gap between activist hopes and real-world outcomes; and that claims about planetary doom are made by some and shrugged off by others. This battle–struggle–contest is the social drama as it is experienced and configured in the lifeworld of mass media consumption and everyday conversation. Within this larger drama are a number of characters with their own narrative arcs. They struggle for attention, make claims, and represent battling perspectives. They are performers whose actions are subject to critique and evaluation. They are people like Al Gore, various leading environmentalists and climate scientists such as James Hansen, organizations like the IPCC, noted skeptics like Nigel Lawson and Michael Crichton, and rogue theorists like Bjorn Lomborg. Their fortunes rise and fall. Climate change can even be thought of as a character itself. Sometimes it is narrated as struggling for recognition – it is a victim in need of help. At other times it looks to be a winner gaining attention and resources. Sometimes it is a bully squeezing out critical discourse and overshadowing more pressing problems. Although the social drama of climate change bubbles along, specific settings and episodes, such as climate conferences, advertising campaigns, scandals, and major new reports from scientists, offer spaces for dramatic intensification, for the identification of *peripeteia* and *anagnorisis*. At such junctures, critics and commentators frequently offer metacommentaries on "what is working," reflecting on the failures of performers and audiences alike. Such reconstructions may or may not be accurate in all their details. Nevertheless, they are effective in shaping public perceptions, motivations, and collective emotions and so are deserving of study.

Plot, Character, and Rhetoric

We have outlined how Turner's view of social drama and Aristotle's *Poetics* can be used for thinking about climate change as this manifests in the public sphere. In what follows we add two intellectual complications to the model. The first of these relates to the availability of romance as a genre-option. It also flags the significant weight placed in contemporary culture on the ethical being and causal force of choice-making individuals. We introduce the second complication in five paragraphs from here.

For Aristotle, tragedy was a serious art form and comedy a more trivial and purely entertaining one. In their original formulations, neither of these provides an attractive template for climate activism, and neither quite captures the narrative structures that we find in activist social movement politics today (see Jacobs and Smith 1997). Tragedy in the ancient Greek mode is never much of an option for mobilization as it keys to fatalism. Whatever we try to do is liable to be undone by the Gods or the absolute power of destiny. A plot anticipating unintended consequences and pointing toward futility does not encourage sacrifice for a cause and collective action but rather the kind of apathy that in the context of climate change leads to conventional, carbon-hungry lifestyles. Aristotelian comedy, meanwhile, suggests that everything will turn out fine in the end regardless of our idiocy and that high motivations (e.g., environmentalist values) are merely our cover for base ones (e.g., getting elected). Again, this is a message to carry on as usual that is rarely seen in serious public discussion. Instead of these nonoptions, climate change activists generally deploy instead the kind of humanist, post-Renaissance reworking of both these genres that we see in other social issue contexts. These depict human effort and choices as pivotal to outcomes rather than the actions of Gods or the cruel twists of fate.

Hegel benchmarked this shift better than any other theorist. Looking to Antigone rather than to Aristotle's beloved Oedipus as the sine qua non of the tragic form, in *Phenomenology of the Spirit*, Hegel suggests that the essence of tragedy lies not in the triumph of a supernatural fate over human will but rather in choice within a difficult situation. The Greek tragic hero, for Hegel, is caught between ethical codes (e.g., duty to the law vs. duty to family) and must knowingly make the choice between them that will bring inevitable negative consequences. This interpretation of the dramatic form in antiquity differs from Aristotle's emphasis on divine intervention, chance, and natural law. It can be considered symptomatic in and of itself as an indicator of a growing sensitivity in modernity to agency and free will in plot. In his later lectures on aesthetics, Hegel goes even further. Here he argues that passions and psychological drivers rather than ethics and divine intervention are pivotal in post-Renaissance drama. He observes with unusual precision a decisive, empirically observable split between the tragic genre of antiquity and that of modernity. Antigone, it turns out, was just an outlying forerunner of a major cultural shift. As Hegel (1975, 1225) puts it, "in modern tragedy" the character is not even driven by ends, whether ideal or material; rather, "what presses for satisfaction is the subjectivity of their heart and mind and the privacy of their own character." In short, the search for inner resolution determines outer events. Consequently, there is heightened attention given to barriers against self-actualization and individuality. Whereas the tragic figures of antiquity represented or embodied ethical positions, they lacked a certain plasticity and psychological depth. In the modern drama – and here Hegel refers mostly to Shakespeare, Schiller, and Goethe – they are rounded sovereign individuals. Even when marked by a dominant character trait that leads to their downfall (jealousy for Othello, indecision for Hamlet, ambition for Macbeth, etc.), the tragic protagonist's internal complexity offers her a perpetual capacity for choice. Now tragedy arises due to action and inaction relative to moral and ethical challenges as these impact on an imperfect and fragmented self. People are responsible for misfortune. Goaded by Iago, a reluctant Othello acts on his perception; Hamlet does not act decisively and the moment is gone; Macbeth vacillates even as he chooses the more evil option time and time again. Likewise in a contemporary social drama – whether on climate change or any other matter – these themes of choice and personality come to the fore. They are deeply imprinted into the dramatic common sense through which we moderns both produce and read public personalities and public events.

The same emphasis on intentional actions and their profound consequences for plot in the modern tragedy can also be found with literary descendants of the comedic genres that Aristotle also analyzed. Of particular relevance here is the fictional mode dubbed "comic romance" or sometimes just "romance" by its most perceptive and influential analyst, Northrop Frye. In romance, a hero goes through a series of adventures, performing exceptional feats and struggling toward victory (Frye 1957, 33, 36–37; 1976, 65–93). Though human, the romantic hero derives his power "from a current of energy which is partly from him and partly outside him" (Frye 1976, 67), moving through a world in which the ordinary laws of nature are "slightly suspended" (Frye 1957, 33). Romance is the stuff of folktales and legends, and in its comic variants, its end is social integration. According to Frye (1976, 68), the literary model of comic romance is the *Odyssey*: a hero returns home after years of dangerous exile, restoring social and natural order. If the overarching theme of Aristotelian comedy is the spontaneous integration of society (Frye 1957, 43), then we might say that the theme of "comic romance" is a heroic struggle for reintegration. This struggle is progressive. Whereas tragedies are about the isolation of a hero from society (or social disintegration), and comedy about the reproduction of stability in existing society, the romance is about the movement from one kind of society to another, with the new form crystallizing around the form and works of the hero (Frye 1957, 163). The creation of this new society is often accompanied by some kind of ritual of reintegration – a wedding, a banquet, and so on – which Frye describes as an "act of communion" with the audience (164). In modern democratic politics, the importance of comic romance cannot be overstated. Without it, most social movements could not exist – or at least they would not know how to describe their mission (indeed, Frye 1976, 77, himself suggested that "an element of social protest is inherent in romance"). Performing in the romantic mode, activists can engender belief in their cause and its possibilities for success, bootstrap feel-good emotions, foster solidarity, and overcome free rider problems (Jacobs and Smith 1997). At its heart, comedy entails a movement toward the real and the good – a movement "from one social center to another not unlike the action of a lawsuit, in which plaintiff and defendant construct different versions of the same situation, one finally being judged as real and the other as illusory" (Frye 1957, 166). Yet unlike high-mimetic heroes, who move in an all-too-human world of social conflict and political intrigue, romantic heroes have access to enchantment. One might say their job is to reenchant the social.

Although conventional Aristotelian readings of comedy and tragedy may well play a small part in metacommentaries about climate change (e.g., fatalistic or lampooning op-eds), the objective of activists is to encourage identification by deploying the cultural structures of post-Enlightenment times we have just been discussing. They suggest that tragedy is a hypothetical future outcome that can only arise if bad choices are made by complex, sovereign decision-making individuals, these agents ranging from world leaders to ordinary citizens. Only if we embrace romance and its associated world-transforming, solidaristic opportunities can we avoid a hot, unjust, and dangerous future. Skeptics and neutrals can set back this storytelling through a process of genre deflation

(Smith 2005) characterized by realist and satiric frames like those of the comedy of Aristotle's time. These prick the balloon of portentous solidarity by suggesting (1) that nothing much is at stake, (2) that the major actors are misguided buffoons, (3) that the problem will solve itself, or (4) that it does not exist. In sum, Aristotle offers clues but not all the answers for our interrogation of culture structures within our social drama.

Our first complication, then, was that the model of drama provided in *Poetics* did not fully recognize the impact of humanism nor the rise of romance in place of the satirical comedy as the preeminent genre for solidaristic expression. Our second complication comes from within Aristotle's own oeuvre and is intended to provide a better understanding of social performance. We pursue this for the next several pages.

The Greek philosopher offered his *Poetics* as a theoretical treatise, critical appreciation, and "how-to" handbook on staged drama. In other words, it is a work of literary criticism concerning a shared and consensual fantasy enterprise. It understands genre as a quality of plot and character and identifies the conventions of both of these. Yet to more fully understand how argument plays out in the confrontational public sphere, we need a different Aristotelian resource, his *Rhetoric*.[6] There is a simple reason for this. Effective staged drama of the kind explored in the *Poetics* involves the actor becoming fully someone else. In the public sphere, effective performance generally involves speaking as oneself, and deeply so. Aristotle was the first great thinker to systematically interrogate and parse this truth, and so in the *Rhetoric* we find yet more tools for exploring dramatic interventions in public life.

Although climate change advocacy works in a variety of speech genres, the one that is most central to its social drama is that which Aristotle terms "political oratory." This has a proscriptive and future orientation. As Aristotle puts it:

Political speaking urges us either to do or not to do something: one of these two courses is always taken by private counselors, as well as by men who address public assemblies.... The political orator aims at establishing the expediency or the harmfulness of a proposed course of action; if he urges its acceptance, he does

---

[6] We rely on two standard translations of Aristotle's *Rhetoric*, Roberts (1954), the most readable, and Kennedy (2007), the most scholarly. All quotations are from Roberts unless otherwise noted. This translation is in the public domain and is widely available online. Other social scientists have drawn on Aristotelian rhetoric to make sense of climate debates (Malone 2009) and sphere-specific climate politics (Roald and Sangolt 2012), but to the best of our knowledge, ours is the first study of climate change to mine his work in an extensive and systematic way.

so on the ground that it will do good; if he urges its rejection, he does so on the ground that it will do harm; and all other points, such as whether the proposal is just or unjust, honorable or dishonorable, he brings in as subsidiary and relative to this main consideration. (1.3.1358b)

We hardly need point out that the social drama of climate change is one that is replete with speakers urging action and occasionally inaction. Dramatic tension emerges around the questions, Will listeners be persuaded? Will they act? And of the speaker, How well did she perform? Such performances, regardless of who is speaking, are evaluated in terms of their capacity to exert oratorical force and to bring about change – or at least signs of change. Although often mined as a brilliant source of observations on microlevel linguistic strategies in debating and practical reason (syllogism, metaphor, praise, quotation, the use of maxims, etc.), for our purposes the more interesting insights of the *Rhetoric* as to what makes for effective persuasion concern not arguments but character. For Aristotle, this was absolutely fundamental to effective public speaking. And as we see later in this book, the narration of character is pivotal to climate change drama. For whether or not she is making a direct attempt at persuasion, the character of an individual somehow stands as a marker of the truth of her ideas.

Persuasion and the Centrality of Character

Just how does this happen? Aside from *logos* (speech or logical argument – the sort of thing that scientists do in their reports), Aristotle identified two other and more influential components of successful rhetoric: *pathos* (or audience sympathy) and *ethos* (the moral character of the speaker). As Aristotle (1.2.4) puts it:

Persuasion is achieved by the speaker's personal character when the speech is so spoken as to make us think him credible. We believe good men more fully and more readily than others: this is true generally whatever the question is, and absolutely true where exact certainty is impossible and opinions are divided.... It is not true, as some writers assume in their treatises on rhetoric, that the personal goodness revealed by the speaker contributes nothing to his power of persuasion; on the contrary, his character may almost be called the most effective means of persuasion he possesses. (1.2.1356a)

It is the combination of these dimensions, the performative fusion of *logos* with *pathos* and *ethos*, that explains why audiences would spontaneously stand and applaud after screenings of Al Gore's *Inconvenient Truth* (see Chapter 4). And it is the inability to fuse these dimensions that explains why so many other attempts to communicate climate change have fallen flat. Indeed, following Aristotle, we might argue that in the case of climate change – a case "where exact certainty is impossible and opinions are divided," if ever one existed – character can be the decisive factor in cultural performance. In this social drama, *logos* and *pathos* arguably exist in abundance. *Ethos*, however, is in short supply. Let's explore this further.

Classicist George Kennedy (1984, 15) defines *ethos* as "the credibility that the author or speaker is able to establish in his work." In Aristotelian theory, *ethos* inheres entirely within speech and is not produced by reputation or social position. Our view is more sociological; we believe that cultural expectations about character type clearly play a crucial role in shaping audience response. Credibility is a performative achievement, but its ingredients are unevenly distributed. Expertise, celebrity, and charismatic authority matter. Money matters. Yet despite these rather obvious positional restrictions, *ethos* is never predetermined and cannot simply be bought. As we will see, authority to speak on climate change can be claimed in various ways. Within the climate denial movement, for example, physicists with little or no background in climate science have become powerful arbiters of scientific truth (Lahsen 2008; Oreskes and Conway 2010). At the opposite extreme, journalists and celebrities often have more prestige than the scientists whose work they champion (Anderson 2011). We note this not in a spirit of skepticism but simply to show that *ethos* is a complex coproduction of established roles and performative prowess. As Wagner-Pacifici (1986, 7) puts it, "the protagonists of the 'social drama' respond to and clothe themselves in their culture's stock of sedimented symbols, archetypal characters, and rhetorical appeals." Working with these tools, virtuosic performers can manipulate and even transcend the expectations of their audience.

From an Aristotelian perspective, credibility and morality are inseparable. To seem credible, Aristotle says, speakers must exhibit three qualities: practical wisdom or good sense (*phronesis*), virtue or moral character (*arête*), and good will (*eunoia*) (2.1.1378a). Without wisdom, we cannot trust speakers to form correct opinions or behave sensibly regardless of how lovable and well intentioned they are. Without virtue we cannot trust them to be honest about their opinions and engage in pro-social self-denial. Without goodwill we cannot trust they have our interests at heart (2.1.1378a). Speakers produce goodwill through their practical knowledge of the emotions; indeed, it is through *eunoia* that the passions enter Aristotelian rhetoric (Garver 1994, 110). Whereas virtue and practical wisdom are characteristics of the speaker as such, goodwill is a "relational property of the speaker relative to an audience" (Garver 1994, 111), and it is forged through the experience of shared emotion – pity, fear, confidence, and so forth. These emotions are not optional add-ons or dirty tricks. On the contrary, they are essential to collective judgment and rational deliberation. As the philosopher Eugene Garver explains, "being too logical and therefore not ethical is a danger specific to the art of rhetoric. . . . Reason can drive out *ethos*" (177, 178). Aristotle was acutely aware of the rhetorical dangers posed by excessive rationality. He was the first person to note an interesting paradox: demonstrations of inescapable logic can actually *undermine* trust.

For Aristotle, pertinent virtues include justice, courage, self-control, magnificence, magnanimity, liberality, gentleness, prudence, and wisdom (1.9.1366b). With an issue such as climate change, where hard evidence and analysis (*logos*) are supposed to be what matters, these virtues might seem immaterial. Who cares if the IPCC or Exxon Mobil are magnanimous? As it turns out, everyone cares, and quite deeply, too. Because climate change has become a metanarrative about the future of global society – a symbol of everything from food security to spiritual salvation (Hulme 2009) – *who* "speaks for the climate" matters tremendously (Boykoff 2011). Even in its low-mimetic incarnations, climate change is inescapably eschatological. It embodies our deepest hopes and fears about the direction of history. Echoing Ulrich Beck's visions of reflexive modernity superseding the "zombie categories" of modernist sociology, the anthropologist Steve Rayner goes so far as to suggest that climate change "has become the key narrative within which political issues from the local to the global are framed," replacing "capital and social class as the organizing theme of political discourse in contemporary society" (Rayner 2009, xxiii). This may be true in Oxford, England, but it is certainly not true in Oxford, Mississippi. Yet the character of climate communicators probably matters more in Mississippi, and precisely because there uncertainty about climate change is far greater than in the cloisters of Headington stone.

When *logos* and *pathos* are contested, *ethos* comes to the fore. For example, it is no accident that in America, where religious faith is seemingly required for full membership in civil society (Weber [1906] 2009), activists on both sides have sought the imprimatur of the pulpit. Gore is just one of many environmentalists who have bent over backward to display their Christian bona fides. He is also just one of many to be branded as a religious fanatic by the Christian Right – or, in the memorable words of Texas governor Rick Perry, "a false prophet of a secular carbon cult" (Shear 2011). As we explain later, this is no category error. Gore's prophetic *ethos* has been carefully crafted and contested.

If underplayed, the importance of character has not been entirely lost on climate change researchers. However, it is typically used as short-hand for psychological type, not performing persona. Anthropologists working with Mary Douglas's grid-group paradigm have long used char-acter as an analytic device by dividing the social world into ideal types: hierarchists, egalitarians, individualists, and fatalists. Aligned with the cornucopian–catastrophist dualism popular since the 1970s (Cotgrove 1982), this schema has produced an ever-more elaborate typology of environmental attitudes (Rayner and Thompson 1998; Thompson, Ellis, and Wildavsky 1990). There are problems here. Empirically, this picture simply does not hold up, especially not in the United States. Many of the players in the longer drama of American environmental politics break these molds in multiple ways, from Thoreau the libertarian romantic to Wendell Berry the evangelical communitarian to Richard Nixon the right-wing environmental regulator.

In science studies, the notion of *ethos* is most familiar from Robert Merton's (1973) famous norms of universalism, communalism, disinter-estedness, and skepticism. His scientific *ethos* was "an emotionally toned complex of rules, prescriptions, mores, beliefs, values and presupposi-tions which are held to be binding upon the scientist" (258n15; on). In the so-called strong program of science and technology studies (STS) and its various offshoots, trust and credibility are even more fundamen-tal. With his seminal history of scientific truth in seventeenth-century England, Steven Shapin (1994) shows how scientists won trust through the performance of gentlemanly honor. In studies of scientific decision making in the present day, scholars such as Brian Wynne and Sheila Jasanoff have repeatedly shown how trust in scientists shapes delibera-tion over environmental risk, including deliberations over climate change (e.g., Jasanoff and Wynne 1998; Wynne 1980, 2010; see also Demeritt 2001; Yearley 1999). For this branch of science studies, it would not be too much to claim, with Shapin (1995, 257–258), that "credibility should not be referred to as a 'fundamental' or 'central' topic . . . [but as] the *only* topic." And as Shapin (2004) has recently argued, trust in experts is not just about expertise; it also has a deeply moral dimension. To be cred-ible, scientists must persuade their audiences (both other scientists and the public) not only that they know what they are talking about but also that they are well intentioned and trying "to do the right thing" (Shapin 2004, 48). In Aristotelian terms, they must display *arête* and *eunoia*.

When the limits of scientific knowledge are in question, "credibility contests" develop (Gieryn 1999). In the case of climate change, the allocation of epistemic authority – in this case, to represent the massively complex and largely invisible workings of the climate – thus hinges not on credentials but on moral boundary work. Again, "in cases where there is not exact knowledge but room for doubt," *ethos* is everything. This is not just true of climate change. As the rhetorician Carolyn Miller (2003) argues, Aristotelian rhetorical theory suggests that in conflict over environmental risks more generally, *ethos* runs the show. Yet, as Miller notes, the moral character of risk analysis is systematically denied in the language games of scientific controversies. Virtue and goodwill are subsumed by technical expertise, *phronēsis* by *episteme* (Miller 2003). Hence an overly rationalistic faith in the wisdom of experts has become the norm in deliberations on risk. It is no wonder that so few people know whom to trust.

Although we draw on these ideas from science and technology studies, our interest in character is far more ecumenical. We wish to examine the *ethoi* of a broad range of actors within the broader attention space defined by climate change: politicians, celebrities, journalists, religious leaders, artists, and even nature itself. STS scholars are primarily concerned with the construction and contestation of scientific knowledge. They want to understand how trust and credibility are generated in a very specific domain of social relations (universities, labs, advisory bodies). This matters to us, too, but we are also interested in the way "trust" is narrated and performed as part of a wider climate drama. We follow the sociologist of science Brian Wynne (2004) in treating "trust" and "credibility" as analytical artifacts that are themselves subject to reflexive narration – not objective cognitive states but social facts that belong in quotation marks. We part ways, however, in seeing these artifacts relevant far beyond the cultural domain and institutional field of science (Sztompka 2007). In important ways, the social drama of climate change that people actually get to see is a story *about* trust. In this sense, it is a story not just about science or nature but about how we know *whom* to believe – artists? politicians? children?

Such a reflexive dimension with its intimations of spectatorship marks a crucial difference between Turner's theory of social drama and the dramaturgical approach of Erving Goffman. Whereas Goffman treated the entire world of social interaction as a domain of gamelike, ritualistic performance, Turner looked at crises or ruptures in the flow of mundane life. Moreover, Goffman saw the theatre of life as something experienced by individuals in strategic face-to-face interaction. For Turner, a drama could also be something overheard and observed from a distance. It enabled society to criticize itself. "Thus," as Turner (1988, 76) puts it, "if daily living is a kind of theatre, social drama is a kind of metatheatre." This does not mean that the two approaches are utterly irreconcilable. Goffmanian interaction rituals may serve as "microlevel guideposts" for actors in social dramas (McFarland 2004, 1250), cuing performances and presenting opportunities for improvisatory redirection. In the world of science, they allow actors to present themselves as trustworthy and credible, both to their colleagues (Shapin 1994) and to broader publics (Hilgartner 2000). Yet they cannot explain how complex, multiscaled, mediatized dramas such as climate change are configured into meaningful narrative wholes. Nor can Goffman's (1959) bleak vision of drama (which Geertz 1983, 24, described as "ping-pong in masks") tells us about the cultural reflexivity of climate change, its capacity to dramatize profound moral and political dilemmas and for those dramatizations to themselves be subject to meta-critique.

An isolated precedent for this position can be found in a one-off essay by the sociologist Ingar Palmlund, "Social Drama and Risk Evaluation," which draws on Douglas, Turner, and Wagner-Pacifici. Written two decades ago, Palmlund's analysis was amazingly prescient. Yet it made only a small dent in studies of risk or social drama, with only sixty-three citations on Google Scholar at the time of writing (some twenty-two years after initial publication). According to Palmlund (1992, 199), "societal evaluation of risk must be seen as a contest, where the participants offer competing views of reality" and where statements about risk serve to build solidarity. Palmlund stresses the central importance of scripted roles in social controversies over risk, especially the roles of "risk bearer" and "risk generator," whose opposing interests generate dramatic tension. She aligns Turner's four diachronic phases of public action (breach, crisis, redressive action, and reintegration/schism) with the conventional phases of risk (identification, assessment, and management) as well as dramatic categories of exposition, complication, crisis, and denouement (207). Breach is initiated by a sudden hazard or accident (Three Mile Island, Bhopal) or new scientific findings (Thalidomide, DDT). In crisis, "attitudes are peeled away to lay bare the underlying values and interests. The crisis appears as a menacing presence in the center of public life itself, challenging the representatives of order, who may wish to ignore it or wish it away, to confront it" (208). Distinguishing between social tragedy and social melodrama, Palmlund claims in a strongly Durkheimian vein that "our interest in social controversy over technological risk may well be a reproduction in modern social settings of earlier generations' anxiety, pity, and excitement surrounding the sacrifice of individuals to further the strength of the group" (212).

This all seems very promising. Yet Palmlund aims too low in terms of ambition at the same time as she sets the bar too high in terms of definition. She continues to work with a restrictive, conventional definition of social drama that excludes certain diffuse and temporally extended phenomena from investigation. So climate change does not make it to the starting gate for dramatic analysis. For Palmlund the problem is that, in this case, breach is not sudden and catastrophic but an abstract pronouncement by social elites. It comes into the public realm as a consequence of "strategic planning," not as a drama "driven by fear and pity." "No victims can be shown. No strongly emotional appeals are associated with the breach. No injured group steps forward with demands or even threats to the establishment" (208). We disagree with this assessment, and not only on the theoretical grounds we laid out earlier in this chapter, as we argued for an expansive view of the social drama. Today at least, a visit to any climate conference will show these claims are also inaccurate. Agents relentlessly engage in dramatic gestures that pluck emotional and social justice chords. More interestingly, the very struggle to find appealing victims, identify villains, increase emotional intensity, and make demands for redress on behalf of nature are part of the drama itself at the level of metanarration. There is much discussion of gambits, representations, and strategy – the rise and fall, success and failure of initiatives in particular and climate change solidarity in general. Palmlund's work did not provoke a serious or sustained response. We are starting afresh by reimagining social drama in more expansive and empirically robust terms.

To offer clarity to readers, earlier we summed up Aristotle's *Poetics* with bullet points. These captured the things we might expect to see in our social drama of climate change – a plot, characters, turning points, and so forth. We are now in a position to do the same for the necessary complications we have added over the past several pages.

- The genre of romance will also be present as a narrative possibility. Themes for debate here will be ideas of cooperation, progress, and solidarity. Romantic narratives will focus on the need to overcome barriers and tests of resolve to build a better world.
- A great emphasis will be placed on the capacity of agents to make choices, the difficulty of these choices, and their causal significance within a wider plot. Commentary will focus on the quality of choices

that are made, for example, whether they are good or bad for advancing the cause of climate change activism and what they reveal about inner character.

- Characters making claims on behalf of climate change will be evaluated not so much in terms of the accuracy of their technical claims but rather on their honor, sincerity, selflessness, wisdom, and capacity to generate positive sentiments in onlookers. A critically acclaimed performance will signal these things and will often be tethered to a romantic genre-outcome.

So climate change enters public life not as a set of scientific facts but rather as a set of collective representations replete with genre, plot, characters with particular attributes, and performative actions that are worthy or unworthy. In the next chapter, we focus on the first of these and show how it is a useful resource for organizing a cultural history of climate change as it emerged as a social drama. We show that representations are structured by genre. In a diagnostic mode, we also suggest that these are linked in turn to risk perceptions and to the relative failure of calls for action.

3

Narrating Global Warming

Scientists usually think of climate change as a material process that requires technology if it is to be understood. With thermometers, satellite systems, weather balloons, and consequent computer modeling, they can come to terms with the chemical and physical process through which the planet heats up. They can measure and predict shifts in rainfall, in extreme weather, and in glacial ice distributions. Scholars involved in political science and social policy analysis look closely at practical human responses to risks. For example, they might explore resource conflicts or the impact of initiatives designed to down our harmful emissions. In the previous chapter we set out another way of seeing climate change. This is to take it not only as the product and producer of social outcomes but also as a meaningful social fact. Climate change is something more than a process involving molecules, energies, oceanic currents and solar radiation, human impacts upon nature, and policy responses. It is also a complex cultural field. To make sense of this qualitatively different, non-material dimension of its existence, the approach of cultural sociology is needed.

From the perspective of cultural sociology the natural event of climate change is subject to communicative translation via binary codes, deeply grounded myths, parables, images, characters, performances, and rituals. Together they add up to the social drama of climate change in which legitimacy is contested, moral authority gained, and public opinion formed. In this chapter we begin our empirical investigations by giving emphasis to one Aristotelian theme to this process: genre. In his *Poetics* Aristotle achieved a major breakthrough by recognizing and documenting the deep structural similarities that underpin various narratives and that lead them to constitute a recognizable genre. Recent work in cultural sociology has built on this insight in three ways that are crucial to our inquiry. First, it has shown that circulating narratives in the public sphere concerning real-world activity often display the same Aristotelian properties as the staged fictional dramas he decoded. Newsworthy events, crises, and civic traumas, for example, are represented through tragic or comic narrations (Baker 2014; Jacobs 2000; Smith 2005). Second, it has been established that these representations have consequences for legitimacy, public opinion, and civic goodwill. They provide or sap energy, sanctify or pollute, bring fatalistic or optimistic thinking. Third, it has been established that genre plays a crucial role in risk perception in times of uncertainty. One might say that it fills in the gaps between isolated facts, actions, and predictions by outlining what is at stake. These three insights come together in the *narrative genre model of risk evaluation*. First developed in the context of wars and foreign policy crises (Smith 2005; see also Ringmar 2006 for an example of theoretical convergence), this offers a systematic and comparative way of looking at the form and structure of storytelling and its consequences for human action. There are several core claims:

1. Uncertain events and real-world facts are "clues." These have little significance in and of themselves. People generally agree on these. They require a "genre guess" to have significance. This guess is vital for the reduction of information complexity, yet it carries with it deep implications for communicative and opinion process.
2. We can see things as low mimetic, romantic, tragic, or apocalyptic. Following Aristotle, the literary theory of Northrop Frye, and others, we can understand each genre as having certain properties. These define the powers of action of players (large or small); likely social outcomes (solidaristic or divisive); appropriate yardsticks for motivation and policy evaluation (pragmatic or business as usual vs. utopian and heroic); and the issues at stake (local and ordinary, or global and epochal).
3. Binary oppositions play a role as building blocks for wider storytelling activity. These are particularly important for marking out good or bad agents within our story or drama.
4. The chosen genre from this cultural repertoire provides a gestalt that retrospectively determines how the clues are put together into a more coherent picture. There is an element of path dependence at work here. Once it has been made, the genre guess works to

close off alternative interpretative possibilities even as it makes the world more meaningful.

5. Some frames escalate perceived risks while others talk them down. Struggles eventuate in which interested parties try to have their stories taken seriously and to falsify or eliminate the stories of others. The combat between frames and their sponsors for interpretative authority is a further important source of social drama. Metanarratives eventuate discussing narrative strategies and speculating on who will prevail.

6. The distribution or adoption of these frames over nations, over time, or over constituencies and interest groups in a civil discourse indirectly shapes political outcomes as well as their timing.

To make this concrete, we can think about war. In the case of the buildup to the 2003 Gulf War, for example, an apocalyptic frame took hold and was promoted in the United States and the United Kingdom. This described Saddam Hussein as a person capable of changing world history, a person of evil motivations, and as a new Hitler who had to be stopped immediately. By contrast, France and other European powers had a low-mimetic narrative in place. This saw the situation in Iraq as containable by means of "business as usual" sanctions, inspections, and diplomacy coordinated by the United Nations (Smith 2005). Fragmented and inconsistent clues about Iraq's "weapons of mass destruction" were seen as believable or as bogus according to the genre guess that was made. Diplomats and intellectuals struggled for interpretative authority over genre within and between nations. Higher-order commentators reflected on these efforts at narrative control in turn, noting the strategies that were used to try to ensure the success of contending visions that preached peril or denounced needless warmongering.

The relevance of such a template to the case of climate change is not something that we need to belabor here. Activists and journalists alike are already aware that this is a context where divergent narratives are fighting for credibility, and that these carry in turn imperatives for action. What theory brings to the table is a certain explanatory distance and conceptual order. The Aristotelian model's specification to a theory of risk perception has relatively close tolerances. It makes knowable in a more reflexive and simple way what everybody knows already. It also provides a tool for a rough and ready history of climate change in which awareness of the problem coincides with institutionalized narrative shifts in representation.

In what follows we sketch out this genre history. But before we do this, some caveats are in order. To say that climate change is storied in patterned or generic ways is not to suggest that everybody has necessarily been paying attention to this story. Nor does it demand that those individuals who do notice find the story compelling. Indeed our argument in this chapter and throughout this book will be that although the social drama of climate change has come into being, it is by no means potent or very well organized as a cultural system. It is a somewhat disorganized drama marked by incoherence, disengagement, and proliferation as much as compression, commitment, and consensus. Our later chapters capture much of these qualities. Here we focus on one particular issue that our reading indicates is pivotal to such dispersed impacts and attenuated force. Put simply, climate change has suffered rather severely from what we might think of as "genre confusion," a confusion that has blocked it from becoming a full-fledged, universal social drama that would compel decisive public action and institutional reform.

Global Warming in the Wilderness

Over the past thirty-odd years, the issues of global warming, climate change, and greenhouse gas emissions have undergone a series of transformations as they entered into public life. First, core concepts have become familiar. They have moved out of the scientific domain and become a commonplace of everyday conversation and even humor. Media sources no longer need to provide little diagrams illustrating the fundamental process, nor provide summaries of key terms, nor put these in quotation marks (e.g., "what scientists are calling the 'greenhouse effect' is caused by levels of the gas carbon dioxide"). Put another way, narrative building blocks have entered the attention space and become cognitively routinized. Second, and despite the environmentalist pushback we note later, there has been a broader narrative shift among political and social elites and within civil discourse toward apocalypticism and away from the low-mimetic forms of narration that once saw the problem as containable with routine policy solutions, or as finger-click solvable by our more technologically advanced descendants. This has translated into a weak sense of crisis and a corresponding ritualized discourse of disappointment at failures to act. Third, there has been a process of sensitization in which more and more aspects of planetary ecology and social experience are tethered in one way or another to this issue cluster. Climate change becomes a sort of master trope for building a comprehensible universe, much as capital and social class once did in the social world (Rayner 2009, xxiii). In the natural world we might make connections so as to explain retreating glaciers, stronger hurricanes, or hotter summers all in one fell swoop. In the same way, individuals now have a new way to think about trading in large SUVs, eating meat, or following up on new gardening and angling possibilities. In governance and social policy, almost every issue has been drawn into the gravitational field of climate change, from national security to regional development to indigenous people's rights. As the discourse of climate change becomes ubiquitous, so do new kinds of ethical subjectivity and behavior come into play as moral yardsticks. We are painting with a broad brush here and admit we are gesturing toward tendencies rather than absolutes. Yet things have undeniably changed. (1) Climate change is socially "visible." (2) It is taken seriously outside of environmentalist and scientific circles and is viewed as a major challenge. (3) It has offered new cultural repertoires and new ways of making sense of the world and ourselves.

Amazingly, none of this was the case just forty years ago. We can see this when we go back and discover that the cultural nexus around climate change that is familiar to us today – the raft of images, anxieties, priorities, gatherings, and exemplary stories that we discuss in this book – was barely in existence. Unlike Marxism, feminism, LGBTQ rights, environmentalism, national identities, personal computing, or most other discursive clusters, the web of meanings surrounding climate change that we have now did not replace any prior edition of itself in public life like some 2.0 reboot that can be captured with the metaphor of waves ("first wave," "second wave," etc.). In recent years it has quite simply come into being. Although people (mostly scientists) had been worrying about the human capacity to influence climate for a very long time, the social drama of climate change had yet to begin.

Until the 1980s, global warming was a sphere-specific issue for a small number of individuals in the scientific community who talked for the most part to each other, sometimes to the governments who funded their research. As historians of climate science have shown, this is a fascinating and culturally complex story in its own right (e.g., Edwards 2010; Fleming 1998; Howe 2014; Weart 2008), some of which has made its way into the contemporary social drama, mostly in the form of prophetic warnings by tragically ignored savants. Popular retellings trace the idea back as far as 1824, when the mathematician Jean Baptiste Joseph Fourier wrote on the balance of energy coming into and leaving the planet and speculated on the role of the atmosphere in preventing the loss of heat through radiation. In the late nineteenth century the British scientist John Tyndall and the Swedish electrochemist Svante Arrhenius put the topic on a more rigorous footing. Arrhenius calculated the relationship between carbon dioxide levels and temperature, suggesting that carbon dioxide fluctuations had been responsible for ice ages, and spoke of the possible role of industry and other human actions in warming the globe. Somewhat interestingly, Arrhenius saw this as potentially a positive thing, yielding a "more equable" climate that could support greater agricultural production (Fleming 1998, 82) – an early indication that a scientific theory or fact does not determine its own broader narration. Even the oceanographer Roger Revelle, who is often called the "grandfather" of global warming theory and was Al Gore's mentor, initially viewed the problem with more curiosity than concern (Howe 2014, 19).

Although there were brief moments of public apprehension about global warming in the late 1940s and 1950s (Fleming 2007, 77–79), and while an increasing number of climate scientists began to raise the alarm in the 1960s (Weart 2010, 71), most people in the developed world saw earth's atmosphere as far too vast and resilient to be fundamentally changed by human activity. With the rise of the modern environmental movement, however, people began to worry about what was happening to the skies. In the early 1970s, the idea of large-scale, human-caused atmospheric change as a looming environmental problem began to enter public debate in America, in part due to widespread concerns over the potential impacts of supersonic jets (Howe 2014, 44–66). It was also during this period that environmentalists and climate scientists began to forge an uneasy alliance, although the former were still preoccupied with "backyard," quality-of-life issues, and the latter with producing "more and better science" (Howe 2014). Still, global warming was vastly overshadowed by problems like overpopulation, water pollution, and wilderness preservation. Although the science was increasingly solid and compelling, it was not until the mid-1970s that journalists began to report on anthropogenic climate change as anything like an established fact, even as they published story after story on badly distorted projections of global cooling. Nonetheless, as the historian Joshua Howe (no relation) convincingly argues, until the 1980s, global warming "remained almost entirely within the purview of the scientific community" (95).

Our own look back at major media sources confirms this claim. A search of "global warming" in the *New York Times* index shows just six stories from before 1980. The items seem remarkably prescient, but they are presented for the most part as quick reports on the talk of scientists in their conventions and publications. The basic science being propounded seems consistent with the one we have today. Yet the items are typically buried somewhere back in the "Science" section and are run in with other ecological stories. This was an issue worthy of being noted, but not an issue worthy of attention in the civil sphere. For example, on December 21, 1969, we find on page 46, column 4 the following compressed and hard-to-understand note:

Physical scientist J O Fletcher warns man has only a few decades to solve problem of global warming caused by pollution, s, Amer Geophysical Union (stet.); notes warming could cause further melting of polar ice caps and affect earth's climate; oceanographic chemist E D Goldberg warns man runs risk of allowing pollution to destroy life in oceans. (*New York Times* 1969)

Toward the end of the 1970s treatments became more extended and have a contemporary feel. For example, an eighteen-hundred-word item in the *Economist* from 1977 covers all the bases that are familiar today in, say, *Economist* features on global warming. There is the difficulty of prediction ("the simplest model has to include 30 variables"); the crucial role of the Arctic and Antarctic ("the polar ice caps are what inflation and money supply are to economists"); an estimate that a "doubling of carbon dioxide" would lead to "global warming of nearly three degrees centigrade"; the possibility of flooding as "the oceans would rise nearly six meters" (*Economist* 1977, 88). The *Economist* (1979) remained agnostic as to the truth of the matter, yet it was unable to see disaster as the end of the line even if the prognostications were true. It wrote a couple of years later:

The results could be relatively attractive: a climate something like that of the warm medieval period from 900 to 1050. There would be winners and losers: e.g., more benign conditions in northern Europe and some of today's arid African regions, but severe winters and frequent drought in eastern Europe. On balance, however, the earth would probably be more productive. (*Economist* 1979, 96)

It is tempting to see this as simply capitalist ideology. To do so would be mistaken. Similar rosy views were held by influential stakeholder institutions at the interface between the laboratory, the political process, and civil society such as the National Academy of Sciences. In 1983 its Carbon Dioxide Assessment Committee made a 496-page report that brought up the usual litany of issues and dangers but concluded:

We do not believe, however, that the evidence at hand about CO_2-induced climate change would support steps to change current fuel-use patterns away from fossil fuels. Such steps may be necessary or desirable at some time in the future, and we should certainly think carefully about costs and benefits of such steps; but the very near future would be better spent improving our knowledge (including knowledge of energy and other processes leading to creation of greenhouse gases) than in changing fuel mix or use. (quoted in excerpts from *New York Times* 1983, 5)

Although this particular report reflected the influence of environmental skeptics in the Reagan administration (Howe 2014, 132–34), its cheerful line of reasoning was consistent with the romantic genre of risk assessment, which had found widespread favor among economists, policy makers, and many others. Based on the principles of what Aristotle termed comedy (Frye 1957), this is the plot structure in which problems appear serious but end up resolving themselves without causing enduring suffering. There was no need to panic, nor even to make a decision. Growing prosperity was not the problem; to the contrary, it would take care of the problem:

Generally, the more well-to-do countries can take in stride what may prove to be a reduction by a few percent in living standards that will likely be greater per capita by more than 100 percent over today's. (National Academy of Sciences quoted in Shabecoff 1983)

Squeezed out by the romantic minimization of risk, a more concerned Environmental Protection Agency report released just a few days before that of the National Academy of Science struggled for attention. It was dubbed "unwarranted and unnecessarily alarmist" by President Reagan's scientific advisor George A. Keyworth III (quoted in Shabecoff 1983).

If off to a poor start, as the 1980s moved on, apocalypticism started to gain traction. To some extent, this reflects the growing influence of environmentalism in everyday thinking as well as the emergence of a broader "risk society" in which sensitivity to self-generated human harms was amplified. There were also more middle-range institutional drivers, including the entrenched antienvironmentalism of Reagan-era conservatives, which galvanized scientists and activists alike (Howe 2014, 118–46). NASA was particularly important here as a genre-entrepreneur, taking advantage of its global remote sensing capabilities to find a new relevance in the post-Apollo age. It coordinated a two-thousand-page report by 150 scientists from around the globe that was released in 1986. This was a prototype for many subsequent reports. Its language is more alarmist than that of the National Academy of Sciences, conjuring up images of unknown futures and chancy gambles: "we should recognize that we are conducting one giant experiment on a global scale by increasing the concentrations of trace gases in the atmosphere without knowing the environmental consequences" (*New York Times* 1986, 11).

The Consolidation of the Apocalyptic Genre

Around the end of the 1980s we see even stronger ethical injunctions emerge, these fueled by growing apocalypticism. The social drama was itself now heating up. Global warming had now created new forms of civic responsibility and subjectivity, these reworking existing environmentalist tropes and converting them into categorical imperatives. The socially constructed representation of a scientific finding was starting to build its normative force in the civil sphere. Scientific projections grew more and more alarming as the decade progressed. By the late 1980s, polls showed that a majority of people in the Western world were worried about the problem, although they still tended to rank it well below other concerns. As their worries grew, so did the influence of industry-funded skeptics, who skillfully used the media and political institutions to sow seeds of scientific doubt. As the genre was consolidated, the cast of characters grew.

Thanks to the growing acceptance of this apocalyptic global warming discourse, a genre of representation that could once be dismissed as a fantasy of the Bay Area's Birkenstock-wearing classes was becoming legitimate on Main Street USA. Now we can find a guest columnist even in the middle- to lowbrow *USA Today* writing that "carbon dioxide and other greenhouse gasses... threaten a disastrous warming of the earth." Hence we needed to "change the whole way we live" with "100% recycling," "public transportation, solar powered cars, bicycles or simply walking" (*USA Today* 1989, 10). As the "problem" of global warming was ratcheted up the genre hierarchy in the next few years, decisions and outcomes became increasingly epochal. So we see a mid-1990s op-ed in the *Christian Science Monitor* setting the stage for a Kyoto environmental summit in terms similar to those we find in the Book of Revelation. One can almost hear John of Patmos intoning his visions of a Day of Judgment. "A warming unprecedented since the dawn of civilization is likely to happen in the coming decades," the *Monitor* warns. This would bring with it "destruction of entire forest systems and watersheds, rising sea levels, flooding, drinking-water shortages and the northward spread of tropical diseases... [there was a] looming threat to geopolitical and environmental stability" (*Christian Science Monitor* 1997, 10). From the standpoint of structural poetics, we can see here the hallmarks of apocalypticism. Greenhouse gases are given extreme powers of action, the consequences of action or inaction are immense, the future of the planet is at stake.

As we often show in this book, it was old-fashioned oratory – not new scientific data nor a sophisticated media spectacle – that helped drive this genre shift. In 1988, the worst heat waves and droughts since the Dust Bowl hit much of the United States. For the first time, journalists asked insistently whether the "greenhouse effect" was to blame (Weart 2008, 150). Then, on a sweltering hot June day, climate scientist James Hansen appeared before Congress at a carefully staged hearing. He announced that he could state "with 99 percent confidence" that global warming was happening. As a *Grist* reporter later recounted:

Seated before the Senate Committee on Energy and Natural Resources, 15 television cameras, and a roomful of reporters, Hansen wiped the sweat from his brow and presented his findings. The charts of global climate all pointed upward. "The Earth is warmer in 1988 than at any time in the history of instrumental measurements," he said. "There is only a 1 percent chance of an accidental warming of this magnitude. . . . The greenhouse effect has been detected, and it is changing our climate now." (Block 2008)

After the hearing, Hansen said it was time to "stop waffling" on climate change (Weart 2008, 150), and his testimony earned front-page coverage in the *New York Times* under the ominous headline "Global Warming Has Begun." This sweaty, anxious episode has been widely credited with putting catastrophic climate change squarely in the public eye. Not long after, *Time* magazine picked "Endangered Earth" as its "planet of the year" instead of its usual person. "This year the earth spoke, like God warning Noah of the deluge," *Time* wrote in its cover story. "Its message was loud and clear, and suddenly people began to listen, to ponder what portents the message held." While conceding that skeptics could be right to dismiss the "dreaded greenhouse effect," the magazine held, "it is far too risky to do nothing while awaiting absolute proof of disaster" (Sancton 1989, 24).

This apocalyptic discourse of global doom set high popular expectations for the 1997 meetings in Kyoto. There were vague hopes for a potlatch ceremony of selfless action in which national interests would be thrown over the cliff. This ritual validation of the apocalyptic worldview might, some hoped, provide the foundation point for a new romantic narrative, one involving sacrifice, sharing, and the pursuit of a common good. Perhaps humanity would prevail. The actual result of the conference was

a further contribution to genre confusion. In the social drama that came
to surround the event we find the narration of a two cheers failed ritual.
Kyoto was historic, but it had also been characterized by horse-trading.
As the event continued and then ended, the word "bargaining" became
used more and more frequently to describe what had happened. From
the apocalyptic viewpoint, what might and indeed should have become a
moment of ritual transcendence had become simply politics and bureaucracy. Possibilities for disillusioned irony presented themselves to onlooking metanarrators. A contributor to the *South China Morning Post* noted
that history could have been made, but instead,

after 10 days of circular and esoteric arguments about gas trading and forest
counting that few understood, and a final dawn-to-dawn session culminating
in negotiators nodding off as clauses were passed, history was on few people's
minds: all most cared about was when it would all end. (*South China Morning
Post* 1997, 10)

Likewise the *Jerusalem Post* contrasted the potential import of the event
with its mundane incarnation:

There are times when the conference itself seems lost in a fog of deceit and
uncontrolled verbal emissions. Most parts of the conference are highly technical
and conducted in a version of United Nations English few English- speakers,
let alone anyone else, can understand. This in itself, rather than the inevitable
disagreements, could yet be the meeting's failure... this supposedly vital 10-
day conference of more than 160 nations started off infected by the numbing
amalgamation of environmental sciences and UN bureaucracy. (*Jerusalem Post*
1997, 8)

Clearly there is a deflation here away from apocalypticism and high-
romantic thinking. But to what? In his *Anatomy of Criticism* Northrop
Frye (1957) identifies a genre of low mimesis. This involves a representation of the world that is devoid of heroic or supernatural elements and
also lacking in comedic and romantic charm. This is the humdrum and
uninspiring world of business as usual that Max Weber described as the
Iron Cage of modernity. In Kyoto, technocracy and diplomacy, the stock-
in-trade of low-mimetic politics, had emerged not only as activities but
also as visible symbols that were themselves a clue to the genre at play.
They were seen to have fended off ritual fusion and so prevented an emotional climax from emerging. Perhaps this reflected not only the Samuel
Beckett–like dynamics of intergovernmental discussions but also the genre
fragmentation of this era expressed in the scientific and technical documentation. For example, the UN's Intergovernmental Panel on Climate

Change itself issued a report in 1995 titled "Economic and Social Dimensions of Climate Change." Here we find amazingly little sense of urgency when compared to its more recent written outputs. The report suggests the problem could be dealt with through "a portfolio of actions aimed at mitigation, adaptation and improvement of knowledge" (IPCC 1995, 2) and draws attention to the widespread availability of "no-regrets" measures to deal with much of the problem. These are defined as "measures worth doing anyway" (IPCC 1995, 16) because they reduce energy costs or local pollution levels.

The prevalence of bureaucratic rationality and low-mimetic metanarration at Kyoto did not prevent moral evaluations of action persisting. True enough, the low-mimetic genre had ruled the roost at the event and pricked the apocalyptic balloon. Still the wider melodrama persisted. To start with, pariahs could be identified. Those who avoiding signing the protocols (the United States, Canada, Australia, New Zealand) were widely narrated as mean-spirited free riders. These were incivil actors driven by selfish motivations such as electoral appeal, saving domestic jobs and preserving entrenched and privileged ways of life. Australia, for example, secured permission for an 8 percent increase in its emissions and for continued land clearing in the bush. Its prime minister John Howard spoke proudly of the need to "protect jobs in the coal industry" and to not "sell out Australia's interests in international forums" (quoted in *Canberra Times* 1997, 6). The angry EU environmental spokesman Peter Jorgensen called Australia's Kyoto deal "wrong and immoral . . . a disgrace" (quoted in *Sydney Morning Herald* 1997, 10). Those who signed up, by contrast, such as the members of the European Union, could undergo a status upgrade. No longer simply polluters, these were now ethically aware global citizens who respected the scientific knowledge base and who realized the time had come to go beyond free rider concerns. Furthermore, the apocalypticists insisted that something concrete had been achieved: global warming was recognized as a legitimate problem deserving of workable solutions at the international and transnational levels.

Fertile soils had been prepared for *An Inconvenient Truth* (Guggenheim 2006). This remarkably successful documentary film of the mid-2000s saw the failed politician Al Gore presenting his slide show on the need to take global warming seriously. We explain in the next chapter exactly how this film achieved its effect. For the time being we note that Gore's genius was to channel and amplify the prevailing mood rather than to create it, and furthermore to provide a utopian moment for activist hope. Scientific and technical reports on global warming make for pretty tedious reading for the general, educated reader. They are larded with caveats, data disputes, and politically correct diplomatic talk that avoids pointing the finger. There are precious few attractive diagrams, no photographs. Warning of catastrophic hurricanes, global flooding that would swamp coastal cities, horrific drought and heat, and wars; backing these up with scientific authority of charts and graphs; flashing up pictures of collapsing ice bergs, wilting trees, and flooded cities; tying this together with a sense of pragmatic possibility, Gore's film intensified the moral drama. Furthermore, it allowed Gore – a longtime global warming campaigner – to be reinvented as a self-sacrificing martyr who had transcended politics and who was prepared to swim against the tide. Caring little for public esteem, here was a pragmatic parrhesiast telling it like it was to people who supposedly didn't want to hear his message. As negotiations came into place for a follow-up to Kyoto, pressure intensified for nonbelievers to get out of the church.

Departing from their earlier moderation, scientific reports of this era became increasingly uniform in their genre-elevated storytelling. The 2006 "Stern Review on the Economics of Climate Change" was the most influential such document to that date (Great Britain 2006). Commissioned by Tony Blair's British government, this sought to price the costs of action and inaction. After reviewing the available evidence in tremendous detail, Stern opted for a more apocalyptic reading of the dangers. These included threats to the water supply of "one sixth of the world's population," "declining crop yields ... (which) could leave hundreds of millions without the ability to produce or purchase food," and "200 million people ... permanently displaced due to rising sea levels, heavier floods and more intense droughts" (Great Britain 2006, Executive Summary, vi). Stern also conjured the image of mass economic collapse along the lines of the Great Depression and the World Wars.

Around this time, governments and bureaucracies that were perceived to be lukewarm in their commitment to tackling the problem were more strongly and widely vilified as mean spirited and shortsighted. More importantly, they were frequently represented as censors of the truth engaging in undemocratic behavior. Their image could be most easily juxtaposed to the image of the hard working, scrupulous, nonpartisan scientist (a representation that was later to take a severe beating during Climategate for reasons we explain in Chapter 6). Hence, in 2006, James Hansen was concerned about pressure from the Bush administration in discussions of risks and solutions. He attracted attention when he noted that speakers from the U.S. National Oceanic and Atmospheric

Administration were followed by "minders": "It seems more like Nazi Germany or the Soviet Union than the United States," he told an audience at the New School (in Eilperin 2006). Likewise, the *New York Times* accused the Bush White House of "censorship on global warming" when it edited out material on the risks of global warming from a U.S. Environmental Protection Agency report, leaving only "some pablum about the complexities of the issue and the research that is needed to resolve the uncertainties" (*New York Times* 2003, 22). The drama was expanding to include a full cast of characters. Those struggling for narrative supremacy were themselves caught up in a wider narration of motivation and morality.

Returning to the genre model of risk perception we set out earlier, we can summarize this story. Very broadly speaking, it is one in which apocalyptic readings of threat have become more strongly institutionalized, particularly among governmental policy elites. They increasingly provide the legitimate or authorized genre of public speech and evidentiary interpretation – even if not followed up by convincing policies. Backed by the authority of a growing scientific knowledge base and institutional brokers such as NASA and the UN, these have slowly edged out low-mimetic readings that envisage a cheap technological fix or that endlessly defer the problem solution until we have more information. They insist on urgent action and establish new categories of deviance. By the mid-2000s, resistance to this shift was framed more and more negatively as something other than the product of ignorance or justifiable doubt.

Apocalypticism Contested

In his landmark study *Risk Society*, written somewhat before climate change was at the center of the attention space of ecological anxieties, Ulrich Beck (1992) suggested that environmental dangers and unknown risks will lead to critical awareness and a new and more democratic global order. As we noted when we reviewed this influential book in the previous chapter, Beck claims that, spurred on by ecological uncertainty, citizens will demand more control over production and consumption processes and push for equity. What Beck missed is the way that this newly contested terrain has generated increased critical reflexivity not only over science, progress, and politics but also over public sphere representations of risks themselves. Crucially, he did not seem to be able to envisage that the emergent ensemble of beliefs, norms, solidarities, and activities he both predicts and endorses could itself become the target of such critical reflexive activity. For example, the very hegemony of the apocalyptic mode allows possibilities for a counterdiscourse. We might think of this as a set of cultural affordances: there are opportunity structures opening up that permit contrarian meaning-motifs and dramatic structures to be taken off the peg. Environmentalists are well aware of the dangers of overreach and of failed prophesy. Their self-critical discourses predict only too well the possibilities for genre confusion as the social drama intensifies into a struggle over representational authority. Yet at the same time, their diffidence compounds the problem. This is a case where the self-imposed regime of two steps forward, one step back leads only to public confusion about the direction of travel.

How does this countercurrent play out? Highly visible skeptics exist who can point to their own "clues" and assemble a different narrative. Media norms requiring a "balanced account" and considering debate and conflict as "newsworthy" provide them with airspace and dramatic influence disproportionate to their numbers. There are qualified scientists here or there who think we are on the wrong track as well as a substantial proportion of the general public who feel the issue has been overblown. Some say global temperature change in recent decades might be due to natural factors. Others claim that global temperatures have flattened out since 1998, yet CO_2 emissions have increased, and that benchmark thermometers at airstrips and in cities are increasingly surrounded by concrete and asphalt leading to heat radiation and heat island effects. Still others claim that natural variations in oceanic circulation may well hold back global warming for decades, this making widely circulating models and predictions hopelessly pessimistic (e.g., Keenlyside 2008; Michaels 2008). The complexity of the climate system makes certainty about the rate and intensity of global warming impossible to attain. The vast majority of nonscientists must simply take what the experts say on trust. That the earth has been hotter in recent centuries – say, the medieval warm period when the Vikings were farming in Greenland – might seem quite relevant to the layperson. When the layperson hears that blizzards are projected to increase in frequency and intensity as a result of overall warming, even highly educated people cannot be blamed for scratching their heads. Such ambivalence about the core science – or at least the possibility for reasonable doubt, and the certainty of confusion – amplifies the importance of a genre selection process involving the leap of interpretative faith that is the genre guess. And even if the human origins of climate change are accepted 100 percent at some future date, this fact still does not tell us how urgent the problem is, nor how much sacrifice we should make to deal with it. Representations filtering information will still play a role in shaping societal responses to ecological information. That is why the social drama matters.

So if the apocalyptic mode is dominant, it is also contested. Narrative struggles are sometimes about data and measures, sometimes about priorities. Genre confusion follows. For example, Bjorn Lomborg (2006) charged that Stern had "cherry-picked" the more severe risks and downside consequences, or underestimated the costs of mitigation, or had imposed an incorrect discounting rate for future costs and benefits of current policy, thus moving him away from more prudent and less costly lines of action. These should include spending relatively small amounts of money in Africa to improve adaptive capacity for the truly disadvantaged. Lomborg's ability to generate genre confusion is well known in activist circles. He is a visible environmentalist and is clearly concerned with social justice. He believes climate change is a real problem, not a hoax. Yet at the same time, he resists genre inflation and intones low-mimetic mantras about cost effectiveness. Confusion could also result from the apparently absurd suggestion that global warming is a good thing. Some claimed the major downside risks we face as a civilization are global cooling and overdue mini ice ages. The climate was unstable and cool spells had wiped out civilizations in the past. In this context the release of carbon dioxide was like insurance against a more serious potential disaster: "it protects us from the unpredictable big freeze that could be far, far worse" (Steel 2002). If we can never live risk-free with a locked-in climate, then our task is to decide which risks we wish to live with. Such arguments are in effect a push for low mimesis grounded in the languages of science and technocracy. That most scientists think they are nonsense is in many ways less relevant than the mere fact that someone, somewhere is making them. What matters is their "truthiness."

Yet efforts at genre shifting need not involve just scientists and their data as they reflect on what Sartre called the practico-inert – that is to say, the material world – and its implications for society. They can also be the work of organic intellectuals speaking to the public sphere about the discursive activity of others. In other words, genre confusion can originate in a complex second-order hermeneutics where players interpret the interpretations and represent the representations. Focusing on the qualities of the words, images, and stories themselves rather than on lower-order "facts," a considerable component of the global warming cultural complex consists of efforts to ironically recast intellectual positions as culturally or ideologically shaped delusions. Hence much of the drama of climate change is about the struggles of representations and their sponsors rather than the movements of thermometers and ice floes.

We trace this activity throughout our book in a number of spheres. For now we note that apocalypticism, as a cosmological stance, has proven vulnerable to genre deflation making use of realism and irony. Through satire, narrations in the elevated mode can be made out to be alarmist, their sponsors fanatics. A column in Ireland's *Sunday Independent* captures the extrascientific possibilities for critique quite neatly for our purposes. After noting that much science was now attributing global warming to nonhuman factors such as solar activity, the witty and cutting Eilis O'Hanlon (2007) explained that the rush of church leaders to "leap on the environmental bandwagon" was because "apocalypse was always their business." Environmentalists for their part are professional "doom mongers" who are "unable to imagine the future as anything other than famine, disease, war, ecological disaster." Human history had shown our species had the ingenuity to triumph over all adversity, yet "the green Cassandras have us all convinced that our descendants will be back in the caves munching on raw thigh bones before Al Gore can say, 'I told you so.'" We need to "all lighten up and have more optimism about mankind's continued ability to solve problems and make life better." Here environmentalism is cast as a fad or fashion ("bandwagon"), one promoted by irrational, narrow-minded individuals who ignore common sense. More accurate, O'Hanlon ventures, would be a romantic genre guess – this is why we need to "lighten up" and be "optimistic." Observe that O'Hanlon does not dispute the facts. She does not speak of sea ice nor average global temperatures. She does not even dispute at length the anthropogenic hypothesis. She simply speaks to the matter of representations, then juxtaposes these against (a particular representation of) human experience.

In his book *An Appeal to Reason: A Cool Look at Global Warming*, former British Chancellor Nigel Lawson (2008) illustrates a more strident and less waggish mode of critique than O'Hanlon. Symbolically polluting his opponents, Lawson detects a closed "eco-fundamentalism" that had eliminated critical thinking. Particularly scathing of the Stern Report, he dubbed this as alarmist. Consistent with the implicit call for genre deflation that was in his book's title, Lawson suggested we should deal with problems as they came along rather than trying to second-guess what they might be. Steady as she goes, one might say. Al Gore became another magnet for criticism. His portrayal of Hurricane Katrina as caused by global warming was denounced as simplistic, his mention of huge sea level rises without a time frame misleading. According to climate-skeptic scientist Richard Lindzen, this was "shrill alarmism" (Broad 2007).

But there is a stronger critique still lurking, one hinting at a drama about knowledge and human interests. It is one that moves beyond allegations of bandwagonism and closed thinking and that inverts the negative representation we saw earlier of climate change skeptics repressing science. Here apocalypticism is not only a bad genre guess that could be mocked but also a hegemonic and antidemocratic force. Allegations were made that climate change skeptics themselves were not being given a fair hearing, while the most negative scenarios were given excessive airtime. Lawson, for example, spoke of the truth monopoly of the UN's climate change panel. Lindzen (2006) wrote in the *Wall Street Journal* alleging that scientists who failed to follow the creed were having their funding cut. Anthropologist and outspoken climate change skeptic Benny Peiser suggested that widespread representations of scientific consensus on the anthropogenic origins of climate change were misleading. Furthermore, he argued that Wikipedia editors had incorrectly written that he had changed his mind on this point and were refusing to let him edit his entry to reflect his still skeptical views (Newman 2008). The Climategate scandal of 2009 proved to many that leading climate change scientists were doctoring their evidence with statistical trickery and censoring opponents through the peer review process. We have a drama involving nefarious human forces as much as climatic ones.

So where are we now? It would seem that the narration of global warming is taking place at two levels. One is the assembly of clues from science and everyday experience into a narrative that includes agents, causes, and consequences and future projections. This discourse is about the relationship of the human and natural worlds. Here we find what the German thinker Niklas Luhmann (1989) calls "ecological communication" being not only shaped by the binary codes he speaks of but also filtered by genres with their consequent narrations of natural process. Technical information becomes storied, and with this colorful storying it becomes relevant to a wider society. The second level of narration is a metadiscourse over and upon that narration. It asks who is doing the narrating, whether we have the right genre, and whether there are costs and consequences to particular collective representations. At both levels, global warming is the theme at the center of a moral and social drama. This is a story where there are good and bad actors, tragic and unintended consequences to action and inaction, foolish and wise choices to be made. Climate change, then, is a complex and layered social fact, both material and ideal, where the cultural translation of scientific information lives alongside reflexivity over those very representations. More than just a series of thermometer readings, it is also a reading of thermometers and then, again, a reading of those readings.

So at the time of writing, climate change activism enjoys a curious and hollow victory. The wine glass is half empty. We have seen that the apocalyptic modality stands as the most legitimate form of public discourse. It carries a certain normative force to talk of the planet as being in peril and of a "we" that must do something urgently about this. For example, heads of state routinely speak in this way. Yet the triumph is somewhat shallow. As we have seen, critical voices can also be heard. The resulting genre confusion has arguably prevented concerted action. Hence a substantial minority believe climate change either does not exist or is not a big problem. Climate change advocates are themselves vulnerable to deflationary interpretations of motivation and rationality. More important still, there seems to be a mismatch between discourse and action. Governments tinker around the edges with their energy policies but seem unable or unwilling to engage in any draconian restructuring. Likewise, most individuals who believe climate change is a real problem do surprisingly little to change their lifestyles or engage in collective action. This failure is remarkable when contrasted with other global threats, notably, in response to terrorism, nuclear proliferation, toxins, or virus outbreaks like SARS and swine flu. Indeed, in many American households, defending against these kinds of insidious, invisible threats has become a whole way of life, especially among self-identified environmentalists (Szasz 2009). Here we see what might be understood as a far stronger correlation of speech and action. If affluent Americans spent half as much time and energy on reducing their carbon footprint as they spend on protecting themselves from trans fats or perfectly clean tap water, climate activists would have a reason to cheer.

What are the possibilities for a breakthrough in which climate change becomes a more coherently organized cultural system with more deeply transformative potentials? On the basis of this chapter, it is tempting to suggest that a deeper institutionalization and discursive dominance of the apocalyptic genre would light the fuse. Yet the genre that would seemingly lead to the most decisive intensification of cultural will is also the most problematic and easily contested. The apocalyptic frame is widely fingered for putting off the public. Indeed, bemoaning its chilling influence has become a cliché in both academic and popular discourse about climate change. Headshaking over "scare tactics" and "doomsday scenarios" has become automatic outside environmental circles. Certainly mainstream apocalyptic environmental rhetoric has been toned down since the "eco-catastrophist" heyday of the late 1960s and 1970s, when green Jeremiahs like Paul Ehrlich and the Club of Rome warned of imminent socioecological collapse. Their neo-Malthusian reverie was undermined by the Green Revolution, female education, and miraculous technologies even those savants and polymaths could not begin to envisage – such as the pill and the condom. Yet the temptation to revert to the (arche)type is ever present. After all, writes Lawrence Buell (1995, 285), "apocalypse is the single most powerful master metaphor that the contemporary environmental imagination has at its disposal." Ecocritics and communications scholars have thoroughly covered this history, and we will not rehash it here (see, in particular, Buell 1995; Foust and O'Shannon 2009; Garrard 2001, 2011; Killingsworth and Palmer 1996; Skrimshire 2010). Suffice it to say the realization has sunk in that the more the apocalyptic card is played, the more it loses value. The genre also has faced critique from critical theory for its abdication of political responsibility. Erik Swyngedouw (2010), for example, asserts that the apocalyptic turn is not merely populist; it also plays into a more general postpolitical condition. By invoking the image that the whole of humanity is threatened, it obfuscates inequality in risk and "forecloses a proper political framing" (219) in which matters of economic redistribution and social trajectory could become issues for debate. Instead, there is a seeking of pragmatic and consensual options that tend to reproduce inertia.

Our principal reservation differs from these and lies in the fact that apocalyptic genre is itself marked by internal genre confusion. The rhetorician Steven O'Leary (1994) provides a very useful framework for understanding this condition. Drawing on Kenneth Burke's (1984) Aristotelian notion of "frames of acceptance," O'Leary shows how tragic and comic frames differ radically in their construction of time and evil:

> The tragic plot conceives of evil in terms of sin or guilt; its mechanism of redemption is victimage, and its plot moves toward the isolation of the evildoer in the "cult of the kill" [cathartic violence]. The comic plot conceives of evil in terms of error, misunderstanding, or ignorance; its mechanism of redemption is recognition, and its plot moves toward exposure of the evildoer's fallibility and his incorporation into society. (200)

Although we do not fully agree with O'Leary's characterization of tragedy (see the previous chapter for what we think is a more nuanced understanding), he makes a good point. When fused with apocalyptic visions of earthly catastrophe, two paths open up. According to O'Leary, the tragic-apocalyptic mode imagines a temporal horizon "beyond which human choice is superfluous" (84), often in the form of a specific date. In the world of climate change, this function is served by parts per million of atmospheric carbon dioxide, where iconic numbers – 350 ppm, 450 ppm, 500 ppm – serve as symbolic shorthand for the "locus of the irreparable." Here we see ecocatastrophist visions of an anti-Edenic afterworld: James Lovelock's notorious image of humanity's last "breeding pairs" huddled in the Arctic, for example. The comic-apocalyptic mode, conversely, makes "the End contingent upon human choice" and "assign[s] to humanity the task of ushering in the millennium" (84). In a rhetorical analysis of press coverage of climate change, communication scholars Christina R. Foust and William O'Shannon Murphy (2009) convincingly argue that the tragic framing of climate apocalypse is more likely to lead to resignation and paralysis, whereas comic framings create space for collective action and social mobilization. Others have reached similar conclusions (e.g., Hulme 2009, and in the sphere of democratic politics, Jacobs and Smith 1997). What is needed, then, is not only a sense that the world is in peril but also a more romantic sensibility that empowers action and generates solidaristic emotional energy. Call it a postmillennial frame. To stitch together doom and hope, one must first thread a very fine needle.

4

An Inconvenient Truth

The Power of Ethos

In 2006, a London-based liberal think tank, the Institute for Public Policy Research, issued a paper arguing that the case for climate change needed to be made more effectively (Ereaut and Segnit 2006). Written by two public relations and marketing specialists, *Warm Words* suggested that the battle for public attention was being lost thanks to mixed messages, contradictory scraps of information, and contending expert opinions in the mass media. Climate change discourse in the United Kingdom was "confusing, contradictory and chaotic" (7). Every argument was met with a counterargument, apocalyptic scenarios were confronted by cheery visions of an emergent British wine industry, and the overall story the public got was that "nobody really knows." It suggested a new strategy was needed by climate change advocacy groups. This would treat "climate-friendly activity as a brand that can be sold" (28). There would be less reference to a top-down "message" from experts and authority sources with the implication of "rational argument." Rather, it urged that "we need to work in a more shrewd and contemporary way, using subtle techniques of engagement" (28). These would include getting the issue onto the "emotional radar" and constructing a myth of "ordinary heroism" in which everyday folk could take on a huge task (8).

It was perhaps imprudent to publish a document, which amounted to an own-goal by activists (we review other clangers in Chapter 6). Critics pounced on it as evidence that the climate change camp is characterized by patronizing and sneaky spin doctors who wish to replace an ongoing rational debate with insidious and patronizing propaganda. The pain of the self-inflicted wound was redoubled by the fact that there was no need to publish. Although far more respectful of science and of the need for debate than *Warm Words*, by the time of the cultural strategy document's appearance, Al Gore's efforts to get climate change taken seriously had already made use of myth, emotion, and those "subtle techniques of engagement."

It is generally agreed that the 2006 film *An Inconvenient Truth* featuring Al Gore and directed by Davis Guggenheim (2006) was a pivotal moment in the history of global warming discourse. Put simply, the bulk of the film consists of extracts from Gore's well-rehearsed auditorium presentation warning of the dangers of climate change. This core is intercut with scenes shot elsewhere. Here Gore talks to camera about his biography and motivation. Such personal themes also appear briefly from time to time in his slide show as asides during the presentation of scientific information. *An Inconvenient Truth* did more than bring attention to an ongoing issue; it persuaded many that the problem of climate change was (1) real, (2) urgent, and (3) solvable. So we might reasonably understand *An Inconvenient Truth* as an effective intervention, production, gesture, or performance. Just how was this impact achieved? We argue here that Aristotle's insights in his *Rhetoric* provide many of the answers. It is so obvious that it can escape observation that this is a film in which one man makes a case to an audience using powers of persuasion. This is a classical scenario with which Aristotle would have been very familiar. He would no doubt have concluded, as we do, that the upshot is a compelling demonstration that *logos* is subordinate to *ethos*. This film is in fact a study of the power of character.

The success of *An Inconvenient Truth* was remarkable and somewhat unexpected, even for its backers. At the Sundance Film Festival release, the producer Laurie David confidently predicted that "none of us are going to make a dime" (quoted in Booth 2006). The prognosis was not unreasonable. In the year 2006, Gore was widely typecast as a political has-been, a man noted by many for blowing his one and only chance to be U.S. president in 2000 when he was narrowly defeated by George W. Bush. After being a sore loser who could not concede defeat with grace, he dropped off the radar. Some Democrats saw things differently. For them Gore was a talented individual who had actually won the popular vote. He had been cheated of the presidency by legal shenanigans and a dubious and partisan Supreme Court ruling that had prematurely halted efforts at a transparent recount (see Dershowitz 2001). Yet even for this group, Gore was a figure of the past at the time of the film's release. They were looking elsewhere for their next intellectually gifted president and were to find him soon thereafter in Barack Obama.

So much for the fading star. As for the film itself, this was a reasonably low-budget documentary lasting ninety-four minutes. As the failed politician thumped his tub, he put up slides showing maps of soil evaporation and cross sections of ice cores. Why would anyone want to watch this? But watch it they did. The film took around $50 million at the box office. It won the Academy Award for best documentary as well as numerous other awards globally. A companion book by Gore reached number one on the American best-seller lists. La Scala, Milan, commissioned an opera based on the film. In 2007 Gore was jointly awarded the Nobel Peace Prize for his work on climate change. The Prize Committee singled him out as the "single individual who has done the most" to generate understanding of the issues. Speculation was soon widespread that Gore would make another run for president.

Other films on global warming have fared poorly by comparison. When an anti–global warming film titled *The Great Global Warming Swindle* (Durkin 2007) was aired on television in the United Kingdom, it generated little interest or controversy, even though it offered a provocative account of a "global warming industry" with a vested interest in fueling alarmism. It saw only a DVD release. One might reasonably have expected this film to become iconic for its latent audience of skeptics and conservatives. It did not. There was also the Discovery Channel documentary *Global Warming: What You Need to Know* (Brown 2006). From the same year as *An Inconvenient Truth*, this was hosted by the avuncular news anchor Tom Brokaw. As we would expect from a Discovery Channel production, this featured high-quality reportage and footage from around the world. The stories presented were said to illustrate the impact of global warming: dying coral reefs in Australia, retreating glaciers in Montana, and so forth. Who remembers this? As for climate maverick Bjorn Lomborg's documentary feature *Cool It* (Timoner 2010), this disappeared almost without a trace beyond the blogosphere, despite its progenitor's basic performative competence and his well-thumbed Rolodex of media contacts.

So how do we explain the extraordinary and unanticipated triumph of *An Inconvenient Truth*? One might think that as a "documentary," *An Inconvenient Truth* has impact because of its use of reason and evidence, its *logos*. On this score, most scientists praised Gore for getting the big picture right, although he was taken to task for mistakes on points of detail and for alarmist tendencies. Others questioned whether there really was the scientific consensus that he depicted (Broad 2007). The evaluation of evidence, however, is not the real game in town here, and we can put this debate aside. The power of the film and the talk lies elsewhere. Gore, remember, did not simply persuade. He got a large number of people interested in a problem in a seemingly effortless way. How? Because Gore and Guggenheim enacted the Aristotelian recipe for effective public speaking. Remember what Aristotle wrote in the *Rhetoric*:

We believe good men more fully and more readily than others: this is true generally whatever the question is, and absolutely true where exact certainty is impossible and opinions are divided. . . . His character may almost be called the most effective means of persuasion he possesses. (1.2.1356a)

It is the combination of these dimensions, the performative fusion of *logos* with *pathos* and *ethos*, that explains why audiences would spontaneously stand and applaud after screenings. Let's explore this further.

We have already noted that Gore's presidential run in 2000 had ended in bitter failure. It had also cemented a particular understanding of Gore that had been growing in the 1990s. There was a perception of "a stolid, capable Vice-President" who was also "a wild exaggerator, ideological chameleon, and total, unforgivable bore." Gore's "monochromatic reputation" as a man without passion included a persona as a "computer nerd." He was one of the "Atari Democrats" who had overhyped the Internet before the dot.com crash of 2000 (Klein 2006). Polls had long reported him as the most boring person in America, with pundits speaking of his near-complete inability to energize crowds (Merinda 1999). Worse than being as soporific as Mr. McGregor's lettuce, Gore had famously insinuated that he had invented the Web itself. Here was a boastful know-it-all who could alienate listeners merely by displaying his formidable historical and scientific erudition. The loss to George W. Bush was often ascribed to the "beer buddy syndrome" (Shapiro 2008) – most voters would prefer to have a hypothetical backyard barbeque with the more genuine and nonelitist Texan than with the wooden, pompous, and overly rehearsed vice president.

The single most important feature of *An Inconvenient Truth* is that it recast Gore, in effect showing a person the public did not really know existed. Viewers at the Sundance Film Festival were amazed to see a Gore who was amusing and entertaining. As the website Real Climate enthused at the time, "this isn't the 'wooden' Gore of the 2000 campaign" (Steig 2006). But there is a little more to it than just being lively and energetic. The conventions of film as a commercial format and as a viewing experience led to a necessary intensification of his personal dimension above and beyond the snippets and asides that Gore already had in his slide show. Gore explained in an interview that the biographical sections of the movie were not his own idea but rather that of director Davis Guggenheim:

[Guggenheim] said that one of the huge differences between a live stage performance and a movie is that when you're in the same room with a live person who's on stage speaking – even if it's me [laughs] – there's an element of dramatic tension and human connection that keeps your attention. And in a movie, that element is just not present.

He explained to me that you have to create that element on screen, by supplying a narrative thread that allows the audience to make a connection with one or more characters. He said, "You've got to be that character." (Roberts 2006)

Guggenheim himself noted elsewhere that global warming was too big and abstract for people to connect to (we disagree; see Chapter 1). He hoped that "if I could tell Al's story in the movie, that perhaps, if we learned about him and learned how he became so invested, then maybe we would too." Interestingly, Guggenheim did not look at other environmental films but rather struck on this strategy by "instinct" (Steffen 2006). Being an outsider to Discovery Channel conventions turned out to be a blessing, for instersubjective identification starts to emerge with this extra, and to some extent off-topic, biographical material. Cinematically, the centrality of Gore-the-protagonist allows *An Inconvenient Truth* to key to some of the key conventions of Hollywood realism and so to become understandable or familiar to the audience. In realist cinema (as opposed, for example, to experimental film), events are generally driven forward in a logical sequence by characters armed with consistent internal motivations acting in more or less predictable ways. Audiences can comprehend what is taking place because they are aware of the reasons for action, perhaps looking back on clues in the early narrative of the film to come to terms with later outcomes and choices. Placing the slide show in the wider biographical context offers a way to answer the otherwise problematic question that would hang over the film: why is he doing this? In *An Inconvenient Truth*, the character-driven story of personal motivations is one that appears intermittently. There is something of a tease going on. The full answer, one that combines duty, hope, and tragedy, is revealed only by the end of the film. The thrust of the cumulative character disclosures is to achieve leveling and yet, paradoxically, also to affirm Gore's status as a privileged interpreter. He is one of us and yet also somehow a chosen one who is above us. As Northrop Frye (1957) pointed out, this kind of actor, who is subject to the laws of nature (unlike the mythical hero) and yet superior to the rest of us, is to be found in the high-mimetic genres of a heroic tenor, notably in romance.

What is curious is that Gore's persona becomes elevated in this way thanks to displays of affability and modesty, which project honesty and humility. This is a character who levels himself down. A crucial moment comes at the beginning of the film. Gore introduces himself to his audience: "I used to be known as the next president of the United States.... I don't find that particularly funny." The structural similarity of his global warming talk to a presidential stump speech offers a foundation for this self-deprecating irony. No longer a contender for high office, the failed Gore now has a reduced status, and he admits it. He implicitly admits to having been hurt by the experience of failure. It is tempting to interpret the success of this play in terms of a contemporary pattern in celebrity culture. This is to reboot a failing career by admitting to emotional trauma, humiliation, or victimhood – say, sexual abuse as a child, or drug or alcohol dependency. True enough, audiences today are often attracted to celebrities who are flawed or who have faced defeat. Yet we would insist here on the classical foundations of this rhetorical move. To present oneself as challenged and perhaps as not worthy of an occasion or task, even when possessing great talent, was a standard feature of ceremonial and political oratory in antiquity. It is found, for example, in that most celebrated of all examples, the Funeral Oration of Pericles. He says, "I wish that the reputations of so many brave men were not to be imperiled in the mouth of a single individual, to stand or fall according as he spoke well or ill," before going on to give the greatest speech in history. It is present too in its leading clone/competitor, Lincoln's Gettysburg Address, where the president laments, "We cannot consecrate, we cannot hallow this ground. The brave men, living and dead, who struggled here, have consecrated it far above our power to add or detract. The world will little note, nor long remember, what we say here."

The leveling theme continues throughout in the many sections where Gore reveals his past. These are shot away from the lecture. Talks to camera are characterized by technical and aesthetic devices that decrease audience distance and suggest informality and authenticity. Gore is sitting in a car or in a barn or on a plane. He looks a little hot and is not wearing a suit. It turns out that Guggenheim and the film production process were again instrumental. Gore later said he was fatigued by a barrage of questions from Guggenheim and became "so exhausted that I didn't care what I said anymore" (quoted in Roberts 2006). The footage is somewhat low grade, perhaps 16mm or camcorder. The camera work is somewhat rough and ready. There is almost no dolly work, panning or zooming, or excess lighting; there is no music. We might think that high fidelity in representation is the bearer of authenticity. Yet often the reverse is the case. In film, low production values have long been associated with truthfulness and witnessing. One thinks of Roberto Rossellini's Italian neorealism in *Roma, Città Aperta* (Rome Open City) (Rossellini 1945), for example, which made use of nonactors, unlit, bombed out street settings, and scavenged, somewhat degraded film stock. One thinks too of the handheld video camera footage from 9/11. For all the talk of the 9/11 attacks being "just like" a special effects sequence in a Hollywood film, viewers could see that the visual surface was in fact very different. The witnessed reality of the events was anchored in the camcorder aesthetics of their representation. The lesson was reinforced with the 2004 Asian Tsunami, an event for which there is no professional footage. We can note also that Guggenheim's location sequences make use of long takes, depth focus, and minimal editing. Each of these characteristics is a feature endorsed by film theorist André Bazin (1967) in his seminal analysis of realism. For Bazin, this representational mode is austere and inherently democratic. It hands over power to viewers. Leveling again.

An Inconvenient Truth skillfully evades mention of Gore's birth into a political dynasty, his privileged upbringing in elite schools and at Harvard – items of information that might have undercut leveling. Instead, as the film unfolds its account of motivation and biography, we discover early on that as a student, Gore was influenced by the pioneering and prescient work of the earth scientist Roger Revelle. He was a man who had predicted and tracked growing levels of atmospheric carbon dioxide. Gore remembers:

Like a lot of young people, I came into contact with intellectual ferment, ideas that I'd never considered in my wildest dreams before. He showed our class the result of these measurements [of CO_2] after only a few years. It was startling to me. He was startled and he made it clear to our class what he felt the significance of it was. I soaked it up like a sponge. He drew the connection between the larger changes in our civilization and this pattern that was now visible in the atmosphere of the entire planet.

He returns to the formative experience again at the end of the film:

There is nothing unusual about what I'm doing. What is unusual is that I had the privilege to be shown it as a young man. It is almost as if a window opened through which the future was very clearly visible.

Now mythopoetics sneakily joins the Aristotelian orator's tool kit. Here we have the classical myth template of early initiation into great mysteries, the sense of calling and an understanding even then that the future of the globe was at stake. At the same time, we have a denial of personal talent. Next we have a litany of failure. Profane worldly forces thwart Gore's uncontaminated ecological vision. These failures can also be understood mythopoetically. They are functional equivalents to the trial or ordeal that tests the resolve of the carrier of a mission, be the carrier Jesus or Hercules.

When I went to the Congress in the middle 1970s I helped organize the first hearings on global warming.... I thought that would have such a big impact we'd be well on the way to solving this problem, but it didn't work out that way.

I actually thought and believed that the story would be compelling enough to cause a real sea change in the way Congress reacted.... I thought they would be startled and they weren't.

In the world of traditional myth the hero meets and defeats serial challenges. Gore, by contrast, is a failure. Here we have a brilliant coup. By failing, he is a person we can pity (leveling again) and recognize in our culture of confession. Yet, by rising above failure, he becomes also a person we can admire. When Congress shrugged off his message, this simply led to an existential crisis followed by renewed resolve: "It just turned my whole world around. How should I spend my time on this Earth?" Even the presidential election defeat might have been ordained. It "brought into clear focus the mission I had been pursuing all these years. I started giving the slide show again."

From each challenge Gore had emerged stronger and with a clearer ethical vision. The bearer of bad tidings, his job had become clear. It was to tell an "inconvenient truth" without worrying about the personal consequences. The mission is followed against the odds.

Cutting against the narrative of Gore the battler and loser is another story that works almost subliminally. This is of Gore the achiever. There is fleeting reference to high-status institutions. The social theorist Edward Shils (1975) argued that there was a "sacred center" to American society consisting of core geographical locations and symbols. These were carriers of a certain charisma. Furthermore, charismatic status could arise by contagion through contact with them. We find Congress, the Senate, the White House, and the presidential election are all mentioned en passant as Gore speaks of his long-standing efforts to get global warming on the political table. Furthermore, we have the backdrop of the family farm as Gore talks to camera. Implicitly, Gore looks at once like part of the center and as an everyman from the periphery.

Mythopoetics helps us to understand the structure of the life narrative that Gore presents and the way that this might appeal to audience sympathies. It also does something else, however, which is to underwrite the truth of his words. We must remember that Gore is situated in a particular rhetorical context vis-à-vis his audience – the one that Aristotle identified as that of "political oratory." He is a person trying to persuade those to whom he is talking about the best course of future action. In so doing, Gore comes to assume or inhabit or speak from the classical position of the parrhesiast (on a closely related character type with an important role in the social drama of climate change, the "whistleblower," see Hamblyn 2009). In the world of social theory we have become familiar with this term thanks to the work of the French thinker Michel Foucault (1983). During his last years and in his final lectures at Berkeley and the College de France he came to see parrhesia as an important resource for the autonomous ethical subject. The parrhesiast can be identified through a number of characteristics. Emerging in the culture of the ancient Greeks, and in particular in the plays of Euripides, this figure is a person who speaks truth to power. Driven by internal psychological forces, they see this truth-telling as a duty or obligation. Often they speak at some risk to themselves from endangering or enraging their interlocutor or the wider community with an unpopular message. The bringer of bad tidings from battle is one kind of parrhesiast. Importantly, the parrhesiast tries to avoid rhetorical tricks. They speak "naturally" and as if the facts of a matter should be allowed to settle the case without the intervention of poetic phrase and emotion. Yet paradoxically from our contemporary perspective, the truth of the parrhesiasts' speech is underwritten by their moral being, not their *logos*. As Foucault (1983) puts it:

When someone has certain moral qualities, then that is the proof that he has access to truth – and vice-versa. The "parrhesiastic game" presupposes that the parrhesiastes is someone who has the moral qualities which are required, first, to know the truth, and secondly, to convey such truth to others. (3)

Courage is the most important of these qualities. To access the subject position of the parrhesiast, something has to be seen to be at stake: perhaps one's life, but also the loss of esteem, friendship, or popularity. Looking just at the title of *An Inconvenient Truth* should be enough to convince that parrhesia is being cited – he is telling us what we don't want to hear. We might hate or mock Al Gore even more than we did after he lost the 2000 election. Courage also has another dimension. According to Foucault, the courage involved is not only in telling the truth to others but also in being able to challenge and question the self, or put another way, to disclose to oneself the truth about oneself through a kind of ascetic discipline and rigorous self-interrogation. Often cited here are the bodily and mental techniques used to cultivate parrhesia by adepts, most often Stoics such as Epictetus, Seneca, or Marcus Aurelius but also some of the Cynics. There is a requirement for relentless self-scrutiny and self-questioning and the need to develop the capacity for endurance and perseverance. Never complacent, the parrhesiast struggles incessantly to separate fact from value, interpretation from what is impressed on the senses involuntarily as brute fact.

According to Foucault, it was an ongoing and practical problem for the Greeks to recognize truth-telling. We might understand the cultural template of the parrhesiast as a set of practical guidelines or instructions for identifying such a person. It is a template that has endured into this day, one that Al Gore and director Davis Guggenheim use citationally to construct a recognizable subject position from which he can speak. The biographical interludes offer up a portrait of endurance, of interior struggle and rigorous self-reflection, of a man telling us the message that we don't want to hear – a portrait of the parrhesiast.

Of course, there are limits to this parrhesiast subject position. For the parrhesiast game, the truth of an utterance is strongly bound up in the character of the speaker. Gore takes a bet each way by also supporting a more positivist discourse in which the self is partially effaced. In the norms of science, the question of who is speaking is rigorously separated out from the truth of what they say. Obviously, this norm does not always hold, as we see in the discussion of Climategate in Chapter 6. However, there is an obligation to "perform" invisibility and deference to objective realities. For this reason, Gore tries to show facts speaking: glaciers are retreating, the hottest years on record are all recent, CO_2 levels are increasing in the atmosphere, and so forth. He speaks of the consensus in the scientific community, in a way distancing his own personal identity from the truth of his utterances.

The parrhesiast moment is also compromised by the specifically prophetic qualities of Gore. As Max Weber (1967) showed long ago in his brilliant analysis of Judaism in biblical texts, the prophet has certain identifiable traits. These are liminal individuals who are part of society and yet outside of society. They spend a period of time in the wilderness. They answer to a higher and sacred calling rather than to worldly masters.

They tell people of the error of their ways, identify sinful behaviors, allocate blame, and call in a more hopeful way for spiritual purification and renewal. Earlier we saw Gore receiving a direct revelation of the truth of global warming. It was as if a window had been opened on the future. We also know he has been a wilderness figure. By analogy, the prophetic mode is an easy fit. And so it is that we find Gore speaking as follows (the words in italics are markers of the prophetic voice):

We are still by far the worse contributor to the crisis. I look around and look for *really meaningful signs* that we are about *to really change.* I don't see it right now.

There can be a *day of reckoning* when you wished you had connected the dots more quickly.

It is *our time to rise again* to procure our future.

Each one of us is a cause of global warming, but *each one of us can make choices to change.*

I have faith that pretty soon *enough minds are changed* that we *cross a threshold.*

Although the concept of parrhesia is not in common use, that of the prophet is part of the familiar lexicon. To underscore our analysis, we might note the extreme frequency with which the term is applied to Gore. In newspaper headlines and captions, for example, Gore is often dubbed a "Global Warming Prophet" or "Climate Change Prophet" when alternatives are available, such as "activist" or "campaigner." Gore is also happy to play up to the role when required. For example, at the New Baptist Covenant Convention in Atlanta, Georgia, Gore was introduced as a "Baptist Prophet" and presented with a green Bible at a special session titled "Stewardship of the Earth" (Roach 2008). Gore's subsequent speech was larded with the prophetic mode of oration ("The signal is on the mountain. The trumpet has blown") and biblical quotations, a performance suggesting that for him this is a familiar cultural template that he has adapted to more secular uses.

In a way, then, we might think of the Al Gore we discover as a hybrid character. He is a failure and an everyman, a mythopoetic hero and a parrhesiast, a prophet. The genius of the film is to construct all of this from just a few minutes of material.

An Inconvenient Truth is a ninety-four-minute film. We believe that most of the heavy lifting for persuasion belongs to about ten of them. Now subtract the credits. What of those remaining eighty minutes? These are less important, but it is useful to quickly review some other features that made for an effective act of communication.

Images

Lectures are often boring. As Davis Guggenheim realized, filmed lectures are even worse. This explains why much vaunted university initiatives with distance learning and remote audiovisual hookups run into problems. Who wants to watch a person behind a podium on television? An effective advantage of *An Inconvenient Truth* is its ability to retain interest through frequent visual switching taking place on top of a monologue that offers continuity. As Gore speaks on any given topic, we are offered long-range, middle-range, and close-up images of Gore. There is also the option to abandon Gore and simply show the slides, again with the talking beneath. A sense of movement and dynamism results from the rapid shifting between these four options. It is enhanced by the possibility of a slow zoom from the back to the front of the auditorium.

Turning to the images, although Gore modestly suggests the film is being made of his "slide show," there is much more to it than that. He uses a range of techniques, including stills, videos, and animations. These subtly shift and mix so as to illustrate or dramatize claims Gore is making as he lectures, often with accompanying voice-over or sound. This sophisticated melange, which moves well beyond the standard PowerPoint presentation, was in fact the product of a makeover by a professional organization, Duarte Design, which often works for major corporations and nonprofits to jazz up the company presidents' keynotes or assist with product launches and campaigns. In 2004 Gore in effect gave them his slides, many dating back to the 1970s, and asked for a refresh. The slick presentation we see, then, is the result of considerable expert work at incorporating narrative with visuals (Quinn 2008).

Many of the most striking still images offer pictures of apocalyptic disorder. Global warming is associated with Dali-esque melting icebergs, crazily tilting trees, and freak storms. These operate at the level of connotation to situate climate change as the bringer, not of civilization (vineyards and beach time), but rather of the unpredictable, bizarre, and catastrophic. It is something about which we might feel anxious and that, in a gothic move, is making nature itself "unnatural." Thanks to human interference, nature is turning against itself in perverse ways. Other presentational features are also important. One is the barrage of these images. Somehow audiences never felt overloaded by the amazing 266 slides Gore uses in his presentation. Looking closely at the images, we find that many are weak in terms of cognitive content. They are primarily illustrative in their functions. Graphs and maps are in the minority.

The rapid succession of illustrative slides suggests the ubiquity of global warming processes and visible evidence. Furthermore, it allows the tempo of the documentary presentation to be speeded up in the manner of an Eisenstein montage. The rhythmic properties of such activity mimic those of ritual, bringing about a sort of entrainment. The technique of redundancy is also relevant here. For example, multiple pictures of melting glaciers are popped on screen in quick succession. Each image is slightly different from the others, yet each time the same point is drilled home – the pictures form a set, but each individual image can be approached with the same narrative as explicandum. Repetition gives a sense of scale and ubiquity, but each image becomes poignant through its particularity. It is not just the case that glaciers are melting but also that this or that particular glacier is doomed. Finally, we note that because the images are mostly free of text, such as the bullets we find in typical PowerPoint presentations, Gore is able to slip rapidly from one to the next without having to wait for the audience to complete the task of reading or interpreting. The use of a remote allows Gore to move around, to get away from the podium and connect with his audience. He appears relaxed and familiar with the material. He chats rather than lectures. He does not rely on a written text but, having delivered the talk hundreds of times, has the lecture hardwired in his brain (Paradi 2009).

The brief animations Gore offers play with emotions – or, better put, conjure them into being. This is most obviously the case with the low-tech animation of the polar bear swimming in search of solid ice, faced with the prospect of drowning. Gore's other images are generally of inanimate objects and landscapes. They generate feelings such as surprise and anxiety and, perhaps when he speaks of flooding and hurricanes, low-level fear. Yet the bear allows for significant intersubjective projection and identification with suffering. As one of the handful of species that have been described as charismatic megafauna, the bear is enabled to be the carrier of *pathos*. This possibility, needless to say, is founded on cultural shifts that have seen sentimental and anthropomorphic views of wildlife becoming widespread. The terrifying Darwinian polar bear – one of the few creatures to stalk humans – is nowhere to be seen.

Audience Subject Positions

An important way in which culture can work is to allocate subject positions or identities to individuals. We have already seen how Al Gore made use of this potential to situate himself. What of his audience? In his discussions on ideology the Marxist theorist Louis Althusser (1971) famously noted that subjects are "interpellated" by language. This means that they are called out or named by others and so able to identify themselves in terms of a repertoire of roles and social locations. Aristotle made much the same point when he spoke of *thymos* – which in Greek means "life," "heart," "spirit," and "courage" (Olmsted 2006, 13), and which we discuss in greater depth in Chapter 5 as the emotional basis of civil solidarity – and of *ethos* as products of the communicative process.

We find that *An Inconvenient Truth* works in subtle ways to shape subjectivities such that believing becomes a logical and ethical consequence of understanding. A major problem for Gore, as for all global warming activists, is to explain why certain people deny the problem. After all, if the evidence is really as clear as they say it is, then only a fool would be in denial. Yet to call people foolish violates a key rule of Aristotelian rhetoric, which is to respect the adversary. To attack an adversary is to generate negative sentiment. This in turn reflects back on the character of the speaker and erodes *thymos*, or collective spirit.

To get around this problem, Gore makes use of analogy – a technique Aristotle recommended as an oblique and yet colorful mode of persuasion. Backed by another somewhat cute animation, he explains that a frog placed in boiling water will jump out. A frog placed in cold water that is slowly heated will cook to death. Importantly, we do not see the frog boiling. It jumps out of the water, there is no harm done. Yet the implicit argument remains that those who deny global warming are somewhat like that frog. They are not evil, simply insufficiently attentive to small signs and gradual change. Thanks to this analogy, the audience to his talk is offered a hidden incentive to believe. It can enjoy an epistemological advantage over skeptics.

Conversion experiences also permit analogy. In one confessional Gore tells us that coming from the South, his family had grown tobacco even after the dangers were widely known from the Surgeon General's Report of 1964. Then his elder sister, a heavy smoker, had died of lung cancer. His father decided to stop growing tobacco: "whatever explanation that seemed to make sense in the past, just didn't cut it anymore." Put another way, there had been a wake-up call to ethical responsibility and an admission of guilt. Another analogy is to history:

There was another storm in the 1930s of a different kind, a horrible unprecedented storm in Continental Europe. Winston Churchill warned the people of England that it was different from anything that had ever happened before, and they had to get ready for it. A lot of people did not want to believe it.

Both these analogies have emotive content relating to death and sacrifice. The resulting *pathos* creates a sense of an ethical rather than simply scientific issue. What is also happening here is a skillful deployment of what Aristotle called the *enthymeme* to lead from premise to consequence. The root of *enthymeme* is *thymos*. Unlike syllogism, which simply leads to a logical conclusion, enthymeme goes "into the heart" of an audience (Olmsted 2006, 13). It works best when making use of shared knowledge and common sense rather than through logical steps being spelled out laboriously. Aristotle writes:

Thus we must not carry its reasoning too far back, or the length of our argument will cause obscurity: nor must we put in all the steps that lead to our conclusion, or we shall waste words in saying what is manifest. (*Rhetoric*, 2.22.1395b)

So Gore leaves it to the listener to join the dots. There is an implicit or hidden induction (*logos*) relating, not to the truth of the dangers of climate change (which is by this point in the film assumed), but rather to the necessity for ethical action. The analogy first indicates that a known or agreed-upon attribute exists in one situation and in another. The transmission of another, more controversial attribute is underwritten by this shared property. As we move through the enthymeme, the statements become more controversial. Anchoring to the original statement allows an inferential sequence to be drawn:

A: The scientific evidence on tobacco harm was strong and not facing up to this was wrong. (Consensus statement to get us started.)

B: The scientific evidence on global warming is a lot like that on tobacco. (Common property asserted. Consensus less certain, but agreement is assumed by this point in the film.)

C: We must stop being in denial and take immediate steps to stop global warming, just as Gore's family did for tobacco. (This is the more controversial and painful consequence.)

And,

A: Denying the evil and danger of Hitler's Germany in the 1930s was foolish.

B: The dangers of climate change are similar to those of Hitler's Germany.

C: Denying the danger of climate change is foolish. Disaster will strike if we are complacent and do not act now.

The power of the technique comes from this ability to combine commonsense, logical inference with the less fully rational symbolic resonance that comes from invoking symbols of evil (Hitler, tobacco) in the course of making an argument. Having made the subject positions for climate change denial uncomfortable (appeaser, tobacco profiteer, frog), Gore sets out a positive identity for the believers. This revolves around themes of common humanity, civilizational achievement, and shared vulnerability. This is anticipated very early in the film when Gore shows a noted picture of the earth taken on the Apollo moon missions. Later he shows a space panorama taken from the Galileo probe in deep space.

GORE: You see that pale, blue dot? That's us. Everything that has ever happened in all of human history, has happened on that pixel. All the triumphs and all the tragedies, all the wars all the famines, all the major advances – it's our only home. And that is what is at stake, our ability to live on planet Earth, to have a future as a civilization. I believe this is a moral issue, it is your time to seize this issue, it is our time to rise again to secure our future.

Let's analyze this. Set against the image we have the conjuring of an apocalyptic scenario (the "ability to live on planet Earth"), a sense of common identity ("our only home"), the translation from fact to value ("a moral issue"), and the emergence of a heroic and enabling subject position ("its our time to rise again"). So as the slide show concludes, Gore offers an uplifting identity for his audience. In contrast to the doom-laden vision he has spent much of the film setting out, he now explains how the problem is fixable. The light at the end of the tunnel involves some political will, some popular pressure, some small sacrifices, and some bold decisions. Many of these will involve increasing the self-restraint and reflexivity of individuals in line with a long-term ecocivilizing process (Rohloff 2011). But there is also a transcendent moment. Gore uses the terms "we" and "us" to generate a sense of collective identity and common purpose. He asks, "Are we as Americans capable of doing great things even though they are difficult? Are we capable of rising above ourselves and above history?" There follows a litany of noncontroversial American triumphs akin to those of the American civil religion that Robert Bellah (1979) has written about: founding a new nation, abolishing slavery, ending segregation and communism alike. Here we see the narrative of the "everyman hero" emerging, the very one urged by the maligned *Warm Words* with which we started this chapter.

Performing Global Warming

Looking closely at *An Inconvenient Truth* provides useful lessons in how culture works when it comes to the consciousness of a "risk society." As Ulrich Beck used it, this term stands as a gloss for a generic set of dispositions, knowledge sensitivities, and anxieties that are scattered throughout a population. This risk awareness is largely the result of a cognitive process of information retrieval, even if that information can sometimes do little more than suggest that "we don't really know" how dangerous something is. The case of Al Gore and the film we have considered in this chapter suggests that something different is going on. Distributed scientific information on dangers plays an incomplete or partial role in this process. As the climate change scientists themselves complain, growing consensus in the science community is only weakly matched by changing public opinion. Sometimes remarkable performative gestures are required for "facts" about "risks" to have meaning or impact outside the academe. Furthermore, our analysis of this one gesture uncovered a surprisingly complex layering of image, narrative, and identity formation – a layering that is unlikely to be decoded by laypeople as they are caught up in watching the film the first time through. We had the luxury of a transcript, the ability to watch the movie multiple times, and the assistance of luminaries such as Aristotle and Foucault. All things considered, we have a film whose power comes from the mobilization of character. This is a triumph of Gore's *ethos*, albeit with some help from other textual and visual elements. This flight from *logos* is a little sneaky given the movie's "documentary" tag. It is also an irony because science has always valued transparency in method. It also tells us that the facts should speak for themselves. If the rules of that game have to be abandoned to get a message over about those facts themselves, this is an irony. We might also say it's an inconvenient truth.

5

Climate Change Art

An Illustrative Failure?

Although emphatic on the pivotal role of character, Aristotle seems to have been in two minds when it comes to the persuasive force of the visual and the visual arts. On one hand, he intimates that the representation of reality is intrinsically fascinating and emotionally energizing for humans:

Objects which in themselves we view with pain, we delight to contemplate when reproduced with minute fidelity: such as the forms of the most ignoble animals and of dead bodies...the reason why men enjoy seeing a likeness is that in contemplating it they find themselves learning or inferring, and saying perhaps, "Ah, that is he." For if you happen not to have seen the original, the pleasure will be due not to the imitation as such, but to the execution, the coloring, or some such other cause. (*Poetics* IV, 3–5)

On the other hand, he subordinates visual representation in the hierarchy of the arts: cultural evolution had given rise to more complex and powerful modes of expression. The human instinct for imitation had been combined with those for harmony and rhythm and eventually "gave birth to Poetry" (*Poetics* IV, 6). Aristotle is clear that this is a more complete art form, especially when it provides the foundation for drama. Within the world of drama itself, he concedes that "Spectacle has, indeed, an emotional attraction of its own" before continuing, "But, of all the parts, it is the least artistic, and connected least with the art of poetry. For the power of Tragedy, we may be sure, is felt even apart from representation and actors. Besides, the production of spectacular effects depends more on the art of the stage machinist than on that of the poet" (*Poetics* VI, 19).

It would seem that for Aristotle, then, the visual can generate superficial pleasures but not a deep and transformative experience. It is too closely tied to immediate experience and sensing, whereas a powerful narrative can exert a more abstract and less context-bound influence. These points are amplified and made more specific later in the *Poetics*. Here again Aristotle gives greater credit to plot than to spectacle for its capacity to generate transformative emotional impacts in audiences:

Fear and Pity may be aroused by spectacular means; but they may also result from the inner structure of the piece, which is the better way, and indicates a superior poet. For the plot ought to be constructed that, even without the aid of the eye, he who hears the tale told will thrill with horror and melt to pity at what takes place. This is the impression we should receive from hearing the story of *Oedipus*. But to produce this effect by mere spectacle is a less artistic method, and dependent on extraneous aids. (XIV, 1–2)

Does Aristotle's argument still make sense in our intensely visual age? Although it seems clear that he places imitative drawing lower than poetry on the hierarchy of the arts, the case might be made that in the context of the *Poetics*, he is chiefly talking about "staging" or even what we today think of as "special effects." The argument might be salvaged that high art (conceptual art, expressive art, abstract art) can rival plot and have equally powerful effects. Moreover, although our analysis in the previous chapter highlighted the narrative and mythic features of *An Inconvenient Truth*, we would have to concede that it simultaneously confirms visual means of communication can be remarkably effective in communicating a message about climate change. A notable check against Aristotle is that we are not aware of any book or speech that has had an equivalent impact. In retrospect, this fact should hardly be surprising. Researchers from education, psychology, marketing, semiotics, and other fields of knowledge have long suggested that visual materials hold attention more strongly than written texts. They offer powerful condensations of meaning that enable comprehension at a glance and can load this with emotional freight as well. More recently, cultural sociology itself has gained a new appreciation of the role of visuality and what it terms "iconicity" as a powerful force in social life (Alexander, Bartmanski, and Giesen 2012; Brighenti 2010). Well aware of the power of imagery, material culture, and artistic representation, the environmentalist community has sought to shape opinion and action through images as well as words. It has used visual means to arouse interest, to suggest a shared fate, to improve public understanding, and to propagate a sense of urgency.

Aristotle's concerns about empty spectacle aside, the theoretical odds look to be stacked in favor of the visual as a force to be reckoned with – and hence as a major component of the social drama of climate change. We turn here to exploring this possibility in its purest form – the laboratory setting of climate change art.

"Climate art" has become a well-established subgenre in recent years and has been subject to plenty of critical review (e.g., Doyle 2011, 145–156; Duxbury 2010; Giannachi 2012; Martin 2006, 2009; Miles 2010; Potter 2012; Ziser and Sze 2007). The possibilities for deep impact seem plausible. For example, campaigns against whaling and seal culls used video and still footage in the 1970s and 1980s to graphically display human violence against relatively helpless animals (Dauvergne and Neville 2011). Images of the earth from the early space missions have also been credited with radically changing sensibilities, these leading to a new set of powerful ecometaphors such as "spaceship earth" (Cosgrove 1994; Henry and Taylor 2009; Jasanoff 2001; Maher 2004). Likewise, there is a substantial track record on the pivotal role of photography in environmental politics, from the formation of America's national parks to oil spills to the antinuclear movement (Cosgrove 2008; Dunaway 2005, 2008; Morse 2012).

Indeed, as the historian Finis Dunaway (2005, xvi) convincingly argues, conservationism has relied on the power of images more than any other American reform movement. True, much of this imagery has been of romantic nature deployed in the cause of wilderness preservation – one thinks of Ansel Adams and Eliot Porter. But the iconography of complex, human-caused ecological degradation also has a prominent history. Even images of regional climate change – in the form of the great Dust Bowl that devastated the Depression-era Plains – are burned into the popular environmental imagination, thanks to filmmakers like Pare Lorentz (*The Plow That Broke the Plains*) and photographer Dorothea Lange, who chronicled the human cost of environmental ruin (Dunaway 2005, 33–59). These producers of visual culture helped make conservation into "a moral crusade, an attempt to reform the basic values and assumptions of American culture" (Dunaway 2005, 34). Why has the same not happened with global climate change?

One common answer is that climate change is just too complicated, both ecologically and politically. Unlike the Dust Bowl, which was the direct, rapid, localized consequence of intensive agriculture (Worster 2004), the causal relations of climate change do not lend themselves to pictorial representation. But if we look beyond the environmental realm to other complex, global-scale tragedies – war, in particular – we see that art *can* cut through similar complexity. Take the Vietnam Veterans Memorial in Washington, D.C., designed by the artist and architectural designer Maya Lin. As the visual culture scholar Kristin Hass (1998, 9) notes, "the deeply controversial nature of the war, its unpopularity, and the reality that it was lost created an enormous void of meaning that compounded the difficult work of memorializing." Yet through her brilliant design, Lin was able to fill that void while forcing a painful public reassessment of American militarism. In the 1980s and 1990s, the AIDS crisis was publicly confronted by famous artists such as Keith Haring and the collective AIDS Coalition to Unleash Power (ACT UP), which helped change the shape of public consciousness of the disease. Even if we set the thresholds for public significance or for "art" much lower, we see that visual culture routinely works this way. Culture-jamming activities of groups like Adbusters suggest that activism can work very efficiently without words and that subversive images are peculiarly well suited to meme-like forms of cost-free replication through the Internet. Moreover representations of Che Guevara, the Nazi Swastika, and the humble national flags of various nations all attest to the solidaristic and motivational properties of visual information.

Yet such easily accessible documentary photography, graphic design, and culture jamming have so far failed to generate for climate change what practitioners call a "mind bomb." "The challenge is to find images of predicted global environmental crises that have the emotional impact of a dust storm rising over an isolated farmstead or of Yosemite emerging as a Claudian dream of arcadia in early morning light," writes the geographer Denis Cosgrove (2008, 1876). Photos of polar bears seem too remote and pathetic (1878). We would add that they also appear clichéd and, as Kathryn Yusoff (2010) observes in a detailed study, are an ethically problematic carrier of the political aesthetics of climate change. Inuit perspectives on the polar bear are often ignored, for example. The act of observation involves the aesthetic capture of the untamed and its facile translation into a banal Anthropocene extinction narrative. Visual representations of climate-related natural disasters, hurricanes, floods, and so forth can be attributed to proximate causes...such as the weather. Campaigns using sex appeal look trivial, and those that aim to shock or amuse, as we will see in the next chapter, are spectacularly risky (Bojanowski 2011). But what about more refined or "higher" forms of visual representation, those claiming the name of "art," that are our focus here?

Recently there has been considerable hope that "art" can be used variously as a means of mobilizing public opinion, adjusting sensibility, or generating new ways of thinking (see Bunting 2009). This might seem a tall task. What first springs to mind for the sociologist are Bourdieu's theories about cultural capital and specifically the barriers that cultural capital puts up against mass appeal. However, it should be remembered that many critically acclaimed artists have acquired widespread popular followings. Images by van Gogh and Warhol, for example, are recognizable throughout the middle classes to the point where not only can they be parodied but the parodies can be recognized as witty. Blockbuster exhibitions sell out. Projects by Christo and Jean-Claude are viewed by millions. The audience for art is hardly microscopic.

The odds for climate art to proliferate in such a way are favored by elective affinities involving institutions, identities, and impression management. The relationship can be thought of as symbiotic rather than exploitative. Galleries need content. They also like to challenge populist understandings of themselves as elitist and as aloof from worldly concerns. Sponsors such as major corporations like to be thought of as socially responsible. So climate change agendas and institutional platforms offer artists a way to have their work noticed and funded. Less instrumentally, climate change themes allow many artists to produce work that conforms to their calling as engaged contributors to an aesthetic public sphere. We can understand this aesthetic public sphere as an arena of artistic activity (in the broad sense of the term) oriented toward a shared consideration and conversation on social, cultural, and political issues. Even if communication is not "rational" within the rubric of analytic philosophy, logical positivism, or Habermasian communicative ethics, the intent is nevertheless to improve societal rationality through encouraging normative and pragmatic reflexivity. A change in subjectivity can come about from phenomenological contact with the artwork in public space. More collectively, it might spring from subsequent discursive activity surrounding the merits of aesthetic objects themselves, and thence to the issues that they purport to bring to the table. New technologies can help. Climate change advocates are especially aware that the Internet can play an important role in this process. Bypassing the need to meet face-to-face in order to to have dialogue as well as the editorial filtering of redacted mass media commentary, the Internet also allows citizens to encounter artworks without traveling. Then they can subsequently share opinions directly and so to develop a grassroots culture of resistance and solidarity though virtual talk – or so many hope.

The dream scenario for art activists would be something like as follows. An exhibition of climate change art achieves high visibility. It has blockbuster attendance and widespread media interest. Certain artworks become famous as pithy, iconic representations of the reality and urgency of climate change. A "climate Guernica" emerges. People encountering the artworks in real or virtual spaces feel emotionally moved. They engage in sustained dialogues over the Internet. These move outward thematically, beginning with discussions about the meaning of certain art pieces and ending with wider themes such as science, technology, ethics, and politics in a context of dealing with climate change. There is also institutional spread. The mainstream media picks up on this chatter. These discussions then radiate out again to influence other spheres of social life, most importantly those of politics and economics. A more modest but not unreasonable expectation is for the artistic enterprise to be noticed by the public and critics and for a contentious but articulate and serious debate to follow about art, environment, and politics, at least among the millions committed to facing up to climate change. Here the positive outcome would be in-group solidarity building and motivation. If this sounds promising as a way forward, the promise has yet to be fulfilled even at this lower threshold.

At first the stumbling block was merely product. A widely cited essay by leading environmental activist and intellectual Bill McKibben (2005) published in the environmentalist flagship *Grist* magazine in 2005 identified this problem several years ago. According to McKibben, whereas AIDS had produced a plethora of artistic exhibits, climate change was failing to inspire creative activity. This was despite that fact that future generations might well see our creeping temperature gains as one of the most significant events in human history. Why had there been a failure of representation? McKibben starts by noting several issues we have remarked upon elsewhere in this book (see Chapter 1). Happening "everywhere all at once," it threatened to become a "backdrop, context, instead of event." Yet when we turn to those events, such as hurricanes, that might have been spawned by climate change, McKibben says, these are so dramatic that they exclude consideration of deeper causal mechanisms. Narrative possibilities are made difficult by the fact that there would be too many villains if "everyone with a car" were held to account. Yet simply bearing witness is too passive. Efforts to generate fear, such as the science fiction movie *The Day after Tomorrow*, in which climate change shifts the Gulf Stream and generates a new Ice Age, just looked silly. All things considered, climate change seemed to be too complex and too much of a challenge for artistic engagement. Artists had not abandoned the field, they had never taken up the gauntlet, McKibben sighed in conclusion.

Just a few years later, McKibben (2009) was reporting back with more enthusiasm that "the immune system of the planet is finally kicking in." Artists, those "antibodies of the cultural bloodstream," had at last found ways to represent climate change. By 2010, this activity had expanded into 350.org's "Earth" initiative, designed to generate art visible from space as well as a wider raft of "artivist" initiatives. Clearly a lot of energy, goodwill, and money had been heading in the direction of climate change art. Still many questions remain. How effective is this antibody activity in generating iconic impacts in the wider mediascape? Did coordinated, thoughtful, and expansive discursive activity cumulate on the back of such aesthetic initiatives? As part of the wider social drama, how were the climate change artists themselves narrated as characters? Finally, is the hope and enthusiasm of McKibben and other climate change art advocates really warranted?

Before answering these questions, it is worth pausing to give a sense of what climate change artworks might look like (see Cook 2007). At the more "objective" or "scientific" end of the spectrum we find relatively unmodified photographic images of ice and glaciers, and also kindred modes such as home movies and satellite pictures. These will often be displayed in aesthetically pleasing ways in gallery spaces to indicate rapid change or to highlight the fragility and beauty of remote locations. Aside from the usual documentary/artistic photos of polar bears and icebergs, the work of James Balog and the Extreme Ice Survey is perhaps best known here (http://www.extremeicesurvey.org/). Placing cameras in remote places for an entire season, they capture the seasonal retreat of glaciers. The resulting sequences sit somewhere between art and science, with Balog striving to show here, as in other parts of his work, the impact of humans on nature – yet with minimal interpretative gestures and authorial presence. Also in a representational genre, we find more actively creative attempts to represent possible future landscapes. These use quasirealist or hyperrealist techniques to generate more or less plausible images of radical transformation, the catastrophe frequently involving either desertification or flooding. *Manifest Destiny* (2004) by Alexis Rockman is a twenty-four-foot-long mural somewhat like a 1970s progressive rock album cover. It shows a postapocalyptic Brooklyn under a glowing red sky. Familiar urban landmarks are underwater and tropical flora and fauna are abundant. Other artworks are more conceptual, but these usually still have a metonymic link to themes of heat, cold, time, and landscape. Tavares Strachan's *The Distance between What We Have and What We Want (Arctic Ice Project)* (2004) is also on display at the Brooklyn Museum. Here a two-and-a-half-ton block of ice extracted by the artist in Alaska is preserved in a solar-powered refrigerator. Artworks with a more general or diffuse interest in the relationship of humans to the environment are also often placed in climate change exhibitions. Expanding McKibben's metaphor, we might think of these as "borrowed antibodies." For example, *Amazonian Field* by Antony Gormley was produced as long ago as 1991. It consists of a room crowded with hundreds of six-inch-high clay figures that gaze up at the viewer wide eyed and open mouthed. The overall sense, according to critics, is of fear and of multitude. The work is not specifically about climate change at all, but nevertheless it was reassembled for a 2009 climate change themed exhibition at the Royal Academy in London.

The emergence of artworks such as these, and their organization into a coherent and self-aware field, was not simply an individual response to the situational conditions of the first decade of the twenty-first century, such as the artist's experience of objective climate change or a growing climate change social movement. The birth of the genre took place against a background of historically entrenched social and cultural factors (Hubbard 2006). One was the existence of a tradition extending back to Romanticism. This has at its core a critique of technology and yearning for ways of being that were more "authentic" and connected to nature. Climate change art could tap into this heritage and sensibility, which seeks the sacred in Nature and views modernity as symbolically as well as literally polluted. A more immediate source of inspiration is the existence of a prior generation of land art or environmental art, this associated with major names like Joseph Beuys, Robert Smithson, and Andy Goldsworthy. Their visibility and status suggested a legitimate, high-end enterprise that can garner critical attention and enter into the wider aesthetic consciousness of a society. Finally, there is the exhaustion of ironic, apolitical, material culture–driven, depthless art associated with names like Damien Hirst or Jeff Koons. By 2010, this was looking to many artists to be facile, even if auction prices were holding up surprisingly well.

Unlike the disinterested "art for art's sake" that dominates galleries and markets – where failure to sell or to find appreciation can be explained away as the cost of fidelity to an artistic vision – an engaged artist has no place to hide. Although "witnessing" offers one legitimate motivation, an activist art hopes mostly for less passive impacts in the form of turnstile movement, Internet clicks, or civic debate. These objective indicators are hard to come by. Our research suggests the wider public does not seem to be especially keen to turn out to view climate change art. When people do show up or click, they should be moved or motivated by the artworks. Yet our examination of blogs and Internet threads tied to art exhibitions shows that scientific or normative debate rarely eventuates. Usually there is zero to minimal discursive response. Sometimes we find brief expressive acts of appreciation. More often, however, discourses fall into place that are only tangentially related to the artworks and to climate change. These *derail* the communicative process in the aesthetic public sphere. Like much other art, the climate change genre has been denounced as obscure, preachy, sentimental, banal, and elitist in some combination. That's one derailing. Added to this are new vulnerabilities to hypocrisy that do not afflict other artists, these focusing on questions of lifestyle and carbon footprint. That's a second. These two response categories might be thought of as ironic resistance to either art in general or climate change art in particular. They deliberately deflate heroic visions and in so doing cut against efforts at genre inflation that insist we are dealing with an apocalyptic issue that needs to be confronted through visionary representation, romantic solidarity, and heroic collective sacrifice. Such responses are to be expected. Far more disturbing is the fact that desired outputs are so often subject to such derailing by otherwise sympathetic individuals. These are not mean-spirited Internet trolls but eco-idealists and artistic fellow travelers. As we will see, often activists and artists spoil possibilities for productive dialogue (what we might think of in an Aristotelian way as "chorus") by pursuing their own agendas and interests. The result might be termed "cacophony." We believe the artistic and activist community viewing and responding to artworks needs to realize that it is itself part of the wider social drama that it witnessed by others. It might think of itself as an "audience" for the art, but to the onlooking global spectator, it is actually player, and it must play its collective part with discipline and in tune.

Aristotle wrote, "The Chorus too should be regarded as one of the actors; it should be an integral part of the whole, and share in the action" (*Poetics* XVIII, 7; see also Weiner 1980). He goes on to suggest that failed dramatic strategies involve weak integration of the chorus with the action of the players: "As for the later poets, their choral songs pertain as little to the subject of the piece as to that of any other tragedy. They are, therefore, sung as mere interludes, a practice first begun by Agathon. Yet what difference is there between introducing such choral interludes, and transferring a speech, or even a whole act, from one play to another" (*Poetics* XVIII, 7). Understood analogously, this problem of thematically disparate, stand-alone choral activity is one that has plagued many climate change activities. The remainder of this chapter illustrates a particular failure to achieve chorus in the specific context of art.

A much noticed essay by the world-renowned British artist and sculptor Antony Gormley (2010) can serve as an exhibit to introduce these themes. In this item published in the British flagship left-of-center broadsheet the *Guardian*, Gormley notes the rise of consumerism and technology. He observes that now we need to "discover our nature within nature" – essentially the keynote theme to all his art. According to Gormley, the time has come to "re-evaluate the function of art within the frame of a sustainable lifestyle," to make us "more aware of the human predicament and of our material and elemental surroundings." The artist, he says, can play a role in this reflexive process. Deeds speak louder than words, so at the end of the essay, Gormley displays how he has changed his own lifestyle and work activity. He notes that he has had his carbon footprint assessed and that he has reduced his number of flights. His studio with seventeen assistants is being insulated and solar panels are being installed. In future, he says, more art materials will be recycled, and he will "investigate the viability of a wind turbine." Art in the era of climate change, it would seem, requires new forms of reflexivity over the production process and new demands for accountability.

Online responses to Gormley posted below his item on the *Guardian*'s website suggest that celebrity artists and major art institutions will find climate change art an especially problematic arena. For many, Gormley's carbon footprint strategies were not enough. Once identified, these offered a prompt for more general critiques of art to fall into place. "I truly like your art," replies Love is Eternal, "but it falls down where all green hand wringers do . . . they won't make the personal sacrifice needed." This was a mild blow; others were harsher: Gormley was like one of those corporations spouting environmental rhetoric to support its bottom line. Whereas the old masters had practiced sustainable art with their "wood stretchers, linen canvases, linseed and walnut oil," this was a pitch for the "continuing survival of Anthony Gormley plc wrapped up in the caring, concerned language of survival of the planet/the human species" (LeeWoods). Worse, he was replaying a tired old ideology. He was "the art version of Harry Potter," advocating "the traditional bourgeois theory of art, the artist as shaman who can change the world of elemental forces. The shaman always decries the big capitalization of art, yet takes the big money to the big bank all the same" (zerozero). Critique was not all personal. In attempting to open the door to a sensitive and ethical engagement with nature, Gormley had also opened the door to an informed but also populist tirade against what was seen as a shallow, bloated, and pretentious modern art establishment. For example, Gormley's essay confirmed the need to "bulldoze the Tate Modern" and to "have the balls to reject the relativism that has corroded notions of value" (SaucyJack). Clearly making an erudite pitch for social and ethical relevance cannot clear climate change art of the usual vulnerabilities of conceptual work, namely, that anybody can do it if she has an outrageous idea; that the art establishment arbitrarily confers recognition on those who can't actually draw; and that remuneration to "startists" is out of line with effort.

What is going on here? Clearly these posted critiques are made by informed individuals interested in the world of the arts. Their vocabulary is complex (e.g., *linseed, shaman, corroded*), and they have taken the time to read a somewhat philosophical opinion item in the *Guardian*, a famously earnest, left-leaning forum. These people certainly don't look like Neanderthal trolls. What has happened? The aesthetic public sphere has derailed its own debate. Rather than taking certain things for granted that would get us started, such as the privileged and socially useful status of the artist as witness and interpreter, and then discussing *how* the artist can become more environmentally aware, *how* art should respond to climate change or *how* humankind relates to the planet, we have set off on a tangent. This is to evaluate and critique Gormley, to ask if he is a hypocrite and to question the nature of art values in toto. We have some critical rationality here, but the chorus is merely expressing rancor and division. The cut and thrust of Gormley's plea is blunted: no onlooker will be inspired.

Antony Gormley's *Guardian* item generated a strong online response. By that measure, at least, we might consider it a success for climate change art. But wait a minute: this prompt was a textual meditation on the relationship of art to climate change and social activism. Responding discursively to discourse is relatively easy. This was not, at the end of the day, the case of an artwork generating a discursive response. Moreover, when it comes to putting climate change art on the map, Gormley is advantaged. He is a world-class figure with high visibility. Sadly, at the same time, he is a target. He is especially ill placed to make a plea for environmental sensitivity given that his signature work, *Event Horizon* of 2007, consisted of multiple life-size statues of himself placed in landscapes or cityscapes, often on rooflines by means of cranes or helicopters. Intended to situate the human in a landscape and to cause meditation on this theme, these seem to many egocentric, obscurantist, and carbon hungry. Perhaps less esoteric projects by seemingly humble, lower-profile figures will elicit the sort of critical discourse that the climate change community is looking for?

Certainly the (few) relatively successful items in the climate change art catalog seem to have been figurative or allegorical items where the artist is not centre stage. The Copenhagen Ice Bear stands out as a case in point. Carved from a nine-ton block of ice by British sculptor Mark Coreth, this 1.8-meter-high sculpture was placed outside the Bella Center conference venue at the time of the 2009 Copenhagen climate talks. The public was allowed to touch the sculpture, their hands contributing to the melting process in a way that was intended to mirror the contribution of everyday life to climate change. As the surface of the bear slowly disappeared, it revealed a bronze inner skeleton. Lit at night, the semitransparent ice gave rise to fascinating visual effects. The Ice Bear can be considered a good idea for three reasons. First, it was copied. Editions appeared soon afterward in London, Quebec City, Ottawa, Montreal, and Toronto. In sociological jargon, it was a "transposable schema." Second, it generated personal involvement among spectators. A visit to Internet photo-sharing sites, for example, reveals a reasonable number of Ice Bear pictures taken by ordinary people. Third, it attracted media attention. The World Wildlife Fund (WWF) issued press releases advertising the photo op and offering interviews with Coreth, other ice sculptors, and scientists. Leading newspapers, television channels, and so forth were tempted by a visually appealing short novelty item with a clear narrative attached. It helped in this respect that the ice bears were all placed in iconic city settings, such as London's Trafalgar Square. The iconically proven combination of incongruity and recognition could be guaranteed. As the World Wildlife Fund 2010) press release noted, the Ice Bear made an "excellent background for TV journalists and weather forecasters." Media friendly, intellectually accessible, and visually arresting, the Ice Bear seems at first glance to have been a step forward.

Unfortunately, we find little evidence of any truly deep public uptake. This is a modest success. Seed images were planted on Flickr and Facebook by the WWF and by the Ice Bear Project. These attracted in turn more images from amateur photographers who uploaded their own pictures to Ice Bear groups and home pages. Yet when we click on "discussion" for such sites, we find no consideration of environmental issues, nor even

Ice Bear aesthetics. The four or five Ice Bear videos on YouTube had attracted about four thousand views a year after they were uploaded in December 2009. The Ice Bear may have been a transposable item of civic sculpture, yet it did not "go viral" in any credible way. Consider briefly that one video of Tillman the skateboarding dog has attracted 20 million hits on YouTube – and counting.

Contrasting with the Ice Bear, the Cape Farewell Project marks a more high-end, somewhat highbrow solution to the question of climate change art.[1] A charity created by artist David Buckland, this undertakes ambitious expeditions to remote locations, usually the Arctic. Once there, invited artists begin to create works inspired by their contact with nature and informed by an awareness of climate change. What's the logic here? Buckland believes that "climate change is a reality... and must move beyond scientific debate. Cape Farewell is committed to the notion that artists can engage the public in this issue through creative insight and vision" (Buckland 2007). So the aim is explicitly to stir up public opinion through the power of art. This, it is hoped, will bring change while governments dither.

A visit to Cape Farewell's very professionally organized website reveals a lot of activity. An impressive list of talented artists, musicians, and performers from several nations have been involved in the expeditions. Many are A-list identities within the culture industries. There is also a film and a touring exhibition that has appeared in museums and galleries in London, Madrid, Hamburg, and Tokyo. Yet looked at closely, the site also reveals the comparative exclusion of climate art from the highest artistic spheres and its problems in attracting an audience.

We were concerned that our Internet sweeps revealed surprisingly little chatter or excitement. Despite a well-maintained, carefully cultivated presence on sites like Facebook and Twitter, and despite a consistently high profile in media reports on climate art, there was little evidence of active public engagement online. That which exists is frequently from

---

[1] At the time of researching this chapter, Cape Farewell had consistently high visibility in Google search results using a variety of search terms. The visits to its web pages on which our analysis was based was made in summer 2010 through to October 2010. (See Brighenti 2010, 96–97, for a nuanced discussion of Google search results as an indicator of visibility, power, and field centrality.) There will, of course, have been changes to Cape Farewell's activities or website by the time our book is published or read. We invite readers to look at the website and see if our analysis still holds. Although our words here might seem harsh, we wish Cape Farewell well. We are merely trying to communicate some sad realities as we see them. We believe our analysis accurately depicts the weak reception of the project within the public sphere at the time of writing.

sources connected in one way or another to Cape Farewell itself, for example, galleries showing the product or exhibition sponsors. This gave the unfortunate impression of an echo chamber in which institutions refer to each other in the quest for legitimacy and status. By contrast, we were all too easily able to find broader public critique of the entire enterprise. It was often argued that it was carbon hostile to ship artistic people to a remote destination. The project was also denounced as elitist. "I'm glad that there seems to be a growing consensus that art (or its practitioners) have a duty of using their abilities towards social ends," writes one online response to an item on environmental art. Yet the "message... is totally undermined when the audience become aware of the ecological cost of such a trip in the first place. It becomes just another ill thought out art junket for the favored few" (guydenning 2006).

There are shades here of the critiques to which Antony Gormley was subject – that this is a world of networked insiders versus outsiders, of gestures versus deeds, of bloated waste and of celebrity hucksterism. The potential for a contrarian reading of Cape Farewell was developed more extensively and wittily by one of those A-list guests, Ian McEwan (2010), in his novel *Solar*. Here, for example, Antony Gormley is transformed into an artist who creates identical ice penguins (no doubt a play on his *Event Horizon* and *Amazonian Field*). The expedition's carbon footprint in terms of snowmobile trips, hot meals, and flights is satirized. The chaos of everyday life on board the hundred-foot expedition boat and the defective personalities at play are contrasted to the worthy sentiments of its members. Again the noble cause appears vulnerable to ironic deflation.[2]

It was worrying that even this well-funded and professionally run flagship effort struggles to demonstrate successful outreach – at least this was the case at the time of writing. For example, the organization's website proudly noted that the Tokyo edition of one of its shows attracted forty-five thousand visitors during its six-week run. This works out at a little over a thousand per day. The figure is somewhat less impressive when we reflect that Japan's art attendances are traditionally very high and that the Japanese public is environmentally engaged. In 2009, there were four Japanese exhibitions attracting more than nine thousand people

---

[2] Perhaps in response to this critique, the emphasis of Cape Farewell's activities seems to have shifted. There is now a greater emphasis on expeditions tracking climate change in less remote locations (e.g., the Scottish Hebrides); on local history and place; on community outreach; and on scientific observation and research. It is possible, however, that this increasing diversity simply reflects growing organizational capacity rather than a response to critique.

per day. The most popular exhibit in Japan in 2010, a postimpression-ism blockbuster, pulled in 777000 (*Art Newspaper* 2011). The Japanese attendance figures also need to be considered in light of the fact that the Cape Farewell exhibit was placed in the context of a larger attraction that offered the true destination for the day-tripper – in this case the Tokyo Museum of Emerging Science and Innovation. People may well have wandered through the exhibit because it was there at the time, and probably free. It is indicative and troubling that the organization also highlighted the statistic of twenty-three hundred people attending an Oslo showing at the Nobel Peace Center on World Environment Day. This is not a bad turnout but still well below the usual attendance of three thousand to five thousand every day for weeks at a time for major special exhibits in major galleries in major Western cities (Collett-White 2010; Kennedy 2001).

Cape Farewell has done well to circulate its art globally. But here again there seem to be problems hitting the most ambitious, high-status, high-visibility targets. The venues are often one tier down the hierarchy. For example, the *Art and Climate Change* exhibition was shown between 2006 and 2010 at the Cranbrook Art Museum, Michigan (not the Art Institute of Chicago); the Fundacion Canal Madrid (not the Bilbao Guggenheim); the Kampnagel Cultural Center, Hamburg (not the Neue Nationalgalerie, Berlin); the Liverpool Biennial (not that of Venice); and the National History Museum, London (not the Tate Modern – although to be fair, Cape Farewell did get a "late at the Tate" slot on February 6, 2009; this would seem to confirm semiperipherality in that it was a discussion evening, not a major dedicated exhibition in a large space).

Still Cape Farewell does have a certain influence. It is certainly well connected and enterprising and can offer vibrant new content to galleries from high-profile artists. *Earth: Art of a Changing World* (December 2009 to January 2010), perhaps its most visible and prestigious showing to date, documents this truth. Held at a top-ranked venue, the Royal Academy of Arts in London, this combined Cape Farewell artworks with older and autonomously created items by high-status figures like Antony Gormley and Tracey Moffatt. Although not a big public hit (see its notable absence from global attendance rankings; *Art Newspaper* 2011), it did manage to attract reviews from leading papers. These are important given the role of critics as mediators of value and generators of interest that has been well documented in the sociology of the arts. The general feeling among critics was of earnest mediocrity rather than peak achievement. According to the *Independent*'s Michael Glover (2009), it was all "a tad too polite, too easy on the eye." For Joanna Pittman (2009) of the *Times*, some artworks were effective, but too many "seem directed at art collectors, at hot trends, at money. Other works dabble in stagnant waters on the mistaken assumption that neglected margins are cutting-edge." These were "slack attempts to shock." For the most part the reviewers chose to write about the non–Cape Farewell materials, especially the historically important *Amazonian Field*. How do we account for this? A problem might be that climate art cannot embody the norm of "art for art's sake" that confers the highest prestige within the artistic field (Bourdieu 1993). It is not a truly pure form of art that privileges the disinterested vision of the artist producing works to fulfill the incessant demands of an inner self (remember Hegel on the modern character in Chapter 2) or responding to the challenges set by peers. This is a form of art responding to a "problem" outside its own sphere and trying to appeal to a general public. It seeks to be popular, not exclusive, engaged and not disengaged. The odds are stacked against an enthusiastic reception in the art world itself – although the case of Banksy suggests that with a mastery of both iconic consciousness and chutzpah, they can be overcome.

Rethink: Contemporary Art and Climate Change was the other major exhibition held around the time of the 2009 Copenhagen climate forum.[3] Backed by heavyweight government sponsorship from the likes of the Danish Arts Council, the Nordic Culture Fund, and the National Gallery of Denmark, it featured works by several regionally and globally recognized artists. Critics were generally sympathetic toward the show, although in a downbeat mode, they wondered about its capacity to actually achieve any real change and noticed that some artists seemed more comfortable documenting personal feelings than demanding action (Bunting 2009) – a paradoxical response in light of the comments we made at the end of the prior paragraph and suggesting a peculiar double-bind for the climate artist. *Rethink* is especially useful for isolating the failure of Internet forums to sustain discourse of the kind that climate change art is hoping for. Whereas Cape Farewell seems (curiously, but as we will see by the end of this chapter, understandably) to avoid offering spaces for public comment and feedback with a somewhat top-down communication strategy, *Rethink* is typically Scandinavian, that is to say, open

---

3 *Rethink* was ranked twelfth in our Google searches for "climate change art" at the time this item was first written (June 2011). Our comments relate to the success and failure of *Rethink* at the time of researching this chapter in summer 2010. Given that this was a couple of years or so after the Copenhagen conference, we feel this was adequate time for the gestation of audience enthusiasm and a critical discourse.

and democratic. For this reason the exhibition was accompanied at some expense by a tidy and professional website aiming for public and media outreach. There we find editor and moderator Lea Schick (2009) tirelessly attempting to stir up reaction or dialogue with a series of prompts, these often based on quotations from artists, descriptions of *Rethink* art projects, and rhetorical questions such as "Is art the only discipline that dares to reveal for us how life will be for us in the future?" A year later most prompts had generated from zero to two responses. One especially poignant example was from a fellow artist:

Hi Lea, I am very interested in your blog and the issues you address and was curious to find out what kind of response you are having, my partner and I are developing a project on the environment and wanted to participate in your blog, but we do not find any comments from anybody. Are we not doing the right thing? Or is the world so apathetic, including the art world? (Yvonne Senouf)

It is worth noting that Senouf is herself an artist with a critical vision of society and the environment, not a member of the general public who has been suddenly enthused through contact with *Rethink*'s artworks and motivated to respond to Lea Schick's meditative provocations. She had discovered a discomforting fact: art was not generating dialogue. A substantial item on *Rethink* published in the professionally produced online zine *ArtCulture* on October 24, 2009 (Norris 2009), suggests that when Internet threads do manage to generate reader-supplied content, this does not mean that content is necessarily valuable.[4] The *ArtCulture* item summarizes the kinds of artworks in the *Rethink* show and expresses how they are intended to offer "new perspectives on some of the complex social issues stemming from climate change." It reproduces representative images and offers brief textual explanations of the themes they address. A thread at the bottom was available for comment. Contributions suggest incoherence more than chorus. The first response is from Peter Hughes. He speaks of his new film about climate change: *Ecoplaza Paradise Oasis.* Calling this "Plan B" to save the world, he touts its leading-edge qualities as a tool for change and asks how he can obtain a venue to show it in Copenhagen. The seven items that follow show disorder more than mutual coordination and respect. A successful thread would be one with a minimal degree of integration in its network of ideas. Postings might refer back to a shared prompt. In this case, that would be the item in *ArtCulture*

---

[4] *ArtCulture* had a Google ranking of 15 for the search "Climate Change Art" in June 2011.

above the thread. They might also refer to each other, creating a web of interchange that would develop ideas and build solidarity. Theory and research on everyday conversation, deliberation in democracy, and even theatrical improvisation suggest that it is important for people to take up the ideas of others and move forward with them, even if they disagree. There is an underlying sense of sociability and complicity in a shared endeavor, in providing a common answer to the question "what is going on here?" This process of "taking up" and "moving on" helps people find creative new ideas and build collective agreement.

In the *ArtCulture* thread we see something very different. Peter Hughes, we have seen, began the process with his puzzling request for a venue for this film and by failing to make a discursive tie to the artworks so generously strewn over the *ArtCulture* web page. He might easily have done this by suggesting briefly that cinema was a kindred spirit to conceptual art before making an advertisement for his film and asking for a venue. For whatever reason, he did not. Where he led others soon followed. A week later (November 5) there arrives contribution number two from a Scott Robinson. This is a descriptive pitch for another artwork. As if cut-and-pasted from a catalog, it says that Angela Carter's "most ambitious and logically challenging work yet" involving a "ghost forest" of rainforest stumps and missing tree trunks will appear in such and such a square in Copenhagen. There is no mention of *Rethink* or even of *Ecoplaza Paradise Oasis*. The posting looks strangely isolated and promotional – indeed rather like an advertisement. With a little Internet searching, we find that Scott Robinson is a donor to the *Ghost Forest* art project. He cares about climate change, but our judgment is that he has derailed the discussion for a second time. The third posting (November 12) is again from *Ecoplaza Paradise Oasis*. They thank *ArtCulture* for posting some details of their film on its website but point out that *ArtCulture* had posted an informal e-mail about the film rather than a more polished and professional blurb. Consequently, there are spelling mistakes, and an e-mail address is missing some capital letters. Could *ArtCulture* please fix up the blurb? So the thread is now being used to communicate practical issues that should be backstage. The fourth contribution looks more promising and on point. Posted on December 2, some six weeks after the original article, this praises the artworks as a "bold statement" by "talented artists" and thanks *ArtCulture* for sharing them. Although we look to be back on track, there is no sustained effort here to talk through interpretations and issues or to invite dialogue on social policy. The post is simply a quick affirmation. This is a pattern that is all too common on climate change art websites (see later). Still this poster understands some basic norms about communication and sociability. Contribution five (December 7) is less helpful and might initially seem incoherent or drunken. This is what it says: "Plan Z to save the human species from extinction circa 2500AD – polar cities. Google them!" The post is from a person called Danny Bloom. "Googling them" takes us to Wikipedia. Here we find that the polar city actually has nothing to do with art. It is a futuristic concept for a refuge for the last humans. This will be underground, on the edges of the thawed out Arctic Ocean. The originator of the polar city idea was the renowned British scientist James Lovelock. Its leading advocate today is one Danny Bloom. Here we have yet more well-intended (self) promotion of a tangential idea. Bloom does not take the trouble to address the climate change art of *Rethink* in so doing. The post seems entirely parasitic, although to Bloom's credit, the mention of Plan Z does cleverly echo the reference to "Plan B" to save the world that is *Ecoplaza Paradise Oasis*. In the sixth entry (December 28), a fan of the artist Phi Phi Oahn from Vietnam, who works with thick semi-opaque glass, has simply cut-and-pasted a quote. The quotation marks give the posting an air of authority, but the source remains obscure. This is all there is:

[...] In Copenhagen this week a group of famous, contemporary artists have installed new art works that in some way reflect on, or comment on, humans and their effect on the planet's fragile environment. Phi Phi Oanh's Specula would have no difficulty in holding its own there. In fact it would be a stand out. She is obviously an artist who will have a successful international future. [...]

Clicking on the name of the poster takes us to an art blog in Hanoi where we can read the entire article about Phi Phi Oanh. It is not clear if the posting was by the author of the item, the editor of the Hanoi e-zine, or the artist herself. It seems self-promoting rather than public spirited, as there is no special effort here to relate this cut-and-paste to the lead article or any other turn in the bulletin board sequence. We believe that a more considerate and public sphere–oriented entry might have begun: "This is a very interesting exhibition. Some of the art works remind me of Phi Phi Oanh's recent installations. A Hanoi critic recently commented..." It didn't. What we have looks like a cuckoo's egg. The seventh entry, from John, arrives on May 6, 2010, some five months after the first. This is a cut-and-paste of turn one – the plea for *Ecoplaza Paradise Oasis* to be shown in Copenhagen – only this time it appears in italics. We often see this in threads when one person takes a lead from a query or comment by another. The cut-and-pasting clarifies that a response is being made to a specific question or comment and adds solidaristic and cognitive density to the communicative network. Here there is no new text. It seems as if John forgot what he was going to say. The final post stands at some distance from its nearest neighbor. On June 4, 2011, a whole year after John's curious cut-and-paste, we find Going Green remarking briefly and appreciatively about the artworks and asking the author of the *ArtCulture* item if he would like to make a guest posting on her site *One World for Us All*. Going Green seems to be looking for artistic solidarity, but the feeling we get after reading the item is of isolation. One wonders if anyone will ever read this request.

The *Rethink* experience suggests that climate change art does not often lead to productive dialogue even within the restricted confines of a self-selecting aesthetic public sphere. Certainly there is no evidence that the Internet has helped build critical rationality of a discursive kind when prompted by such art. Rather than working cooperatively and in a focused way to foster dialogue about art and climate change (result = chorus), it would seem that Internet spaces for dialogue have free rider problems and issues with unclear or unenforceable norms as to their use (result = cacophony). Without proper gatekeeping, these are characterized by puzzling statements coming out of nowhere that require considerable ethnomethodological problem-solving activity by readers. We have to be creative to answer the questions "What are they thinking?" or "What is going on here?" and hence make sense of the postings. Effective public communication should be about the ideas themselves. Here our efforts are arguably sidetracked and wasted by trying to make sense of it all.

More populist efforts than *Rethink* seem to do a little better when it comes to the length of their threads. Yet these also fail to attain global reach and can sustain only meager and impoverished discourses. Consider CoolClimate. This event of 2010 allowed artists to submit entries online in a global art competition. The aim was not so much to encourage the avant-garde as "to generate iconic images that capture the impact of climate change" (CoolClimate 2010). The winning entries were to be distributed to environmental activists, showcased at 350.org's annual event (350.org campaigns to have atmospheric carbon levels limited to 350 parts per million), and made generally available in the effort to enhance awareness of the issues. There were more than one thousand entries from all around the globe. First, a preselection was made by anonymous CoolClimate staff. Then a jury consisting of art experts, green experts, and concerned but seemingly unqualified celebrities – the soft rock singer

Jackson Browne ("Take It Easy"; "Running on Empty") and veteran comic actor Chevy Chase (*Fletch, National Lampoon's Vacation*) – would further reduce these. The most popular five images would be voted on at the *Huffington Post*. Looking over the art, we see a number of graphically striking items, many of them Photoshopped images envisioning a hot or drowning future planet or creatively punning on climate change themes. The short list included a little girl holding her hand over the chimney of a power station to keep the pollution in, a deflated balloon with a wrinkled and distorted earth upon it, and a scuba diver swimming through a kelp forest past the head of the Statue of Liberty. As befits a global and Internet-based initiative, the CoolClimate website encouraged public participation with a space for posting comments (Deviant Art 2010a).

In contrast to the highbrow world of the gallery, here we have a democratic, freely available resource that will generate a passionate global discussion along with a series of unpretentious and chat-worthy art items. Or do we? To begin with, we find that there were fewer online comments than entries. Put another way, artists like to produce artistic material rather than offer feedback. True enough, there were plentiful affirmations of ecological and artistic values, yet these were brief and without analytic complexity. For example, the winning entry (the girl stopping the smoke of the power station with her hand) received comments such as "Its cool!!!!" (heiserova), "A fantastic message to the world...STOP" (Murawski), "Brilliant!" (Visionart), and "It's great" (daf-mark) (Deviant Art 2010b). Most of the comments appeared to be from artists already logged into the Deviant Art web community that had been the virtual host for the CoolClimate event. The activity seems to have energized hobbyists and lower-order professionals into dialogue but not a wider public sphere. Nor had it generated deep thinking on climate change. Still the feedback will no doubt have reassured artists that a small community of sympathetic viewers was out there. In short we seem to have a situation of artists talking to artists, and generally in offhand, if sincere, ways. This echo chamber of thin peer support might be mocked by some, but at least it is a start.

Less useful was derailing. Some posters quibbled about the scientific status or plausibility of what was shown, in effect spoiling the shared mood of celebration and aesthetic appreciation with points of nitpicking detail: "Hey, that's not pollution, it's just steam isn't it? It's a nuclear power plant and isn't one of our big potential sources of energy to replace crude oil nuclear power?" (RiiAqua). The comment was backed up by Nero-53: "The cooling towers don't pollute. That's just steam." All this led the Greek artist Christos Lamprianidis to reply politely, "I know it. This is symbolic not realistic neither photojournalism" (Deviant Art 2010b). Others used the winner's page to ask technical questions: "You know the photo effect, the colors. I believe you changed the colors of this picture with Photoshop, and my question is how?" (EgzonNikqi). Lamprianidis helpfully replied that he had used "Nik Software Vivenza plugin for Photoshop." Such feedback is unlikely to generate *thymos* and inspiration.

As might be expected with a grassroots activity that is also a competition, large numbers of people grumbled about the process as insufficiently democratic and open. Such comments were particularly important in derailing CoolClimate home page discussion away from the substantive issues of artistic values, pollution, and global solidarity (the following are taken from Deviant Art 2010a). The anonymous preselection of items for the high-status jury to review was considered especially problematic by competitors. For example, One Billion Moons seemingly felt excluded or cheated: "This is the oddest way to judge one art competition I have come across. Even in the most renowned art competitions the official judges, judge every work submitted." Pandabase agreed this was "a bit of an unusual and not very transparent way of judging an art competition." Bymarty hinted at a conspiracy: "I'm with you 100% that's why they call selves deviants. I think they are connected with the SF Art Academy and there [sic] agenda is to give the classmates dibbs on there [sic] art careers." H-o-l-t followed up, "I agree with all 3 of you and have now taken my submissions out. Never thought about it, until I read those messages. Thanks." Another grumble: a small amount of prize money was announced, but this could only go to U.S. entries (we presume for tax reasons). Mohanadtaiy: "I'm just wondering why you have an international gallery, when only United States Finalists will win money. I think it is unfair to those of us who are not from the US to believe that we can participate in the challenge and get some prizes." Yet other postings to the home page were about technical issues and bureaucratic processes. Pandabase again: "Is this the official list of semifinalists? I thought they weren't meant to be announced until October." Irucrem: "It was indicated that my submission was accepted (before the end date). However my work is not showing. It appears in my Deviant folder but not in my contest folder." Who, looking on, could be inspired by any of this? We have, not a community of discourse, but a community of complaint.

To be even-handed with CoolClimate, the high-end conceptual art that makes it to galleries also generates banal Internet comments rather than more complex meditations on art, science, and politics. "Those are some batteries," writes one person in response to a behind-the-scenes look at the installation of Tavares Strachan's *The Distance between What We Have and What We Want* posted on Flickr by the Brooklyn Museum. They seem more impressed by the technology of the exhibit, which used solar energy to keep a block of Arctic ice frozen, than by the imminent threat of climate change. Another art item by Jane Marsching involved seating made from recycled materials and some laptops where visitors could access a blog on climate change issues. One sympathetic journalist reported, "The blog was successful as a clearing house for links to online eco-information, but I'd hoped for more discussion and new ideas arising from cross-pollination among the heterogeneous contributors" (Cook 2007). This diagnosis matches the one presented in this chapter: reception of climate change art is overly passive and shallow. True dialogue and communication are elusive. Further proof: at the time of writing, Marsching's own ongoing blog, which considers art and climate change largely in the context of her artwork, was likewise overwhelmingly characterized by posts without responses (see http://www.janemarsching .com/).

On the eve of submitting this manuscript to the publishers, we performed a routine checkup of McKibben's artistic "immune system" as a check on our own interpretations, these formulated a couple of years before. This brief foray online confirmed that this is a rapidly evolving, dynamic field, yet one still plagued by systemic problems of churn, public inattention, internal disorganization, and discursive fragmentation. Some of the efforts we discussed in this chapter have receded far into the background, leaving little online trace. Once near the top of the list, they now appear well down any search hierarchy. Others have been overshadowed by new but similarly toothless efforts to put climate change at the front of the art world's agenda. Take the website *Artists and Climate Change* (http://artistsandclimatechange.com/), through which the New York–based playwright Chantal Bilodeau monitors climate art from around the country and the world. Bilodeau, who writes and promotes dramatic works about climate change, catalogs mounting artistic activity in a variety of genres and media. Things are clearly happening. Yet, as of September 8, 2014, almost two years after the site's founding, this tireless aggregator of artistic activity had only garnered 157 "likes" on Facebook. It seems hard to blame this on Bilodeau. Imagine2020 (http://www.imagine2020.eu/), a much slicker, European Union–funded consortium of performing arts venues and festivals that promote art about climate change, has done slightly better, earning 613 Facebook "likes" and 114 Twitter followers. This is hardly the stuff of digital uprising, however. Although bloggers and media outlets continue to trumpet the arrival of breakthrough exhibitions and visionary climate change artists, these communicators are still struggling to command sustained, urgent public attention. Much like the latest scientific report warning that things are getting worse and worse every day, climate art appears to have become routine rather than truly disruptive.

A Failed Project?

We do not intend to be naysayers and ironists in this chapter. On the contrary, our faith in the social power of visual representation leads us to suspect that breakthrough climate art is inevitable, at least within the art world. Moreover, it seems like only a matter of time before Hollywood makes a "serious" climate change drama that generates popular debate.[5] And from small beginnings, "high" climate change art has logged some successes. Exhibitions have been held, including many since the writing of this book. These have been visited by thousands and reviewed in the major press. They had some visibility. These exhibitions have a substantial online presence. Competitions have received lots of entries. The concept

[5] Indeed, Darren Aronofsky's biblical epic *Noah* (2014) was billed as just such an event: the first serious, big-budget movie about climate change. It seemed to have all its dramatic ducks in a row: a critically acclaimed director with art-house credibility; a massive budget for special effects and A-list action stars like Russell Crowe; a story that everyone knows; and an environmental theme – "stewardship versus dominion" – that even hard-right Christian fundamentalists could accept as worthy of discussion. What is more, Aronofsky made no bones about his agenda. "There is a huge statement in the film," he said, "a strong message about the coming flood from global warming. Noah has been a silly-old-guy-with-a-white-beard story, but really it's the first apocalypse" (Friend 2014). Yet even here, chorus was elusive. Much of the critical and popular response to the film focused not on climate change but on Aronofsky's proselytizing for vegetarianism, agrarianism, and animal rights. He was easily branded as a farmer's market radical, not a spokesman for civil society. Worse, he was viewed by some as a Malthusian misanthrope, the kiss of death in mainstream environmental politics. Writing in the *New Yorker*, the film critic David Denby (2014) described the film as "an epic farrago of tumultuous water, digital battle, and environmentalist rage (think of Al Gore glaring at the apocalypse)." Writing for *Slate*, another left-leaning magazine, the journalist David Plotz (2014) excoriated its "vile message condemning both humanity and civilization" and its "nostalgic, unsophisticated view" of the good society, which would consist of "glowering, friendless farmers living miles and miles from one another." So much for moral solidarity. Nevertheless, the film grossed more than $350 million worldwide, suggesting at least that some of the sociological barriers we described in this chapter are eroding.

of "climate change art" itself seems natural rather than contrived. Yet we must consider the success modest. Furthermore, we must ask whether this modesty is symptomatic of a chronic condition. Critical responses to exhibitions have been ho-hum. Attendance has been very slim relative to those of familiar blockbusters on van Gogh or ancient Egypt. An iconic standard-bearer has not yet emerged. Judging from Internet threads and online discussion, climate change art has not generated a culture of critical discourse in the art world, let alone the wider public sphere. The most promising discourse we can find is shallow, even if it is sincere. Much of the rest appears off point or self-serving.

How do we explain all this? The minimal impact of conceptual climate change art is reasonably explicable. High-end contemporary art appeals to a limited constituency of people with elite cultural capital. These are art consumers who are attuned with great sensitivity to the aesthetic codes at play and who feel engaged. It would be unreasonable to expect any powerful wider social impacts. Organizations like Cape Farewell have come to this realization in recent years and have diversified their programs and offerings. Vocabularies of motive speaking to the intrinsic value of art activity or, in the case of activist art, to the importance of "witnessing" rather than changing can be considered a partial response to the gap between hope and reality. So can the new turn toward more bleak artworks. The *Dark Optimism* exhibit at New York's MoMA PS1 (note that, consistent with our observations on Cape Farewell, this is not the famous MoMA of 53rd Street but a satellite gallery on the 'wrong' side of the East River) saw the Triple Canopy collective riffing on "the sentiment of being on the edge of an apocalypse" (Kelsey 2013) rather than seeking to offer iconic inspiration or solutions (for an eco-art-world critique documenting this point, see Spaid 2013). Such responses resolve the cognitive dissonance that would otherwise attend to failure: McKibben's antibodies have become more like MRIs or X-rays that analogically and imagistically reproduce a cancer rather than fighting back and curing it.

More troubling and perplexing than the failure of the highbrow top end is the relative indifference shown by a wider public toward more accessible figurative offerings such as those of CoolClimate or the Ice Bear. These might be reasonably expected to have iconic or viral qualities like those of the Abu Grahib photographs, a Banksy visual pun, or Tillman the skateboarding dog. They don't. More worrying still is the inability of the art field to generate a critical discourse with itself, whether operating with top-end or more populist materials. It seems as though even those equipped with enthusiasm and sensibility have amazingly little to say about the works of others. We presented in this chapter evidence from some Internet threads as well as looking at countless others during our research process. Let's be clear: these did not suffer from the invasive acts of incivil anonymous trolls and bots, such as those that recently led *Popular Science* to shut down its comments option (LaBarre 2013). The problems seemed internal to the field and related to effort and coordination. We found threads that quickly died out, failed to start, were characterized by weak or banal expressions of agreement, or were hijacked by technical or self-promotional statements by fellow believers. This failure is made all the more embarrassing by the ability of the science community to sustain high-level, moderated debate using the Internet. Consider RealClimate, a site where scientists offer commentary and debate for the general public.[6] Written by NASA scientist Gavin Schmidt (2006), an article called "Art and Climate" would seem to be particularly appropriate as a fair point of contrast. This discussed the merits of artworks as indicators of past climate change. The thread that followed had sixty-one contributions within two months. These consider the claims made by Schmidt in his essay and soon range into various technical matters to do with the measurement of historical climate. The contributors refer to other posts by number and debate each other on points of fact and interpretation: What about oral history as an alternative resource? To what extent do artistic conventions influence what is to be found in pictures? How reliable are our other records of past temperature? This is an organized and energetic discussion with a purpose. Thematic integrity was further assured by active moderation. Although arguably incivil and undemocratic in that skeptical voices based on what was deemed "bad science" were excluded, this editing permits things to stay on track within the organized discourse community of climate scientists and science followers. As Gavin Schmidt posted when responding to one disgruntled individual advocating the climate-skeptical views of science fiction author Michael Crichton, "This blog tries to keep discussion focused and with a reasonably high signal to noise ratio. Each time that a thread degenerates into tired old arguments that are off-topic and that just provoke a wave of extremely predictable point and counter-point we lose an opportunity to actually have any communication." Signal to noise: well said. That's what it is all about. Of course such moderation is a luxury made possible by an active community of high-quality posters.

[6] At the time of writing, this item by Gavin Schmidt was the number 1 hit for the search "Climate Change Art." As our chapter shows, this is no accident.

It's easy to point a finger at the communicative incompetence of the climate art community. But perhaps there is more to it. If the scientists can debate "art and climate change" efficiently but the art world cannot, perhaps this reflects interpretative norms. It might also say something about the difference between art understood as an expressive medium and art taken to be an unobtrusive measure. Certainly, when it comes to aesthetic reception and public communication, there are some thorny issues. It is rarely clear what exactly is being asserted by artists. Artworks are often said in catalogs and promotional materials to be "gestures," "reflections," "meditations," or "commentaries" that aim at shaping awareness or sensibility. When questioned, artists themselves scrupulously avoid statements on the precise meanings of their works. The artworks seem to be there as provocations or to make connections, but not as truth claims in any conventional or logical positivist sense. They are analogous to poems. As one climate change artist put it, "the kind of education too subtle to be put on a syllabus: that's the important role of art" (Keith Tyson, as cited in Bunting 2009). Susanne Langer (1957) writes helpfully on the form this education through the ineffable takes:

A work of art presents feeling (in the broad sense I mentioned before, as everything that can be felt) for our contemplation, making it visible or audible or in some way perceivable through a symbol, not inferable from a symptom. Artistic form is congruent with the dynamic forms of our direct sensuous, mental, and emotional life; works of art ... are images of feeling, that formulate it for our cognition. What is artistically good is whatever articulates and presents feeling for our understanding. (661–662)

Feelings are important. As Langer points out, elaborating on Cassirer, they are a foundational source of nondiscursive cognition. One can understand the temptation to tap this spring. Yet it could well be the case that art, especially in its more abstract forms, is not helpful at all when it comes to thinking through climate change. In part because it can be taken to be speculation and fiction, or to license personal responses, it may encourage some of the derailing we have bemoaned. The discursive work of the public sphere is perhaps best provoked by arguments that are propositional in form, or at least relatively disambiguated. These lay themselves open to factual contestation or reasoned disagreement over normative or pragmatic specifics. They encourage public dialogue over private contemplation and demand judgments be matched with justifications. Art, for the most part, moves with a contrary logic to debate.

The case against this retreatist position and for the power of the visual in the public sphere is usually made with reference to iconic photographs. These operate to fix emotions, become widely known, and are pivot points for debate. Yet the truth is that they generally work with a very different logic from most contemporary art. Iconic photographs, especially those related to newsworthy events and epochal crises, often have strong implicit narratives behind them. We are able to reconstruct what has just happened (a soldier has just defected and is jumping barbed wire; a man has been shot and so is falling; a girl has been hit by napalm and is running and screaming). Each image captures or condenses the essence of a wider symbolic field into a concrete exemplar (communism is evil, war is tragic, Vietnam is America's shame). Furthermore, such images frequently feature dramatic scenes of great emotional intensity (risking all for freedom, dying, pain). Thanks to a theory of mind, viewers are able to project emotions onto characters and, in the act of so projecting, come to be captured by the images themselves. Iconic photos actually work in very Aristotelian ways. They make plot visible. On top of this dramatic quality, we know that the photograph captured something that really happened at a real moment in time. This ontological fixing offers the frisson of *pathos* and recognition that Roland Barthes famously dubbed "punctum."

Climate change art, by contrast with iconic realist photography, is radically disadvantaged. The sculpture, installations, and paintings of contemporary high-end artistic production are overwhelmingly nonnarrative or even antinarrative. At the end of the day, they are not read as "real" but rather as contrived or constructed. The artist has intervened in the fixing of reality. Unless the artist herself is represented (through narrative!) as prophetic or charismatic – like, say, van Gogh, who is attributed greater powers to "see" than we ourselves have – this mediation fosters emotional cooling. The artist does not help as she stands between ourselves and the "real" itself, and punctum is lost.

So the problem of failed communication is not simply a case of deficient cultural capital. Indeed, perhaps the converse is the case. Thriving on small differences and without apparent rationality, the more refined aesthetic response to art might stand against the sort of reductive or causal explanation that might make for a productive, cumulative exchange of pragmatic ideas of a familiar public sphere kind (see Wittgenstein 1966). Norms of art consumption, for example those captured by Langer herself, permit or expect the viewer to inhabit the realm of the nonrational, immediate, and nondiscursive. For once in our lives, here are choices and feelings where there is no strong social expectation of explicit reasoned justification and elaboration. This is precisely the pleasure of art. You like it, or you don't. Enough said. Unless, that is, you are a critic.

At the end of the day, it is not clear what kind of extended communicative moment could be called out in the viewer by an exhibition of climate change art. Perhaps the short affirmative posts on CoolClimate that we talked down as shallow can be better understood as documenting a complete and tacit internalization of art appreciation norms. If we are wrong about all this and elaborated debate is normatively or practically permissible, there remains one last hurdle for discourse to emerge. Even if the intent and capacity are present in the viewer for a shift of register toward a more maximal discourse, what exactly are the rules or schemas of procedure for converting an articulated aesthetic response into rationally accountable public dialogue on politics, economics, or science? There is a huge disconnect in language games. It requires a virtuoso such as Kant or De Quincy to move seamlessly and unpretentiously between aesthetic, normative, and scientific registers – or to collapse such distinctions altogether. Isn't it easier and arguably more socially appropriate in most settings to simply say, "That's cool"?

It is no accident that the two more successful exemplars in this chapter were discursive and had a stronger, simpler claims-making quality. In fact, they sidestep the aesthetic altogether. Antony Gormley wrote about the need for art to address environmental issues. This was a claim that could be contested or endorsed. Discussion could emerge, even if the result was perhaps not one for which Gormley would have wished. In our second positive example, scientists addressed the (written) suggestion from Gavin Schmidt that art might be used to evaluate past climate. This led in turn to an informed exchange on the reliability of various measures and historical scenarios. Here a factual claim (art can be useful for climate science as an indicator) starts debate moving. A debate follows organized largely around the evaluation of fact by a community equipped through training with the norms and schemas for this very activity.

So talk leads to talk. Art is in a different register. It is experienced. This is a case of fire and ice, of elemental differences. But there is more to it than this. Applying Aristotelian categories to our case, we see that some basic properties of successful drama and oratory are missing. Unlike Al Gore, the artists are unable to present themselves as republicans representing the general interest with clear oratory as they sacrifice their own advancement. Rather, the image that emerges from and permeates the social drama narrative is of hypocrites struggling for attention: they enter competitions; they seek prestige; they speak in mysterious allusions, not plain facts. Moreover, for the onlooker, there is no visible evidence of enthusiasm connecting the art world audience to its artists. The general public sees solipsistic narcissism and chaos, not an upwelling of community-level *pathos*. Even if the invitation is extended, who would wish to come to the party? If art specifically has failed as a strategy to raise awareness and generate a critical dialogue across spheres, that is not to say that climate change activism has failed altogether in this respect. Indeed, the next chapter explores some moments when climate change did make it to the attention space of public life. There we look at moments when passionate activism and creative activity engendered elaborated normative and political responses. Unfortunately, as we will see, this has all too often been in the context of scandal, debacle, and apology.

6

Climategate and Other Controversies

We have seen that films and artworks are a significant path along which climate change activists attempt to arrive at public visibility. These are deliberately articulated attempts to stoke the fires of the social drama and to inject passion into what activists fear is perceived as a dull issue. Yet perhaps the most important and direct route of transition from background noise to the center of the social attention space is through the circuits of "news" production and consumption. A capacity to be newsworthy is of the utmost importance along many dimensions. Simply being selected out for news coverage marks climate change as a significant issue worthy of priority relative to the panoply of problems every society faces. Whether critical or benign, talk about climate change in a "news" forum gives an implicit ranking to this ecological problem, making it visible as a public issue. It is also significant to note that the news reaches a numerically large and socially dispersed audience. Films and artworks appeal to limited social constituencies. As we have seen, even within those constituencies, only a small proportion of people will find the time or energy (or in some cases have the basic social competence?) to thoughtfully engage with such creative products. By contrast, exposure to whatever is in the news is somewhat nonelective and is robotically embedded in daily routines – reading the paper on the train, listening to the radio on the drive to work, checking out CNN, the BBC, or Democracy Now! online during the lunch break, and so forth. In addition, the field of "news" tends to reach over social barriers. To a substantial extent, the same "important" or "newsworthy" events are carried in highbrow and lowbrow formats, on radio, television, print, and the Internet. A final plus to getting into the news is that coverage is cost free. Considered in terms of advertising dollars, any news attention given over to climate change is an immense potential boon for climate activism.

So the news sounds like a golden opportunity: it is inescapable, free, consumed promiscuously, and confers the status that comes with visibility. That said, climate change's appearance in this paramount sphere of social drama has often been unfortunate, problematic, or mismanaged. Media and communication scholars have identified a wide variety of reasons for this troubled entry into the public sphere (e.g., Lewis and Boyce 2009; Eide et al. 2010; Lester and Hutchins 2013), but they have tended to miss the scripted, ritualized quality of the process, relying instead on the rubric of static cultural "frames." If we switch to the analytical lens of cultural performance, we see that when climate change appears within the frames of "scandal," "outrage," and "blunder," it is because basic structural elements of successful social drama – especially the emotional identification of audience with performer – are missing. As a result, most of the stories "with legs" have jumped the track that runs toward a possibility of romantic solidarity. We explore some examples of such dramatic derailing in this chapter, arguing that making it into the news can often be a curse rather than a blessing.

Activists often wish this were not the case and insist that more attention should be given to facts than to moral and personal failings. Why is climate science so unappealing to the news media? There are, in fact, frequent reports of new scientific findings about global temperatures, melt rates, the extent of sea ice, carbon sequestering estimates, and so forth. Often culled from the prestigious journals *Science* and *Nature* and reduced to three or four paragraphs, these rarely survive more than one or two news cycles. Even IPCC assessment reports suffer a similar fate. In part this is because there is generally not much to say once the finding has been reported and aligned with other estimates of the speed of climate change. Scientific advances on climate change make for "bad news" so far as the news desk is concerned. A core component of news is surprise. But for the most part, any new scientific finding will confirm what is already known: climate change is happening – or, if you are a skeptic, scientists "still believe" climate change is happening. Often there is a rider – the change is happening "faster than expected" or "ahead of schedule." This too is becoming too familiar to be interesting.

Possibly the cultural tide is against science here. In his cross-national comparative study, Gabriel Ignatow (2007, 116) shows that "modern environmentalism was scientistic from the start, and early on developed a scientistic and universalizing vocabulary." Put another way, notwithstanding the enduring power of romanticism, there was also an unreflexive and uncritical belief in the power of the scientific worldview. Times have changed. So-called postmodern environmentalisms place greater emphasis on religious, nationalist, personal, and aesthetic themes than on data and measurement. Faith in reason is less central to decision making today. We can add that more proximate institutional factors also weight the dice: it does not help that stories on basic science are amazingly resistant to emplotment within conventional news genres that emphasize discord and contestation within the context of an "event" (Schudson 2007). Ironically enough given the theoretical approach we take in this book, the most powerful and sustained news events (a strike, a war, an election, a trial) offer an unfolding tableau of characters, performances, struggles, strategies, and outcomes that more easily comport to the expected contours of a social drama than climate change. Each drama moves toward a resolution (a pay rise, an invasion, a victory, a verdict) that is unknown until after history has unfolded. We follow the news to find out what happens next, or in the case of disasters and accidents, in a forensic way to see how what happened came to have happened. As Simon Cottle (2013) points out, natural disasters hold synergies with this template. They are unexpected "events" involving victims, suffering, struggle, triumph, and so forth and are amenable to representation through mediatized rituals that give birth to solidaristic and cosmopolitan moments. Not so climate change. By contrast with compelling news items that have formal similarities to a drama or detective story, a conventional scientific finding on climate change does not provide what the literary theorist Roland Barthes (1975) called the "pleasure of the text" – the sense of emotionally engaged and titillating suspense that attends to tracking something toward its denouement. In a science report, there are no developed characters to love or hate, no moral loadings to project – and we never get to the end of it. This is why scientific findings on climate change are boring, at least to most people. It is also why activists try so hard to link stories about climate science to those traumatic, unpredictable events of which Cottle speaks – droughts, wildfires, floods, and so on. Even when a shallow victory is attained, it usually does not amount to an unequivocal step forward.

Norms of public reason sometimes make things worse. As Max and Jules Boykoff (2004; see also Boykoff and Boykoff 2007) have shown, the long-standing practice of giving equal time to skeptical viewpoints and exaggerating disagreement (in part due to journalistic norms of "impartiality") has helped distort public understanding of what the vast majority of scientists actually think about climate change. Polls still show that Americans believe the issue to be much more hotly contested than it actually is. In the United Kingdom, despite increasingly sophisticated media coverage emphasizing scientific consensus, many people still believed the basic science was up for debate as recently as 2007, when the IPCC reported that the evidence of global warming was "unequivocal" (Butler and Pidgeon 2009). So to report a "scientific controversy" over climate change is to destabilize a core message: climate change is a "fact," not a "theory" that is disputed. This puts climate scientists and activists in a very difficult spot. Without drama, they cannot get the public to care; with it, they risk making climate change seem like just another endless struggle between special interests – the fallout being a descent into metadrama and a detached spectatorship position for the public as they watch the spokespersons slug it out. Moreover, drama is associated with the manipulation of emotion and the subversion of reason. To reduce risks of symbolic pollution, scientists stick to a dry delivery.

So climate change makes it to the news briefly as science, problematically as drama. In the latter case, the focus switches to events (controversies, conferences), people (activists, politicians, occasionally scientists), motivations (honest, sneaky, civil, incivil), and the relationship between these, not to "findings" about nature itself. There is often a further meta-narration that goes with each such episode. This concerns the controversial event's implications for wider struggles over climate change opinion, its impact on strategy and impression management. This is commentary on the metadrama. For the most part, climate change activism has performed badly in this complex environment, with the news essentially reproducing what Northrop Frye (1976, 97–126) called "themes of descent." These stories involve the status degradation of protagonists and the loss of *pathos*. There is an erosion of the social, with emphasis given over to fatalistic coverage of failed campaigns, futile attempts at cooperation, defective institutions, and problematic judgments. As we outlined in Chapter 3, this pattern corresponds to the Aristotelian mode of tragedy in which humans are feeble or misguided. Even when they have good intentions, fate is stronger than they are. The tragic is a genre that sucks energy and motivation from a social movement (Jacobs and Smith 1997).

This is why an increasing number of environmentalists are calling for more positive news stories. They suggest that a romantic struggle for social justice (Hulme 2009), green energy (Nordhaus and Shellenberger 2007), or local autonomy (McKibben 2010) should be promoted to the media in place of the tragic model. Here again the struggle will be harder than it first appears. As Garret Hardin's (1968) famous parable of "the commons" illustrates, the cultural logic of tragedy is deeply ingrained in the American environmental imagination. Environmentalists must fight the default conviction that we live in an irredeemably polluted world (Buell 2003; Szasz 2009). Using science to combat this environmental fatalism is both necessary and fraught with difficulty. As the historian Stephen Bocking (2004, 30) notes, "controversies ... cast a harsh, unflattering light on scientific knowledge. Uncertainty is viewed as inadequacy, interpretation as mere opinion, lack of consensus as evidence that science cannot yet justify any action." Indeed, some of the most effective environmental communicators – Rachel Carson and Lois Gibbs come to mind – have used this vulnerability to their advantage, casting themselves as insurgent critics of the "cult of expertise." Speaking on behalf of ecological common sense and the precautionary principle, they challenged the hegemony of men in white lab coats who assured us that everything was understood and under control. Environmental science, at its most dramatic and compelling, has often fought *against* consensus, not for it. In the case of climate change, it does not help that only a small number of scientists truly understand the computer models on which the entire edifice of contemporary climate knowledge rests. As the historian Paul Edwards (2010) shows, the public perception that models are arcane and "unreal," involving subjectively cherry-picked estimators, has been used effectively to claim that projections of dangerous climate change are not grounded in "hard," empirically verifiable data. Climate scientists are thus easily forced into the same dramatic role as hedge fund managers, political consultants, and advertising executives – elite practitioners of a voodoo-like predictive "black art," thus enemies of "sound science" and transparent common sense.

The hope that "positive" science can provide the basis for a narrative shift in climate news reporting must also endure a further reality check. This lies in internal differentiation within the climate community. Scientists and "science" are not the only source for stories. Activists, government bodies, and others are also caught up in the news cycle. What little space is available for climate news might be taken up by distractions coming out of left field. Newsworthy scientific activity and opinion are replaced by newsworthy events emerging from other sources. In recent years, controversial advertising campaigns stand out as a major competitor. Here the focus is not on science – whether good or bad, optimistic or fatalistic – but rather on matters of taste, civics, and character. The news genre of the "scandal" takes over, with a normative breach reported and its implications assessed. Information as such becomes irrelevant. *Motivation* is everything.

The long and the short of it in this chapter will be as follows. News values that focus on normative breaches tend to assure that both the "science" story and the "PR campaign" story often result in damage to *ethos* and losing a character war. To understand this deeper rhetorical failure, we must look to the second leg of Aristotle's rhetorical tripod, *pathos*. As Eugene Garver (1994) argues, *ethos* and *pathos* exist in a relationship of close interdependence. Recall Aristotle's admonition in the *Rhetoric* that "it adds much to an orator's influence that his own character should look right and that he should be thought to entertain the right feelings towards his hearers; and also that his hearers themselves should be in the right frame of mind" (2.1.1378a). In other words, how a speaker is thought to *feel* – both about his subject and about his audience – matters a lot. To win their trust, he must seem, not only reasonable and intelligent, but also made of the right emotional stuff: amiable, generous, empathetic, kind. According to Garver, it is hard to overstate the importance of this emotional attunement in building *ethos*. "The *Rhetoric*," he asserts (Garver 1994, 108), "is about civic emotions." That is to say, it is about the emotions proper to citizens, and thus about the emotional basis of civic life.

For Aristotle, shared emotions are an essential ingredient of deliberative rationality (Garver 1994, 104–38). When reason does not lead to an obvious conclusion, emotion fills the gap. Indeed, as Garver stresses, judging and deliberating are impossible without passion. "*Pathos* is not an accessory to argument, but a part of it" (Garver 1994, 110). Moreover, without practical knowledge of the passions, an orator cannot generate *eunoia*, or goodwill. "The speaker shows himself to be trustworthy . . . when he shares pleasures and pains, and so expectations and evaluations, with his audience. The emotions, then, are part of the art of rhetoric because understanding them provides the speaker with ways of exhibiting *eunoia*, in that they enable him, and deliberators and judges in the audience, to apprehend the relevant particulars for sound ethical decision and *phronesis*" (111). In ancient Greek terms, the emotional faculty that makes *eunoia* possible is *thymos* (also often spelled *thumos*), or "spiritedness," which Garver defines as that which makes us angry toward enemies and welcoming toward friends (113). (A colleague in classics defined it more colorfully as "umph.") *Thymos* is the quintessential political emotion. It was famously criticized by Francis Fukuyama

(1992) as the atavistic or "tribal" desire for recognition, a feeling that emerges from the inflated value that one places on one's self and one's group in relation to outsiders. Closely linked to feelings of pride and indignation, for Fukuyama *thymos* "is something like an innate human sense of justice: people believe they have a certain worth, and when other people act as if they are worth less – when they do not *recognize* their worth at its correct value – then they become angry" (165). Following Aristotle in the direction of Durkheim's late work on collective "effervescence," we take a more constructive view of *thymos*. It does not degrade deliberative rationality but rather infuses it. Without the emotional glue it provides, social solidarity – and thus civic rationality – fall apart.

That said, within the cultural discourse of democratic civil society, *thymos* must always be carefully contained. Fanatical patriotism and territorial groupthink point to anticivil motives and undemocratic institutions. Especially when the future is fearful and uncertain, the orator must navigate treacherous emotional waters. She must evoke *thymos* without allowing it to overwhelm her performance. Understanding this balancing act is key to our Aristotelian theory of democratic social drama. For Aristotle, emotions do not simply operate in the background by guiding an audience toward particular conclusions. Like character, emotions are objects of knowledge *and* subjects of argument. To persuade an audience, a speaker must not just make her audience experience particular emotions; she must acknowledge the emotions proper to right-thinking, rational, even-keeled people. She must be able to demonstrate why some people can be trusted and why others cannot. Evoking the noble indignation of *thymos*, she must show who belongs at the center and who at the periphery. She must perform citizenship. We might think of this dimension of social drama as "emotional reflexivity."

Again, Aristotle helps us understand just how this is done. In his famous discussion of emotions in Book 2 of the *Rhetoric*, he (2.4.1381a) argues that people are friendly toward people who are, among other things, just and self-controlled. They are friendly also toward those who are "good-tempered, and those who are not too ready to show us our mistakes, and those who are not cantankerous or quarrelsome" (2.4.1381a). We are also friendly toward "those who do not reproach us with what we have done amiss to them or they have done to help us, for both actions show a tendency to criticize us" (2.4.1381b). Conversely, we feel anger toward those who show contempt for things that we take seriously and toward those who take pleasure in others' misfortune (2.2.1379b). Slighting, which Aristotle defines as "the actively entertained opinion of something as obviously of no importance" (2.2.1378b), takes three main forms: contempt, spite, and insolence. "Clearly," he writes, "the orator will have to speak so as to bring his hearers into a frame of mind that will dispose them to anger, and to represent his adversaries as open to such charges and possessed of such qualities as to make people angry" (2.2.1380a). In other words, to stir up anger toward an enemy, a speaker must depict that enemy as unjustly contemptuous of what her audience holds dear. At the same time, she herself must appear just and level headed. This is what performing the binaries of civil emotion is all about.

This is a tall order in environmental politics, where "the enemy," as Pogo famously said, turns out to be "us." How do you mobilize an audience to feel righteous anger toward itself? What kind of *ethos* do you project, and which genre do you use? Attempts to solve this puzzle are extremely risky. Consider an example from the United Kingdom that adopts an ironic stance and uses the conventions of satire to critique "us." This became newsworthy for the wrong reasons. As Aristotle recognized, taking pleasure in others' misfortune, especially when those others are "just like us," is not a recipe for gaining trust.

10:10 and Other Disasters

It is easy to blame the news establishment for not reporting climate change responsibly. Sometimes, however, the fault lies not in the stars but within ourselves. Perhaps the most dramatic example of a failure that did not need to happen was a 10:10 advertisement campaign that ran in the United Kingdom in fall 2010. The 10:10 organization started out in 2009. It seeks to have individuals and collectivities cut their carbon emissions by 10 percent in a year. This is understood to be a more practical and meaningful step than the long-term targets mandated by governments who will not be around long enough to have to make tough decisions. Individuals and organizations around the world have been asked to pledge. By and large, 10:10 has done well. It boasts some significant and high-status sign-ups. These include major corporations and organizations (e.g., Oxford University, Microsoft France), cities (e.g., Paris, Lille, Oslo), and sporting organizations (e.g., the French Tennis Federation, Tottenham Football Team). According to its professional website, more than one hundred thousand pledges had been made by the middle of 2011. With its manageable targets, social networking qualities, and widespread reach, 10:10 looks to be a success story. Still, everyone makes mistakes.

At the end of September 2010, 10:10 launched a major new advertising initiative: "No Pressure." The signs were propitious. The four ads were scripted by leading romantic comedy and satirical writer Richard Curtis (*Four Weddings and a Funeral, Notting Hill, Blackadder*) and directed by highly regarded advertising expert Dougal Wilson. They featured attention-grabbing guest spots by noted and concerned sports and entertainment stars such as David Ginola and Peter Crouch (soccer), Gillian Anderson (actress, perhaps unfairly still best known for *The X-Files*), and a sound track by the somewhat intellectual rock band Radiohead. The flaw came with misplaced humor. At the end of each ad, the person who is not prepared to pledge to 10:10 is blown up; blood, clothing, and flesh are strewn about. The accompanying squelching sound suggests liquefied body parts falling to the ground. In one ad, a former Tottenham player, the talented David Ginola, learns about 10:10 from teammates at a training ground. They talk about low-energy floodlights, public transport options for fans, and so forth as being important to the club's 10:10 agenda. Ginola replies with disinterest and in a passive-aggressive way: "Whatever. I wouldn't do it. It seems like a distraction from football to me." A player replies cheerfully, "That's just fine, David. You don't have to join in. Just ignore it. No pressure." He then, like Wiley Coyote, presses a red button on a black box with attached wires, and Ginola explodes. Another commercial with Gillian Anderson has her doing a voice-over for a 10:10 commercial in a sound studio. At the end of the recording, the (male) sound engineer asks her what she is prepared to do herself to reduce her carbon footprint. She explains that she thought doing the voice-over was her contribution to the environment. "Right, absolutely, no pressure," replies the sound guy. He hits the red button, and a second later blood splatters all over the glass of the recording booth. Two other versions of the advertisement were made. A middle-aged male figure representing the affable face of contemporary management talks about 10:10 to his team. At the end of the ad, he blows up three employees who are lukewarm about implementing the 10:10 idea in their workplace. The most problematic advert featured two schoolchildren who failed to pledge like the rest of their class. They are blown up in front of their peers by a seemingly benign teacher. The other children look shocked as they are spattered with blood and flesh.

Reviewing the advertisements on YouTube, one can sense the comedic structure trying to get out. There is the shared visual catch of the box with the red button. There is an element of surrealism and disproportion rather as in a Monty Python sketch, as well as the gross humor of

South Park. Very importantly, those cool toward 10:10 are portrayed, not in a stereotyped way as evil, but simply as weak willed and apathetic. From an Aristotelian point of view, this is a smart move, as the potential audience for conversion retains *thymos*. Furthermore, there is an element of absurdity and self-parody in the contrast between the sociable atmosphere of each scene and the violent act that ends it. This is a light reminder, not a lecture. Still, the makers of 10:10 would have been well advised to remember Aristotle's remarks:

> Your language will be *appropriate* if it expresses emotion and character, and if it corresponds to its subject. "Correspondence to subject" means that we must neither speak casually about weighty matters, nor solemnly about trivial ones.... This aptness of language is one thing that makes people believe in the truth of your story. (*Rhetoric*, 3.7.1408a)

Climate change is a serious business. Trying to make it something else was not a good idea. On the day of the launch, the *Guardian Online* seemingly bragged when it spoke of its exclusive scoop from its "friends at 10:10" (Carrington 2010). It acknowledged that the videos were "edgy." It quoted 10:10 founder Franny Armstrong quipping that "doing nothing about climate change is a common affliction," that such people were "threatening everybody's existence on this planet" before suggesting that "maybe a little amputating would be a good place to start." No doubt she thought she was being humorous. Within a few hours of this announcement, the video had been taken down from the *Guardian*, 10:10, and YouTube websites (it can still be found posted by other users, generally climate skeptics), and 10:10 was issuing apologies. What had been interpreted as "funny" by 10:10 and the producers of the short films (one imagines due to some sort of writing room groupthink) was being seen in a very different way by many members of the public. In a 6:00 P.M. update posted below the "scoop" article we find a statement from 10:10. Franny Armstrong explains here, "We wanted to find a way to bring this issue back to the headlines while making people laugh." In other words, a risky strategy had been chosen to get into the attention space. She said that many had indeed found the videos funny, but "unfortunately some didn't." Now she wished to "sincerely apologize to anybody we have offended." Climate change was in the headlines for the wrong reason. In attempting not to offend the apathetic "we" that was its target it had ended up offending many. The protagonists who were punished in the ads seemed undeserving, and *pathos* was lost. Who now would want to be like these self-important, self-satisfied, out-of-touch creative types from Notting Hill and Moseley? Now we had a social drama, and so themes of morality, culpability, and character came into play that made No Pressure newsworthy.

Reading through posts under the article at the *Guardian*, it is hard to see initially where the problem lies. There are some positives. For example, in contrast to weak interest in climate change art, we documented in the previous chapter, by October 3, there had been 884 responses by *Guardian* readers. Some wrote that they found the film funny or even hysterical. Others were concerned in an instrumental vein that it would be interpreted the wrong way: it seemed authoritarian, to patronize skeptics, and would in the end help sustain their prejudiced views about environmentalists as ecoterrorists. Some saw the film as embarrassing and as a propaganda "own-goal." Only a minority, although a substantial one, identified what was to emerge as the major problem for the wider community: the film was offensive and chilling. It featured decent people (including women and children) in everyday situations being suddenly blown up in frighteningly real detail.

Fears of an own-goal were well placed. Sponsoring corporations and charities rushed to distance themselves from the product. As we have already noted, the video was pulled only to pop up again on sites associated with climate and ecoskepticism as smoking-gun evidence of evil intent. Interest continued. A column on the debacle by the conservative *Daily Telegraph*'s provocative climate skeptic James Delingpole (2010) was much referred to in the general media and Internet chatter. On top of this, it received an amazing 1,541 posted comments direct from the public. According to Delingpole, the environmentalist video "revealed the snarling, wicked, homicidal misanthropy beneath its cloak of gentle, bunny-hugging righteousness." His readers – confirming the fears of *Guardian* bloggers – eagerly agreed in posts below his provocative op-ed. The video seemed to be advocating extreme violence: "They make videos advocating blowing up our children for not believing in their scam and they accuse us of unfounded paranoia. Unbeeffingbelievable!" (Catweazle). We might expect this sort of response from the *Telegraph*'s famously older, male, and conservative readers. It is notable, however, that over at the profession-oriented *Marketing Week*, bloggers also tapped the eerie resonance with real-world terrorism. "Yeah, really funny. Blowing up people that don't agree with your politically motivated ideas. I guess I've been missing the 'dark humor' of the Taliban and Al Qaida all this time" (Lance). Or perhaps thoughts of Nazism were triggered: "It is pure fascism. Just replace the dissenters with Jews, gypsies and the disabled to understand the real message" (Kenny). More simply, the problem could be stepping beyond the bounds of decency: "It's as simple as this: you produced a film that showed 2 young children being blown up" (Parolalista).

Because climate activists were unwilling to step forward to defend the videos (perhaps believing in the maxim "least said soonest mended"), climate skeptics had control of the space of opinion to present their version of events. For example, in the United States, the Fox News (2010) television channel ran a feature on the "violent climate change video." After mentioning with indignation that 10:10 did not want to come onto Fox to defend the video, the daytime anchor Megyn Kelly performed visible outrage as she turned to climate skeptic Marc Morano of Climatedepot.com. "The global warming fear promoters are in desperation right now," he tells her, noting the failure of President Obama, the United Nations, and others to carry the torch. "Their idea to get attention was to blow up schoolchildren in as gory and disgusting a manner as possible," he continued. The anchor asks a leading question: would this video perhaps inspire some deranged individual to commit acts of violence in the name of climate change? Morano, as one might expect, endorses this fear (Fox News 2010). Climate activists were equally unhappy at 10:10. Bill McKibben of 350.org lashed out: "It's the kind of stupidity that hurts our side, reinforcing in people's minds a series of preconceived notions, not the least of which is that we're out-of-control and out of touch – not to mention off the wall" (quoted in Kaufman 2010). After a couple of days, it was clear that more damage control was needed. The initial apology by Franny Armstrong (mentioned earlier) was problematic as a public performance. It appeared to be blaming those who did not find the video funny for not finding it so. In addition, it had a flip, "whatever" feel to it. "We live and learn," Armstong had said. The writer Richard Curtis had himself offered an explanation rather than an apology in a statement. Rather than "simply drift into disaster," it was worth the risk of "trying to write something unexpected" (McVeigh 2010). A further attempt at damage control came on October 4. Yet even this apology by 10:10 UK Director Eugenie Harvey was problematic. It seemed like a memo that was directed not toward the general public but rather to the internal solidaristic needs of the 10:10 community: employees, stakeholders, and sponsors. The backlash against the campaign, it said, had been a damaging distraction, and improved processes would be put in place within the organization to prevent this sort of mistake from happening again (Harvey 2010). We are uncomfortably reminded of the much-criticized pseudo-apology of cyclist Lance Armstrong in an interview with Oprah Winfrey. Rather than expressing humble regret to his fans and the general public for years of arrogant deception about drug cheating, and also for bullying his accusers (what everybody actually wanted to hear), he often chose to focus on offering contexts and explanations for past actions. He admitted to various harmful deeds but seemed to find it difficult actually to use the word 'sorry' (see Kador 2013). Here was a man who had not truly learned his lesson: it was evident that he just didn't get it.

A comparative case suggests that shock videos will always have a hard time once they become caught up in the news cycle. They tend to be seen as emotionally manipulative and hectoring, or as appealing to irrational fears or to the subconscious rather than critical thought. Consider the case of Plane Stupid. This organization campaigns against air travel on environmental grounds. Short-haul flights associated with low-cost airlines come in for special critique given that functional alternatives (bus, train) exist (or might come to exist with a little political will) and that such aviation crowds the skies. Their controversial November 2009 advert featured a deserted business district with skyscrapers. It might be 5:00 A.M. There is the sound of a whining jet engine. Blobs appear falling from the sky. These become recognizable as polar bears. They thud and bounce off the buildings and eventually splat on the pavement. A voice-over explains that each short-haul flight generates four hundred kilograms of carbon, which is the weight of a polar bear.

Although it gained news attention, as with the 10:10 campaign, all the attention was about the merits of the advertising campaign and the motivations of the people who produced it. In short, *the social drama of climate change was newsworthy; climate change was not.* Worse, the step to metadramatic analysis was made. This involved making sense of the ad campaign by foregrounding the larger battle over climate change as a context for the interpretation of this one item. This is another example of "derailing" that we also saw in the case of responses to climate change art. Evaluation took place, but largely with regard to the following sorts of issues. Was the campaign effective? Was it in good taste? Did the ad make sense? Would shock tactics work? What did this reveal about the desperation of the anti–global warming activists? In this case the answer to the questions was generally no, no, no, no, and yes, they are getting desperate. For what it is worth, the ad was also widely interpreted in negative ways as "ridiculous," as "plain stupid," or as "propaganda" because it manipulated emotions through sentimentality (e.g., see Gillespie 2009 and subsequent posted comments). Like 10:10's No Pressure, the campaign became a news event but did not lead to much by way of productive discussion on the issue of short-haul air travel. Instead, a distracting set of commentaries on persuasion and good taste took over.

Even before Plane Stupid's falling bears, this discursive pattern had been visible with the response to the so-called drowning puppy video produced by the United Kingdom's Department of Energy and Climate Change. Here a father is reading a bedtime story to his young daughter that turns out to be about climate change. The story turns dark as it cuts to watercolor illustrations from the children's book: a puppy seemingly drowns, a kitten is marooned on a kitchen table, and a rabbit cries in the desert. The ad had been aimed at adults, allegedly prompted by a survey showing that most people felt that climate change would not impact on them personally. Presumably the intent was to generate some guilt about intergenerational impacts. Still protests immediately eventuated to the watchdog advertising standards authority claiming that the advert was terrifying children and that this was a totalitarian attempt at brainwashing innocents (Revoir 2009).

What is the story here? It would seem that advertising campaigns can indeed leverage climate change into the news pages, web pages, and broadcasts. These provide the increased visibility and free publicity that climate change activism so desperately seeks. Yet the circumstances under which this takes place are suboptimal. The story is essentially a drama of deviance, not of policy, nor climate science, nor planetary survival. The reported consensus is that organizations and individuals committed to climate change have made a mistake, gone too far, exposed their problematic inner thoughts, violated acceptable social norms. Commentary identifies and accounts for this deviance. Climate change and the policy needed to deal with this challenge are no longer the talking point. Rather, as our theory has predicted in this book from the start, it is the background against which a compelling and more human drama plays out.

Climategate: Trust, Tribalism, and Anticivil Science

The 10:10 disaster was indeed an own-goal. It was also an instructive one. Like Plane Stupid and the Drowning Puppy, it illustrates the rhetorical risks involved in making "us" a problem as well as an audience. It got into the news, but for all the wrong reasons. Questions were asked about motivations and rationality of environmental activists, about their civility and their basic social competence. Questions were not asked about climate policy. Still the damage was limited. Once the videos were pulled and a mistake clumsily admitted, the furor rapidly died out. Far more problematic as an enduring news event was the Climategate scandal. This went to the heart of the matter by suggesting that the science of climate change was itself bogus. Like 10:10, Climategate hinged on questions of emotion and character. At the end of the day, it was not the science itself that created a crisis of trust but the perceived motivations of climate scientists.[1]

The figure of the scientist is one with peculiar iconic power in contemporary culture. At the far end of the scale, as Roland Barthes (1972) shows, are mythologized figures like Albert Einstein. Vastly superior to us in intellect, they have God-like capacities to understand the mysteries of the universe and the consequent right to pronounce on existential and moral issues. Although few scientists can hold this aura of intense sacrality, most can lay claim to a more diffuse consecration. Like priests and doctors, research scientists are ethical beings who float a little above the contamination of everyday life. They gain prestige and authority from their representation as ascetic and disinterested truth seekers. Those working in academic settings are deemed to have turned down large salaries and worldly gains in the search for knowledge. They are monklike figures whose social authority comes from their unworldly study of the world, their capacity to speak truth to power. A reminder of the leverage this subject position can give came in the wake of the 2003 War in Iraq. The British prime minister Tony Blair had made a case for war based on a published dossier of intelligence concerning Iraq's alleged weapons of mass destruction. Leaks to the media from the Ministry of Defense scientist Dr. David Kelly caused the accuracy of the dossier to be questioned. Dr. Kelly's name was itself leaked (seemingly in revenge), and he was later found dead. News reports of this tragic event represented Kelly as a man who was compelled to tell the truth owing to a sacred

---

[1] Not surprisingly, those who study the social dimensions of climate change have taken great interest in Climategate. For an exhaustive journalistic account, see Fred Pearce's (2010) *The Climate Files*; for surveys of the academic literature, see Grundmann (2012a, 2012b). Although a number of scholars have focused on the critical dimensions of character and credibility (e.g., Grundmann 2012b; Jasanoff 2010; Wynne 2010), they have looked at the event in the narrow context of scientific practice and communication. They have missed how climate skeptics used Climategate to change the broader trajectory of the social drama by renarrating climate change.

sense of duty. He had been pressured toward suicide by insidious political forces and by exposure to impurities of the mundane, partisan world. In this case the identity of "scientist" was relentlessly applied to Kelly as a badge that testified to his honorable nature. He was a quiet man who wished only to serve his country. Standing by facts was in his very nature. By contrast, the politicians and spin doctors of Blair's government were seen as a secretive camarilla. They had manipulated data and had hung scientist Kelly out to dry by feeding his identity to the press (see Smith 2005, 191). For climate activists the saintly qualities of such a free-floating, truth-speaking, socially detached "scientist" subject position are a great potential resource in that they make space for this kind of binary discourse that would separate truth from politics. Somehow it has never quite stuck, and Climategate was to remove the card from the deck.

The origin of Climategate lies in the still mysterious hacking of e-mail files, documents, and a source code in November 2009 at the Climate Research Unit (CRU) at the University of East Anglia in the United Kingdom. Extracts soon appeared on the Internet, where climate skeptics claimed they had found smoking-gun evidence of scientific fraud at one of the leading global centers for climate change research. The East Anglia scientists seemed to be talking about how to massage their data, cover anomalies, silence critics, and explain away embarrassing evidence that contradicted their theories. Certain quotes from the e-mails became sound bites for skeptics globally, such as the celebrity-politician Sarah Palin, and Senator Jim Inhofe in the United States. "The fact is that we can't account for the lack of warming at the moment and it is a travesty that we can't," wrote one scientist. Another e-mail spoke of a "trick" needed to "hide" a decline in temperatures. Several e-mails showed that the scientists were unwilling to share their data with climate-skeptic researchers who had made Freedom of Information Act requests. The e-mails mentioned boycotting a refereed journal that had published climate-skeptical research, trying to "contain" the outlying impact of the medieval warm period, deleting certain e-mails before a Freedom of Information Act request made them available, and being tempted to "beat the crap" out of the skeptic Pat Michaels.

Subsequent independent inquiries showed that reasonable explanations could be found for most of these backstage comments. For example, the "trick" was about a narrow technical issue to do with the statistical alignment and effective presentation of data rather than an outright deceit. There were no smoking guns that demonstrated concerted scientific fraud on an unprecedented scale, nor the hiding of data, although the e-mails did show the scientists being "rude or dismissive," according to Factcheck.org (Henig 2009). Indeed, no less than six independent commissions were established in the United Kingdom and United States to investigate the affair, all of which concluded that the scientists had not committed fraud or scientific misconduct – although one, invoking the Mertonian ethos, identified "a consistent pattern of failing to display the proper degree of openness."[2]

Nevertheless, certain words had been used and the damage was done. Climate skeptics easily steered the media and the public toward biased, sensationalistic coverage of the hacking scandal, exploiting "old" media's increasing reliance on outlets like the Drudge Report (Cox 2013). Whereas 10:10 gives the impression of climate activists who are either out of touch with the mainstream, desperate for attention, or expressing violent neoterrorist fantasies, here a different set of negative images came into view. Backstage communication, when made public, gives the sense of a cabal. This in turn allows the discourse of civil society to mobilize established tropes about conspiracy. Like President Nixon and his so-called plumbers at the time of Watergate, the climate scientists looked like a secretive, paranoid, and mean-spirited group engaging in deviant activities for their own advantage. Moreover, it appeared that the hard data that were supposed to document the irrefutable reality of climate change looked somewhat soft in crucial places. Data analytic choices that were invisible in published research were moved to the front of the stage once public scrutiny demanded accountability. The grand narrative of climate change seemed to be determining how climate sequences were reconstructed from raw data – rather than the reverse. In a telling choice of words, the centrist skeptic Roger Pielke (2009) described "the trick" not as fraud but as scientists "stage managing their presentation of climate science for the greatest possible effect." The mainstream scientific community organized to try to combat the damage. Public statements from the American Association for the Advancement of Science, the American Meteorological Society, and other scientific bodies attested to the reality of climate change and the validity of the scientific knowledge base. At the same time, the researchers and scientists at the center of the scandal – Phil Jones, Keith Briffa, and Michael Mann – were portrayed by their supporters as scientific martyrs.

If 10:10 and Plane Stupid illustrate bad offense, Climategate shows us what bad defense looks like. For weeks after the hacking, climate

---

[2] http://www.cce-review.org/.

scientists and environmentalists seemed helpless against the critical onslaught. Although the story never became a major scandal in the United States, it fed a wave of deepening skepticism about climate change. Surveys by Anthony Leiserowitz and his colleagues found that 29 percent of Americans were aware of the story, and 25 percent claimed to have followed it in the news. Within this quarter of the population, 47 percent said the story had made them somewhat or much more certain that "global warming is not happening," and 53 percent said it had caused them to have somewhat less (24 percent) or much less (29 percent) trust in climate scientists. "Thus, in total, approximately 6 weeks after the story first broke, nearly 13% of American adults said that the event made them more certain that global warming is not happening, and reduced their trust in climate scientists" (Maibach et al. 2012, 290). Given the dismally small number of Americans who pay attention to science reporting, this number seems quite significant, especially when we consider that subsequent surveys showed that self-identified Tea Party members – that is, the people most likely to turn out to vote, to discuss the issue on talk radio or in the comments section of newspaper websites – were far more likely than other groups to know about the fiasco, alongside weathercasters and TV news directors (Maibach et al. 2012). Even so, survey data cannot show the real cultural impact of a story such as this. It is not simply that Climategate made conservative Americans even more skeptical about climate science. It became part of the social drama, a scene or episode that "everyone knows." All sides, skeptics and true believers, must now include it in their narration of global warming.

On its surface, Climategate was all about data integrity. But it was really a character war. It was a struggle to define the *ethos* of a handful of climatologists who became in effect metonymic proxies for the IPCC, climate science, and global environmentalism more generally. If we examine how these scientists and their accusers were depicted in what Jacobs and Townsley (2011) call "the space of opinion" during the weeks and months following the e-mails' publication, we see two narratives vying for dominance.[3] The first of these itself appeared in two versions, one for

---

[3] Jacobs and Townsley (2011, 13) define the space of opinion as "that part of the public communicative infrastructure in which the elites of our huge, complex societies debate matters of common concern." Born of journalism but not confined to it, the space of opinion exists at the overlapping border of several cultural fields: media, think tanks and advocacy groups, and academia. Yet its original and still-archetypal home is the newspaper opinion page, which is what we focus on here. Although editorials, op-eds, and letters to the editor form one small piece of today's complex opinion space, they still

right-wing audiences and another for centrists. In conservative and especially evangelical circles, the scientists were depicted as "high priests" of a millennial cult and apostles of a Green World Order. In the mainstream press, they were depicted as a greedy and tribalistic faction of scientific thugs, more gangsters than fanatics. These tropes of cultishness and criminality often shaded into each other. Defenders, meanwhile, attempted to derail the skeptics' melodrama with a low-mimetic tale of academic backbiting and professional rivalry. *Scientists are only human*, they said, *but the science is still unassailable.* Yet this story seemed to fall on deaf ears. Only when they began to turn the tables on the skeptics by portraying them as the Grand Inquisitors of climate science did they gain rhetorical traction.

But we are getting ahead of ourselves. To first understand how the American skeptical community made its characterizations stick, we need a more detailed accounting of the semiotic codes in its arsenal. Two tropes did the most work: cultishness and corruption. Let's start with cultishness first.

Christian conservatives have long portrayed environmentalism as a doomsday cult (Buell 2003, 18–21; Taylor and Globus 2011), and Climategate presented a perfect opportunity to make this portrayal stick. As linguist Brigitte Nerlich (2010) shows, religious metaphors suffused commentary on Climategate in the skeptical blogosphere. They also appeared prominently in the right-wing press. The most outspoken exponent in the United States was the *Washington Times*, which published a steady stream of articles and editorials on Climategate, far more than any other American newspaper.[4] In a series of ferocious editorials, it blasted the "global warming theocracy" and the "doomsaying" of "climate theology's leading high priests" (*Washington Times* 2009a, 2009b, 2009c). These epithets were clearly intended to resonate with an established narrative emanating from the Christian Right, which painted environmentalism (and environmental science) as a neopagan cult bent on world domination. In an interview on Climategate with the *Dallas Morning News*

---

occupy a privileged position as the place where intellectual elites and experts speak to the public. They are an important (if slightly dusty) stage for the social drama of climate change.

[4] A search of major world publications for the term "Climategate" on LexisNexis got 1,290 hits (August 9, 2012), 701 in the United States. The papers with the greatest number of hits were the Canadian *National Post* (146), the *Australian* (107), and the *Washington Times* (104). Next on the list were the *Financial Times of London* with fifty-four references and the *Guardian* with forty-nine. By contrast, it appeared in the *New York Times* a mere seventeen times.

(2009), Senator Jim Inhofe, the government's most outspoken climate denier, alluded darkly to the United Nation's role in perpetuating the "hoax" of global warming and pointed to "far-left environmentalists" infiltrating America's churches (a reference to the so-called Creation Care movement). "I think what's happening is what we see in Romans 1:25," Inhofe said, "the idea that there would be people who 'changed the truth of God into a lie, and worshipped and served the creature more than the Creator.'" For evangelicals, this was a key scriptural reference, often invoked by antienvironmental groups like the Cornwall Alliance to represent the rise of climate science as a sign of the end times (Barkun 2003; Boyer 1992; Kearns 2011; McCammack 2007). In this apocalyptic discourse, Climategate was more than just a conspiracy to defraud the public; it was part of a plot to destroy the world.

This explicitly scriptural narrative had less traction outside Christian Right circles, but other religious tropes circulated widely. More secular conservatives used them in a deeply ironic mode, painting climate scientists, not as demonic Others, but as members of a laughably paranoid, fanatical subculture – more as objects of scorn than of fear. The beauty of this discourse has always been its ability to unite conservative Protestants and secular libertarians by fusing the legacies of anti-Catholic and anti-communist rhetoric. Responding to Climategate ("the greatest scandal in modern science"), *Washington Times* columnist and radio host Jeffrey Kuhner (2009) wrote, "The myth of global warming along with the Environmental Protection Agency have become the hammer and sickle of eco-Marxism – the new green-red alliance that seeks to destroy capitalism and the sovereign nation-state." "Just like the communists before them, radical environmentalists are driven by secular utopianism. They are followers of a pseudo-religion, except salvation is to be found in this world rather than the next. They demonstrate the irrationalism and imperviousness to facts and empirical evidence akin to a cult." Linking the CRU scientists to the Jim Jones of Warmism, Al Gore, Kuhner concludes that the lie of global warming "must be propagated at all costs to maintain the faith in Gaea, the ancient pagan goddess of the Earth."

On both sides of the debate, the trope of tribalism played an equally prominent role. Designating anticivil or, better yet, *pre*-civil behavior, this trope points to an undemocratic, Dionysian excess of *thymos*. Conservative commentators located this excess squarely in the scientific camp. Science-minded environmentalists saw it everywhere and lamented its distorting effect on rational debate. For example, the first chapter of British environmental journalist Fred Pearce's (2010) chronicle of Climategate, *The Climate Files*, is titled – no doubt with intertextual reference to the

Frankie Goes to Hollywood hit of 1984 and its iconic mass-brawl video – "Two Tribes Go to War." In his account, *thymos* explains almost everything. "As I read the emails in the days after they were made public," he writes (5), "it became clear to me that sniping over many years between mainstream climate researchers and their critics, many of them running climate-skeptic blogs, had degenerated into a secret and corrupting conflict." This conflict, Pearce continues, was "a battle for ownership of data" and "to open up the closed world of scientific peer review to challenge by outsiders." It was thus a "battle for the soul of science." For Pearce, this battle takes the form of ironic tragedy. It is "dark" and there are "few heroes"; it is a tale of how "tea-room tittle-tattle" became "the preferred mode of communication among some respected scientists" (11). "The bunker mentality – of climate scientists faced with the mob trying to take over their labs – is brutally exposed in the emails," he writes (13). "But so too is the opportunism of the outsiders, and the confusion caused in the labs by their efforts to question what was going on." In the story Pearce tells, both sides begin with reasonable motives – one to ensure quality control in the scientific literature, the other to make the scientific debate more open and democratic. But anger and paranoia polluted these motives, making sane deliberation impossible. Tribalism trumped deliberative rationality. *Thymos*, whose dangerous volatility we noted a few pages ago, ran riot.

Whereas cultishness and tribalism invoked premodern threats, criminality and corruption invoked contemporary dangers. The CRU scientists were frequently accused of "cooking the books," which, following the financial collapse of 2008, linked them symbolically to corporate greed. Here was yet another clique of brainy elites using fuzzy math to defraud the public. According to this narrative, their motives were simple: greed and prestige. "Global warming alarmism has become a gravy train for scientists, bureaucrats and corporations who profit from the billions of taxpayer dollars spent researching and fighting climate change," wrote H. Sterling Burnett (2010, A11), a senior fellow with the National Center for Policy Analysis, a conservative think tank. Often this line of argument merged with the religious. Writing on the *Wall Street Journal* opinion page, Bret Stephens (2009) explained that if one "follows the money," an entire "ecosystem" of universities, research institutes, and advocacy groups emerges, feeding at the government trough. "All of them have been on the receiving end of climate change–related funding," Stephens concludes, "so all of them must believe in the reality (and catastrophic imminence) of global warming just as a priest must believe in the existence of God" – or as a made man must believe in *cosa nostra*. As the Lowell

Sun (2009) put it, following a well-established line of attack, the CRU scientists were guilty of a "mafia-like suppression of dissent, suppression of evidence and methods."

Climategate allowed skeptics to act as high-minded defenders of scientific objectivity. Believers, conversely, were forced to play the cynical realists. This was not a winning position. Their attempts to deflate the crisis by divorcing unsavory scientists from unassailable science rang hollow. Once again, they doubled down on *logos* and ignored *ethos*. By arguing that "everyone knows" that science is a nasty political game, they appeared to cede the moral high ground to their opponents. Writing on the *Wall Street Journal* opinion page, Pat Michaels (2009) likened the CRU's behavior to "filtering what goes in the Bible" – that is, the peer-reviewed scientific literature. In the *Detroit News* (2009), editor Nolan Finley clucked, "Research skeptical of climate change is denounced as quackery. But science should never be 'settled,' as the global warming industry has declared this matter to be. Nor should it be cause driven, massaged to align with popular movements. It should be cold, impassive and willing to prove itself against dissenting theories. It should welcome new evidence, even if it alters its assumptions." Even sympathetic skeptics piled on the moral opprobrium. "Dissent was stifled, facts were suppressed, scrutiny was blocked, and the free flow of information was choked off," opined Bjorn Lomborg (2009). The "real tragedy," he continued, was that by toeing the "party line" and "substituting spin for scientific rigor," the CRU scientists have given skeptics a reason not to care about global warming. "This unsavory glimpse of scientists trying to cook the data could be just the excuse too many people are waiting for to tune it all out," Lomborg warned.

When the *New York Times* (2009) finally weighed in with its editorial page on December 6, it dismissed the controversy as mere "noise." The scientists might have been "mean-spirited" and "intemperate," but that did not change "the underlying scientific facts about climate change." According to the *Washington Post* (2011), the scientists were simply "catty." The *St. Louis Post-Dispatch* (2009) argued that many great scientists have behaved badly, noting that Isaac Newton "badly overreacted to critics and dabbled in alchemy." Sounding an almost desperately deflationary note, Peter Frumhoff (2009), director of science and policy at the Union of Concerned Scientists and a lead author of the IPCC's Fourth Assessment Report, said in a statement, "What the e-mails show are simply scientists at work, grappling with key issues, and displaying the full range of emotions and motivations characteristic of any urgent endeavor." In a late-arriving op-ed denouncing America's conservative "thought police," Paul Krugman (2011) tried a more aggressive line of defense: "Nothing in the correspondence suggested any kind of scientific impropriety; at most, we learned – I know this will shock you – that scientists are human beings, who occasionally say snide things about people they dislike." Centrist media outlets were less knowing and more alarmed. A *USA Today* (2009) editorial wrote of a "disturbing level of pettiness, groupthink and willingness to disguise inconvenient data among leading climate scientists." For this paper, as for many others, the lesson of Climategate was that science needs more "transparency." As the *San Jose Mercury News* (2009) argued, "scientists by nature are not great communicators. They prefer to conduct their business in private, partly to avoid embarrassment to colleagues whose theories and projects are discredited. But frank, clear communication is crucial when public policy and precious funding is [*sic*] at stake." Against a near-constant barrage of references to "Mike's Nature Trick" and Ben Santer's desire to "beat the crap" out of Pat Michaels, it is no wonder that this insipid, school-marmish message failed to make a dent. That left-of-center publications like the *New York Times* generally dismissed the scandal only reinforced the Right's belief in a massive cover-up. In the *Ottawa Citizen*, Canadian columnist David Warren (2009) accused the so-called mainstream media of "maintaining the silence of Iago on the revelations."

Climategate finally seemed to sputter out in spring 2010. Attempting to capitalize on the lingering storm of skeptical outrage, however, conservative politicians went after the scientists. In April 2010, Virginia attorney general Ken Cuccinelli demanded that the University of Virginia hand over a wide range of records relating to grant applications by Mann, a former faculty member. Cuccinelli said he was looking for evidence of fraud. The ACLU and the American Association of University Professors rushed to Mann's defense, and the university successfully fought Cuccinelli in court. Soon it was clear that Cuccinelli's move had backfired. Howard Becker (1967) writes of a "hierarchy of credibility" that favors the institutionally powerful over the less powerful. In this case, however, a different principle was at play: faith in the attorney general seemed to be trumped by the signs of "professor" and "scientist." An editorial in the *Richmond Times-Dispatch* (2010) declared, "Among laymen, the debate over global warming has ceased to be about the science. It is now a team-sport contest involving the politics of personal destruction, in which points are scored by proxy. What a shame that Cuccinelli – whose engineering background should make him more, rather than less, appreciative of scientific rigor – should participate in the sordid game."

The *Roanoke Times* (2010) called Cuccinelli "the commonwealth's inquisitor general," comparing him to Galileo's Catholic persecutors. Virginia Sierra Club director Glen Besa (2010) wondered in the *Richmond Times-Dispatch* if Cuccinelli was funded by "Big Oil and the other polluters that have bankrolled a decades-long disinformation campaign meant to protect their profits by confusing the public enough to stop progress toward a clean energy future." The *Washington Post* (2010) castigated the attorney general's "witch hunt," arguing that "science progresses when researchers can propose ideas freely, differ in their methods and argue about the interpretations of their results." The journal *Nature* (2010) weighed in, calling Cuccinelli's campaign an "ideologically motivated inquisition that harasses and intimidates climate scientists." Even some skeptics felt compelled to condemn him. After keeping up the skeptical drumbeat in the early days of Climategate, *Richmond Times-Dispatch* columnist A. Barton Hinkle (2010) ended up defending Mann against what he depicted as Cuccinelli's McArthyite crusade. Echoing the words of Pastor Martin Niemoller, the title for his column said it all: "First They Came for the Climatologists..."

Cuccinelli ended up losing his legal battle and inadvertently allowed Mann and his supporters to seize the moral high ground. This was largely a local victory, however. Whereas Mann and the CRU have become permanent players in the social drama of climate change, Cuccinelli plays a bit part at best. Still, one has to wonder how all this would have played out had environmentalists not waited for his subpoena to link Climategate with McCarthy, Salem, and the Inquisition. Rather than pollute the identities of their adversaries, they stuck to their rationalist guns. Was this a missed opportunity to turn the tables on skeptics? According to a March 2012 study by the Yale Project on Climate Change Communication, most Americans trust climate scientists (73 percent) more than other kinds of scientists (65 percent) as sources of information on global warming. But among those the study calls "dismissive," the opposite is true: only 29 percent trust climate scientists and 39 percent trust other kinds of scientists. The only group with lower levels of trust are fossil fuel companies (Leiserowitz et al. 2013).

Trust, Romance, and Environmental Melodrama

Environmentalists have every right to be outraged by the way science was distorted in the wake of Climategate. Although it is true that the CRU was an important generator of climate data, anyone with even the most basic understanding of climate science would have understood that misdeeds by a handful of prominent scientists could not fatally damage the consensus achieved by thousands of researchers working in dozens of fields, corroborating, criticizing, and reproducing each other's results in numerous ways. As the historian of science Paul Edwards (2010, 429) puts it, "there are too many models, there are too many controls on the data, too much scrutiny of every possibility, and there is too much integrity in the IPCC process" for groupthink, systematic errors, or scientific elitism to form the basis of agreement. Indeed, as Edwards notes at the end of his book (439), some scientists think we may *never* have more accurate projections than we have now, because future warming will permanently skew the historical baseline.

But to many, if not most, Americans, none of this matters. Reading through the spate of post-Climategate commentary from both the Right and Left, it is remarkable how rarely the actual details of the controversy are debated. Much like the science itself, the scientists' e-mails seem to have interested a small minority of inside players. What mattered to everyone else was character. *What kind of people are these scientists, their defenders and their critics? What makes them tick?* As Aristotelian theory predicts, this was and still is the central question wherever climate change becomes a social drama.

It is important to recognize that skeptics did not just sully the character of climate scientists. They forced a genre shift. Acting as a chorus, bloggers, political pundits, and journalists performed a virtuosic feat: they turned the romance of the IPCC (heroic scientists from around the world battling ignorance and greed in a jamboree of public-spirited truth finding) into what Frye called "irony." This is a mode in which the audience feels it is "looking down on a scene of bondage, frustration, or absurdity" (Frye 1957, 34). More specifically, they turned it into an ironic melodrama. "In melodrama two themes are important," writes Frye (47), "the triumph of moral virtue over villainy, and the consequent idealizing of the moral views assumed to be held by the audience." In its most lurid incarnations (think CSI-type crime shows with serial-killer pedophiles), melodrama induces what Frye calls "the pure self-righteousness of the lynching mob" (47). Mainstream narrations of Climategate moved in a slightly different direction, closer to ironic comedy. Climate science was renarrated as a morally repugnant game played by treacherous ideologues. Far from repudiating science, the chorus cast itself as the true defender of the scientific *ethos*. It thus put the audience in the position of knowing better than the scientists of guarding "sound science" against its debasers. "Cultivated people go to a melodrama to hiss the villain with an air of condescension," Frye (47) writes: "they are making a point of the fact that they cannot take his villainy seriously." By scapegoating the CRU researchers, skeptics staged just such a melodrama, one sufficiently layered to attract an ideologically diverse audience. Credibility was lost.

By portraying climate scientists as venal and absurd, skeptics mapped the discursive binaries of civil society onto scientific terrain. Through a ritual of "inverse stigmatization" (Alexander 2006a, 232), they marked the science of global warming as "anticivil science." As Alexander and Smith (1993) demonstrate, for at least two centuries, anticivil or counterdemocratic actors have been represented as hysterical or deranged; in their behavior toward other community members they are secretive, suspicious, self-interested, deceitful, calculating, and conspiratorial, and they build institutions that are arbitrary, hierarchical, and exclusive. The goal of any contestant in a democratic social drama is to place the audience on the side of civility, to make them feel like defenders of the democratic code. Where low-mimetic dramas shade into ironic melodramas, this shared sense of moral solidarity can become frighteningly intense. Yet in complex, pluralistic societies, pushing this shift from solidarity to scapegoating can easily backfire. Moral crusades can quickly become Inquisitions. In the discourse of democratic civil society, crusaders are acceptable; inquisitors are not.

In the case of Climategate, skeptics successfully portrayed climate science (and environmental science in general) as "tribal," "corrupt," and even "cultish." In America, these characterizations resonated with longstanding anxieties about the ideological dangers of environmentalism, anxieties most often articulated in religious terms. But when the skeptics appeared to go beyond moral condemnation by persecuting individual scientists, they encountered resistance from the political center. The result, we suggest, was to reinforce the romantic narrative among environmentalists. For them, Climategate proved that science was "under assault" by a McCarthyite cabal of free-market capitalists and religious fundamentalists. This hardening and polarizing of positions may be an inevitable consequence of the melodramatic frame (Schwarze 2006).[5]

---

[5] Schwarze (2006, 239–240) persuasively argues that melodrama's ubiquity in environmental politics "stems from its capacity to provide a coherent, synthetic response to several of the persistent rhetorical obstacles facing environmental advocates. It can transform ambiguous and unrecognized environmental conditions into public problems; it can call attention to how distorted notions of the public interest conceal environmental degradation; and, it can overcome public indifference to environmental problems by amplifying their moral and emotional dimensions." Whereas Schwarze emphasizes the utility of melodrama for environmental activists, we would argue that it can be just as useful for their opponents.

Culturally attuned observers understood that Climategate was all about trust (e.g., Hulme and Ravetz 2009). They also understood that climate science and activism as a whole suffer from a deficit of trust, and that this deficit – more than ignorance, fear, or denial – is what prevents Americans from agreeing that global warming is real and dangerous. What they have yet to explain fully is *how* this deficit has been generated and maintained. In this chapter, we have shown that battles over trust turn on genre choices and the projection of character. Moreover, we have shown that both genre and character depend on the projection of *feeling*. Flawed advertising campaigns were unable to generate a sense of *thymos* in their audiences. They hectored them and seemed to treat them with contempt. They were evidence that climate activists were out-of-touch zealots who preyed on emotions and were prepared to ignore norms of civil decency. Climategate was a complex genre war that hinged on how the emotional dispositions of its antagonists were perceived. By casting climate scientists as the skulking villains of an environmental melodrama, skeptics and their supporters convened a hissing, sanctimonious public that could feel good about itself as it clamored on behalf of "real science." *Ethos* was lost. Scientists and their defenders fought back with a low-mimetic nonstory consisting of disconnected, itsy-bitsy justifications for each individual infraction. This checking-off-of-boxes response did nothing to restore trust. Only when they cast the scientists as the embattled protagonists of a romantic struggle against paranoid inquisitors were they able to stem the bleeding.

Climate science has long claimed that it does not receive enough attention in the media. Perhaps it should remember the saying "be careful what you wish for."

7

The Climate Conference as Theatre

We have spoken throughout this book of climate change as amenable to fruitful analysis as a drama. Nowhere is this claim more obvious than in the case of climate change conferences. Yet as we show in this chapter, the theatricality of climate conferences is surprisingly multifaceted and marked by a high degree of what Victor Turner called "performative reflexivity" (see Chapter 2). These are no mere dog-and-pony shows. Of course, such meetings have bureaucratic and legislative activities that are to some extent hidden or "backstage," and policy experts are apt to depict this backstage deal making as "where the action really happens." Still the drama analogy holds along a surprising number of dimensions. We begin by noting that conventions and conferences have ritual aspects. As Lyn Spillman (2012) shows in her discussion of American business association annual meetings, even the most humdrum get together of concrete engineers or rubber glove makers will have a solidaristic and civic component. This is enacted and reproduced through performative gestures like memorials, award ceremonies, charity auctions, and dinner cruises. She writes that in such events, "many contemporary associations demonstrate camaraderie well above and beyond the pursuit of shared interests" (169). So conferences and congresses are like rituals. And from ritual to drama is but a short step, as Nietzsche – echoing Aristotle's prior analysis – showed in his interpretation of Greek civilization.

The analogies are manifold. Indeed, strictly considered, they are not even analogies but shared properties. Like staged dramas, conferences take place in a defined location (a city, a convention center) and exist for a predetermined period of time. These are places where people perform to each other to make claims and to demonstrate their good character.

The guaranteed presence of the global mass media makes the effort involved in performing well an even better investment. So politicians and activists work hard to tell stories, to display competence and talent, and to relay facts to the onlooking global audience. There are even cultural scripts that allow these performances to be both improvised and understood. For example, one can enact moral indignation, pragmatism, aspiration, or victimhood by turning to the playbook for each of these subject positions and rhetorical stances. It is important to observe that the cast of motivated performers includes both official and invited delegates and others on the fringe of the event who wish to express their views or gain global attention. For this reason, nongovernmental organizations (NGOs), protestors, artists, and climate change celebrities can often be found attempting to take a slice of the attention space that the conference will have claimed within the global civil society. Finally we should note the presence of those we call reluctant performers: police and security services, caterers and cleaners, local citizens going about their business, and so forth. These groups most likely wish to remain out of the limelight, but they can find themselves caught up in a dramatic episode or subject to narration as components of a wider story of success or failure.

Clearly the legal agreements and protocols arising from a conference are a major measure of its "success": true enough they are often displayed as landmarks by activists and politicians. Yet this is a narrow and somewhat uninteresting metric from the perspective of cultural sociology. We wish to suggest here that other registers of evaluation can be equally visible and significant in shaping readings of any particular conference. These involve meanings that are both "given" and, more importantly, "given off" by the conference, to invoke Goffman's distinction between direct and indirect, motivated and accidental signification. Like a music competition (McCormick 2009), the most culturally effective climate conference is one with the capacity to transcend its own genre. The best music competitions are no longer "competitions" of isolated individuals but at the end of the day consume their own purpose to become something much more: they become celebrations offering ritual fusion with the transcendent power of music over politics and difference, with the deep time of the musical tradition or the vitality of youth. International conferences are formally understood as instrumental meetings organized around treaty formation and, to a lesser extent, information and opinion exchange. Yet the most effective conferences in terms of cultural power are those redescribed in a meta-narrative as ritual celebrations of human unity, of problem-solving capacity, and of planetary solidarity. This status must be contingently achieved by participants and then communicated to outsiders through distant spectatorship or critical commentary. Importantly, the transcendent event can carry with it the ritual energies required for sacrificial activity where particularistic interests are burned on the altar of the general good. Alternatively, a conference might be downgraded. A routine event can become a farce or tragedy in which the participants are unable to perform as expected and attain even low-mimetic goals. The conference becomes associated with Victor Turner's phase of "breach" more so than with "resolution." Indeed, it can come to seem like an incessantly recurring breach, a skipping record on the political turntable.

Considered as a social drama, the distant, mediated experience of a conference is as worthy of study as its diplomatic and technocratic outcomes. This is all the more so because any particular event can potentially become a generalized symbol or shorthand that exerts totemic power over distant spans of time and space. We know this can be the case for festivals. Woodstock was not just an event in the 1960s. It became a defining event of the 1960s and so came in time to define what the 1960s themselves were all about (Smith 2012). Woodstock was powerful as a motivating force and collective memory not only for those who were there but also for many of a certain generation and in subsequent generations. It suggested possibility by example – and indeed has been replicated in various contexts. As Adam Rome (2013) shows in his richly detailed history of Earth Week, environmental politics have worked in much the same way. Standard environmental histories of the early 1970s focus on the passage of landmark legislation such as the Clean Water Act (1972). But Rome clearly shows that the street theatre, speeches, marches, and musical performances of Earth Week were not just surface-level responses to underlying shifts in environmental attitudes but in fact helped produce those shifts.

In a similar way, a single heroic climate conference has the potential to bootstrap itself from a localized pragmatic encounter toward becoming a paradigm exemplar that can drive future climate change agendas as a motivator and template. Even by simply becoming a named "event," the climate conference does important cultural work by demonstrating to the world that "something is happening." The stakes are high not simply administratively but also culturally, precisely because each named conference has a remote chance of becoming a powerful symbol for social justice, human cooperation, and collective wisdom. The world is watching.

What are the narrative forms, tropes, and images we might expect to find associated with positive and negative representations of the climate conference ritual encounter?

Liberally interpreted, Aristotle offers some clues. As we noted in Chapter 5, he indicates that spectacle (*Poetics* VI) has some emotional attractions, but these are weak and superficial when contrasted to those of higher forms of art involving language and narrative. An echo of this point was made by Frederic Jameson (1984) in his famous critique of postmodernity. He saw this as involving the waning of affect and the substitution of the insubstantial image for auratic, narrative communication. Taking these theorists as indicators of a prevailing binary normative discourse rather than as analysts of empirical truths, we surmise that the culturally successful conference will be described as involving authentic emotions and genuine communicative activity rather than simply as a media event, or grandstand for the famous – in short as an empty spectacle. The growth of well-intentioned fringe activities around climate change conferences (arts festivals, Eco-villages, protests, and so forth) has in fact been a dangerous trend that amplifies possibilities for an emptying out of ritual energy and the substitution of such impertinent metaphors – "sideshow" and "circus" being perhaps the most common of these. As we showed in our analysis of 10:10, appearing to mock or belittle serious concerns can quickly demote a performer – and her cause – in the eyes of an audience.

The next set of themes relates to human motivation. In a successful conference, we will see reports of gestures of sacrifice and solidarity associated with romance. As Northrop Frye points out, the idea here is that there is a net increase in sociality when we contrast the end with the start of the dramatic sequence. Such narrations emphasize higher motivations for action and the capacity of humans to triumph through concerted acts of the will and through ethical choices. At the level of embodied activity, Durkheimian ritual theory predicts rhythmic entrainment: applause, touching, chanting. There will also be a sense of sustained attention to the major conference themes and dedication to a particular space rather than a diffusion of energy and attention. Although the interaction ritual theory of Randall Collins (2004) sees these as objective features of successful ritual, we note that they are also indicators that can be recognized as such by distant audiences. In a sense they are discourse tokens or items of mediated evidence that can be used to leverage a particular interpretation of a particular dramatic episode.

A failed conference will be associated with tragedy and satire. These modes reflect the futility of human life. In the former case, as we discussed in Chapter 2, noble characters are dragged low by fate, make poor choices, or are caught in lose-lose dilemmas. The result is a dissolution of the social. In a traditional drama, this means death, murder, or factionalism are outcomes of plot movement. Whereas tragic figures might have high motivations, in satire characters are driven by base motivations such as lust and greed. They are inferior to spectators and are dependent on selfish urges and emotions. Rather than being autonomous actors, they are controlled and consumed by passions and biological forces over which they have no control. Within the satire, there is usually an amusing or worrying disjuncture between the high motivations that people profess and the true nature of their actions. As with tragedy, the net result is a deflation of the emotional energies that can lead to cooperative and innovative actions, not only among participants, but also among spectators. Collinsian objective indicators may well be invoked to support this reading. We will find mention of delegates looking for food stands or falling asleep; of talks given to empty sessions and of emotions such as boredom triumphing over more heroic and romantic ones.

These tropes and themes combine to answer the core question that is asked of each conference within the wider social drama of climate change: Was this a step forward or a step back?

Copenhagen

In Chapter 3 we touched on the 1996 Kyoto Conference. This had fallen short of providing a romantic narrative not simply in the petty and bean-counting details of its treaty but also in its more general media representation. Coverage of Kyoto had focused on selfish national behaviors – especially those of killjoy nonsignatories – and the wearying combination of bureaucratic- and science-speak that suffocated any sense of a festival atmosphere. Visual images often showed delegates asleep at their desks, not smiling or hugging. Still, something had been achieved: the question with which we ended the prior paragraph could be answered – yes, there had been a measured and bureaucratic step forward.

More than a decade later, interim conferences had achieved little. Altogether larger in scale than Kyoto, Copenhagen in 2009 was intended to break through the impasse and push the climate change international cooperation to a new level. Considerable groundwork by so-called

Sherpas took place backstage. These invisible technocrats and diplomats were intended to fix the ladders for treaty formation. At the level of cultural process, lessons had been learned too. The complex meaning-rich possibilities of the climate conference were well recognized by the organizers of the 2009 Copenhagen conference. A raft of fringe events, a series of high-profile speakers, and resources for the global mass media indicate a serious concern, not only with treaty formation, but also with wider communicative and expressive agendas. Unlike exclusive G-8 meetings and Davos-type forums of self-congratulatory plutocrats that had dominated in the 1990s (and received negative narrations of the kind evoked by our word choice in the first part of this sentence), here a platform was provided for the Global South to speak as well as the major players of the polluting economies. What would go on display, it was hoped, would be a celebration of cosmopolitan and ecological solidarity.

Ironically enough, for all this detailed cultural work, no other conference has done so poorly as an item of motivational theatre. One problem seemed to be vulnerability to recoding as spectacle by cynics deploying the negative side of the binary code we sketched out earlier. Fox News (2009), for example, quoted the prominent climate skeptic Myron Ebell as dubbing the event a "circus" and lampooning fringe activities such as Brahma Kumaris World Spiritual University, with its intent to "explore how thoughts affect matter and how a shift in consciousness can transform current deteriorating conditions" for the environment. Ebell also speared efforts by women activists to eliminate quantitative benchmarks and targets. Radical critics also mobilized this imagery: "the Copenhagen climate talks were a bright green spectacle that ultimately moved global climate policy backwards" wrote Doyle Canning (2010) on the *Left Turn* website. However, analogies to distracting entertainment were less significant in the end than those relating to human discord. These were propagated in a somewhat sordid low-mimetic mode that morphed imperceptibly into the tragic pattern: poor choices were being made, chances were being missed, bad outcomes were eventuating. Commentators remarkably early on wrote that this was an event turning sour.

The sense that themes of disunity would trump those relating to unity began toward the start of the conference with various protests by activists and motivated citizens. On December 12, a huge demonstration saw more than forty thousand people take to the streets of the Danish capital. Reports of what happened, even when attempting to be neutral, flattered nobody. According to the BBC (2009), "bolt cutters and gas masks had been found inside a lorry at the front of the march," and "protesters threw bricks and smashed windows in the city center, while others set off fireworks." The impression here is of both organized and disorganized violence. Meanwhile, in the same report, the authorities looked repressive as they adopted the package of militaristic policing strategies for crowd control that have diffused globally (see Graham 2011). It was noted that protestors had been forced to sit in lines on the ground with their hands tied before being taken away. The BBC quoted Mel Evans from Climate Justice Action: "They weren't able to have any medical attention, any water, and weren't allowed to have any toilet facilities. People were there in freezing conditions urinating on themselves and being held in lines like, essentially like animals." Television and Internet images showed the corralled ranks of protestors, the police in riot gear, and barking police dogs. The overall impression was of an ugly spectacle featuring a rent-a-mob versus the goon squad. Humans were being systematically degraded. This was not an environment in which pro-social, public-spirited gestures could become visible, never mind contagious. (For a detailed cross-national analysis of media coverage of Copenhagen, see Eide, Kunelius, and Kumpu 2010.)

Over the next few days, further reports emerged from protestors of seemingly undemocratic and unjust policing actions. These in turn reinforced the impression that the climate change conference was anything but universalistic, inclusive, and democratic. Like the global economic conferences at Davos and Seattle, this seemed once again to be an event for an elites or oligarchs, not the people. Protestors spoke of police infiltrators (nearly always identifiable by their clichéd Palestinian-style scarves), of random searches and beatings. It came to light that there was a detention center with wire cages called "Guantanamo Junior" even by the Danish police themselves. Protestors were pepper-sprayed when they attempted to break the cages. In court, details came out of wiretaps on noted activists (van der Zee 2009). Newspapers reported how difficult it was to actually access the conference center, which was surrounded by several layers of security. The overall impression was not of the peaceful and affluent Scandinavian social democracy of liberal mythology but of a secretive conference under siege working with the tools of the police state. Importantly, it was the conference itself that had generated these outcomes: it had motivated the wiretaps, the cages, the aggressive policing, the introduction of security cordons. Not simply another manifestation of preexisting characteristics of Denmark, the conference was like a cancer eating away at the fundamental way of life within that society. It had polluted a nation.

The orchestrated high point of Copenhagen was the arrival of more than one hundred heads of state toward the end of the conference. This was intended to energize the process and to allow high-level decisions to be made quickly. These visits were interpreted differently, and often in a negative light. Direct meetings between key heads of state took place away from the main conference forum. This opened up visions of backroom deals that excluded the minor and vulnerable nations in the auditorium who had been symbolically positioned as the main "victims" and carriers of risk. Such talks were seen as subverting the United Nations's focus on visible diplomacy and devalued the core ritual activity of the front stage conference, which relentlessly stressed equality and solidarity. According to Yvo de Boer, the UN's soon-to-be-disgruntled-and-bypassed climate change diplomat, "rumor and intrigue" took over from any accountable and transparent process. More importantly, few of the heads of state were seen as acting in good faith. They had come to Copenhagen so as to appear to be taking the issue seriously, or simply to appear to be a globally important person by bathing in the reflected glory of other, more truly important people. The *New Scientist*, for example, pointed to the amount of precious time each leader took up with speeches relayed to big screens. It skewered bad science, theatrical and attention-seeking behavior, hypocrisy, and sentimentality in second-tier leaders such as Zimbabwe's Robert Mugabe, Canada's Stephen Harper, and Australia's Kevin Rudd (Pearce and Brahic 2009). Put another way, these players were debasing the event through spectacle and egotism rather than demonstrating *ethos*. Meanwhile, poorer nations stalled events with procedural objections (Walsh 2009). Although arguably valid, these were interpreted as petty and obstructionist. As noted in Chapter 5, a rule of successful improv theatre and conversation alike is that you take what is offered and run with it. Here there were a series of refusals to play. Much as we found with the failing threads in climate change art forums, this is a failure of the chorus that merely diluted *thymos*.

Once it was clear that years of footwork would not result in a new Kyoto, some face saving was required to justify the energy, expense, and visibility of the conference, especially after the apparent involvement of various heads of state in direct negotiations (Dimitrov 2010). All that emerged was a toothless nonbinding accord signed by some, but not all, nations. This was without any specific targets or deadlines. It was mentioned that climate change was a problem and that steps should be taken to deal with it, little more. Journalists reported world leaders leaving before the final plenary session when this tentative and feeble document was to be voted on. Commentators suggested they had skulked off to avoid humiliation, full of shame. "'Copenhagen is a crime scene tonight,' an angry Greenpeace official declared, 'with the guilty men and women fleeing to the airport'" (quoted in McKibben 2012a).

There followed a highly visible blame game that merely fostered the impression that climate change was too tough to handle and that democratic deliberation was impossible. The Danish hosts were blamed for undemocratically excluding many smaller countries from key sessions and for railroading with a draft agreement in an effort to streamline the negotiation process. Emerging economies, especially India and China, were blamed for demanding the same right to pollute as developed nations had before them. Africa was blamed for seeking aid handouts. The United States and developed economies were blamed for having double standards by demanding that others not be allowed to pollute as they had in the past and were still doing at present (see Vidal 2009a, 2009b).

What is important for our purposes is not just that the preceding litany of events happened; nor why; nor whether they really happened the way we have narrated them. What is crucial is that critics and commentators noticed them in just such a way. They were taken up as key indicators of a miserable example of a human failure to cooperate. *Time* magazine, for example, quoted at length a frustrated Saudi Arabian delegate:

I am working without break for 48 hours now. I do not see in the future, a situation where we can adopt a legally binding [agreement]. This is without exception the worst plenary I have ever attended, including the management of the process, the timing, everything. (Walsh 2009)

Media images focused on protestors and on visions of fatigued participants. For example, the *Guardian*'s report of December 8, 2009, was full of diplomatic and technical information, but the picture at the top was captioned "A Haitian Delegate Rests before the Second Day Session Begins in Copenhagen" (Vidal 2009a). It showed a woman with her face in her hands and her elbows on a table. She appears to be taking a catnap. The suggestion is not that she is lazy, rather that people are trying hard, but that the process is simply not efficient or inspiring. The willing are burned out and frustrated. A search of Internet photo sites shows the "sleeping delegate" photo is an established genre that has been recognized even by stock photograph agencies. Copenhagen provided some of its masterworks. Another visual genre familiar from global economic meetings was also imported: instead of delegates and speeches, this showed violent protestors clashing with violent police officers. Such images often appeared at the top of the main feature – even when the following text was mostly about going on within the conference venue.

In a famous essay on the power of images, Stuart Hall (1973) observes that news photographs can be used to ideological effect. For example, in the case of street protests, they can position one party or the other as a violent aggressor. Typically, he says, protestors are seen acting unreasonably toward authority. Contra Hall, what is interesting about the Copenhagen photographs is that neither side looks good. In the manner of artworks depicting close combat in the context of a disintegrating sixteenth-century pike phalanx – we are somewhat reminded here of Holbein's *"Schlechten Krieg"* – there is a melee of compacted, pushing bodies. The product suggests a deindividuated Hobbesian world where might determines right rather than a Habermasian one of egalitarian solidarity and communicative reason (e.g., Associated Press 2009).

Now we are back in the tragic scenario where the protagonist's efforts are futile. In sum, Copenhagen was a missed opportunity not only for binding international agreements but even – in the absence of these – for positive messages to emerge about potential solidarity, community, and political will. At the end of the day, the event transmitted images of discord, not harmony. It seemed to be secretive, hierarchical, and repressive rather then open and democratic. Motivations look shallow, not utopian. The gravitational pull of routine politics had not been overcome.

Cancun

Against Copenhagen stands the case of Cancun. Copenhagen was a disaster not only because it failed to produce a meaningful agreement but also because it sent out the wrong signals. This was a bloated, exclusionary, and antidemocratic event that had squandered its historic opportunity. Somehow it left a sour taste. That "somehow" is not a black box. We have shown it has the properties predicted by Aristotle and his followers. It consists of attributing low motivations to actors, relaying narratives of discord suggesting an end to the social and representing the conference as an empty spectacle rather than a meaningful ritual.

Copenhagen was predicted to be a success and ended a failure. A year later, a minor event in Cancun reversed the equation. Held in December 2010, this conference led to an agreement to keep temperature increases to 2 degrees Celsius over preindustrial levels and set emissions goals for all major polluting economies. A fund was set up to support developing nations, especially those that did not cut down forests. This was a major legal and diplomatic achievement. Equally important was the message that Cancun sent out as an observed ritual. The event was narrated as a triumph of low-key diplomacy. As the *New York Times* put it (Friedman and Chemnick 2010), "hysteria seems to have taken a holiday from the U.N. climate change treaty talks." There was a focus on "small practical steps" and "a positive and pragmatic approach," wrote a commentator in the usually disappointed ecozine *Grist* (Stavins 2011). Sitting beneath this was the narration of what Northrop Frye calls "themes of ascent," suggesting by way of contrast with Copenhagen a human capacity for growth and rationality. Cancun had an "unrelenting positive mood" (*Daily Telegraph* 2010). "Participants showed encouraging signs of learning to navigate through the unproductive squabbling between developed and developing countries that derailed the Copenhagen talks"; "China and the United States set a civil, productive tone, in contrast to the Copenhagen finger-pointing" (Stavins 2011). According to climate ethicist Benito Müller (2011), "a senior diplomat – being British not prone to emotional exaggerations – described the final night of the recent Cancun climate change conference as 'cathartic,' a healing experience for the multilateral climate change process." Whereas Copenhagen had foundered on the old logic that "divided the world into competing economic camps," Cancun had started to "move beyond the old Kyoto divide" that separated the world into warring developed and developing nations.

Importantly, visible embodied signs of ritual energy generated by the participants (Collins 2004) could be cited as evidence to anchor this new vision for distant spectators. Reports are marked by sequences such as the following:

Applause, standing ovations, cheers and even some teary eyes followed each speech, as country after country rose to demand that the Conference of the Parties (COP) accept the final negotiating text as an official decision.... More important than the deal itself was the intangible effects of what happened in Cancun, witnessed by the thunderous applause on the plenary floor. (Jervey 2011)

It's hard to explain how exciting it felt to be in that room.... Applause and even spontaneous cheering are really quite unprecedented. For the first time since the Copenhagen conference one year ago I am genuinely confident that this process can prove to the world that it can be successful. (Stark 2010)

The image here is of collective empowerment through growing solidarity. Notice Stark's interesting last sentence. Consistent with our social drama argument, his point was not that anything was achieved, nor that it would be achieved at some point in the near future, but rather a message had got out that a future message might get out ("can prove to the world") that change was a possibility. The real triumph of Cancun was in fact a signal of a hypothetical related to communication and mood. Even when the substantive diplomatic and technical achievement is talked down, this solidaristic/optimistic residue can remain. So for the *New York Times*, this was an event where "serious questions remain" about any capability to reduce greenhouse gases. Nevertheless, it spoke of delegates "embracing one another and patting colleagues on the back" and gave most of its attention to the fact that the process was not broken or disrupted as it had been in Copenhagen (Chemnick and Friedman 2010).

It is notable that discussions of Cancun usually positioned it in relation to the events that had gone before. In so doing, it was not understood as an isolated episode but rather as a plot point in the wider narrative or social drama of climate change. In this way, it became recognizable as a potential turning point. Aristotle wrote that the turning point, or what he called the *peripeteia*, was the most emotionally effective moment in a good drama. It is where there is a reversal of fortunes, from good to bad or vice versa. Narratives also indicated the presence of learning. Copenhagen had been a disaster, Cancun showed people had grown up. Much as it had done for Al Gore when he realized his time on earth had a purpose, *anagnorisis* had taken place. Perhaps, in retrospect, Copenhagen had been a necessary evil. Orienting Cancun to this narrative, discussions seeking to anchor *anagnorisis* engaged in relentless binary contrasts.

Copenhagen	Cancun
Undemocratic	Democratic
Secretive	Open
Disorganized	Coordinated
Mean spirited	Public spirited
Exclusionary	Inclusive

The new coding found embodiment in the character of Patricia Espinosa. The Mexican foreign minister was described as chairing the meeting with efficiency and charm. She was dubbed a "goddess" by the Indian minister and was credited by many as single-handedly changing the mood of negotiations. Again a process of learning from the past seemed to be involved. "Most of the credit for the summit's success rests with her [Espinosa] and the Mexican government's inclusive, flexible and open approach: they seemed to have studied the Danes' disastrous conduct of Copenhagen so as to do the precise opposite," wrote a surprisingly enthusiastic commentator in England's usually climate-cynical *Daily Telegraph* (Lean 2010).

While the Danish had been busy "masterminding... closed door 'secret text' negotiations" (Jervey 2011), Espinosa was open and approachable.

Looking back to public discussions on Copenhagen just after that event, and reading closely, we see the possibility for collective *anagnorisis* foreshadowed. Even before Cancun, Copenhagen had been narrated as a learning moment and a turning point. According to *Time*, for example, the Scandinavian conference had in fact demonstrated that "climate diplomacy has finally come of age." Failure was interpreted as a sign of harsh reality starting to bite – this was a reality check caused by the need to make tough decisions and sacrifices for the first time. There had been a transition toward a "climate realpolitik, which eschews hot air for real action" and signals that "global climate talks have moved beyond symbolic rhetoric" (Walsh 2009). In this formulation Copenhagen is translated into a portent. As they say, the darkest moment comes just before the dawn.

Durban and Doha

In 1999, the Climate Action Network (CAN), an international alliance of environmental NGOs, began giving its "Fossil of the Day" award to countries that performed badly in climate change negotiations (see Lipschutz and McKendry 2011). The ironic award has since become a routine emblem of international failure. After the Rio +20 meetings in June 2012, which produced yet another toothless declaration, the group threw up its hands in despair and gave the award to all of the governments at the conference. Rather than disrupt the predictably mundane flow of conference time, the award has come simply to reinforce an all-encompassing narrative of stasis, recalcitrance, and corruption. It has also come to highlight a key symbolic opposition in the climate conference meta-narrative: young versus old. As the moral standard-bearers of civil society, young people – most notably young women – have displayed a special capacity to steer this narrative in the direction of romance. Yet we will see that they have also faced special performative challenges.

At the 2011 meetings in Durban, South Africa, one American college student jolted the dominant low-mimetic narrative, if only for a moment. As chief U.S. climate negotiator Todd Stern mounted the podium to address the conference for the first time, Abigail Borah, a twenty-one-year-old biology major at Middlebury College in Vermont, interrupted the proceedings. Dressed primly and professionally in a black skirt and yellow blouse, hair clipped back, Borah announced in a thin, almost childlike voice:

2020 is too late to wait. We need an urgent path to a fair, ambitious and legally binding treaty. You must take responsibility to act now, or you will threaten the lives of the youth and the world's most vulnerable. You must set aside partisan politics and let science dictate decisions. You must pledge ambitious targets to lower emissions, not expectations. 2020 is too late to wait. (Democracy Now 2011)

Mohammad Al-Sabban, the senior economic advisor to Saudi Arabia's Ministry of Petroleum and Mineral Resources, who was presiding over the session, attempted to cut Borah off. "No one is listening to you," he said as Stern smiled sheepishly, waiting at the podium for security guards to escort Borah from the hall. But everyone *was* listening. Delegates and observers gave Borah a standing ovation, and news outlets from around the world led their daily reports with her outburst. As National Public Radio's Lynn Neary put it, "U.N. climate talks are, like many negotiations, a blend of dead seriousness and theater. Today, at the talks in Durban, South Africa, an American college student provided the theater" (Harris 2011). *Der Spiegel Online International* ran a story on Borah with the headline "Rebelling against the Climate Change Dinosaurs" (Schwägerl 2011). The influential climate change blog *Think Progress* (Johnson 2011) called Borah a "climate hero," and the left-wing *Daily Kos* (EdMass 2011) praised her for "speaking truth to power" and giving Stern a "shellacking."

After her interruption, Stern called a press conference to rebut the allegation that America was dragging its feet. "I've heard this from everywhere from ministers to press reports, to the very sincere and passionate young woman who was in the hall when I was giving my remarks. I just wanted to be on the record to say that that's just a mistake. It's not true." Yet in the same breath Stern seemed to endorse a European Union plan to adopt a road map for future discussions, something he had only tepidly supported in the past. The media widely reported this "change in tone" as a concession to increasingly frustrated delegates, shamed by Borah to do something substantive (Broder 2011).

At the same conference, another student from an American college, Anjali Appadurai of the College of the Atlantic, made headlines when she gave an indignant and confrontational speech on behalf of youth NGOs. "You've been negotiating all my life," she protested, focusing on the plight of developing nations. Appadurai continued:

There is real ambition in this room, but it's been dismissed as radical, deemed not "politically possible." *Stand with Africa*. Long-term thinking is not radical. What's radical is to completely alter the planet's climate, to betray the future of my generation, and to condemn millions to death by climate change. What's radical is to write off the fact that change *is* within our reach. 2011 was the year in which the silent majority found their voice, the year when the bottom shook the top. Twenty-eleven was the year when the radical became reality. Common but differentiated and historical responsibility are [*sic*] *not* up for debate. *Respect* the foundational principles of this convention. *Respect* the integral values of humanity. Respect the future of your descendants. Mandela said, "It always seems impossible, until it's done." So, distinguished delegates and governments around the world – governments of the developed world: *Deep cuts now. Get it done.* (YouTube 2011)

Appadurai then walked to the front of the stage, dropped her notes, and with the help of other youth activists at the back of the hall, led a "mic check," the call-and-response technique popularized by the Occupy Wall Street protests. "Equity now!" and "Get it done!" they chanted. After her speech, acting COP president Artur Runge-Metzger, chair of the European negotiating team, reminded the audience that Appadurai was speaking for half of the world's population. "And on a purely personal note," he added, "I wonder why we let not speak half of the world's population first in this conference, but only last." Yet by performing the mic check, Appadurai had violated the UN's strict rules regarding demonstrations, and she was subsequently stripped of her conference badge. A year later, she was banned from the UN conference in Doha, then readmitted following a Twitter storm directed at UN climate chief Christiana Figueres. Though lionized by many on the Left (Naomi Klein called her a "hero" on Twitter), the impact of Appadurai's activism was unclear. Had she galvanized civil society by speaking truth to power, or had she simply confirmed that young activists are strident, self-righteous, and easily marginalized? Her *ethos* appeared to remain undecided.

These flare-ups stand in sharp contrast with the best-known instance of youth conference activism. In 1992, twelve-year-old Severn Cullis-Suzuki gave a moving speech on behalf of children at the Earth Summit in Rio. Standing before world leaders in a floral dress and slightly frowzy hair, Cullis-Suzuki, a Canadian, calmly and confidently announced that she had "come five thousand miles to tell you adults you must change your ways." What followed was a rhetorical tour de force – a masterful interweaving of *ethos* and *pathos*. "Coming up here today, I have no hidden agenda," Cullis-Suzuki said. "I am fighting for my future":

Losing my future is not like losing an election, or a few points on the stock market. I am here to speak for all generations to come. I am here to speak on behalf of the starving children around the world whose cries go unheard. I am here to speak for the countless animals dying across this planet because they have nowhere left to go.

In video of her speech (YouTube 2008), delegates are shown listening raptly, faces pensive. "Here you may be delegates of your government, business people, organizers, reporters, or politicians. But really you are mothers and fathers, sisters and brothers, aunts and uncles, and *all of you are someone's child.*" Cullis-Suzuki spoke broadly of species going extinct, the hole in the ozone layer, and children starving in the favelas of Rio. She spoke of Western greed and disregard for nature. "You grownups say you love us," she concluded. "But I challenge you, please, make your actions reflect your words." Her speech received a standing ovation. Al Gore shook her hand and said it was the best speech given at the conference (McIlroy 2003). Cullis-Suzuki became an instant environmental celebrity, a gift she has parlayed into a successful career as an activist, author, and television personality.

It turns out that Cullis-Suzuki was well prepared for her performance. Her father, the scientist David Suzuki, is one of Canada's best-known environmental activists and host of a popular CBC Television science show, *The Nature of Things*. But her speech was so powerful precisely because it seemed to come from a place of complete innocence and apolitical purity. According to the *Toronto Star* (Landsberg 1992), "at U.N. headquarters in New York – where they didn't even know at first that she was the daughter of a renowned environmentalist – the name of Severn Suzuki is now being mentioned with something close to awe." The year 1992 was not the end of the story. In 2008, her speech was posted on YouTube by one Kim Seong Lee. It is telling to note that Lee appears to be a typical YouTube user, not a professional environmental organizer with slick marketing skills. The video is buried among Lee's holiday footage (circa five hundred views each) and an amusing song about memory loss by the folk singer Tom Rush (circa twelve hundred views). Lee seems to have lost interest in YouTube with no recent posts after a spurt of initial activity. Who would bother to follow Lee's channel? The version of Severn Suzuki's speech uploaded is of poor quality and has Portuguese subtitles as if pirated from Brazilian TV (YouTube 2008). Who would want to watch that? Lee dubbed it "The Girl Who Silenced the World for 5 Minutes." As of August 2014, it had been viewed 28,103,438 times and received 63,270 comments. These statistics suggest an effective intervention when compared to that of the Ice Bear we reviewed in Chapter 5. It even bests our benchmark of Internet virality, Tillman the skateboarding bulldog (21 million views). In so doing, it draws our attention to the power of the Internet to keep issues and performances alive in what one of the anonymous reviewers of our manuscript called a "whack-a-mole" manner. The web transcends routine news cycles and permits sleeper and slow-burn effects to play out. The Cullis-Suzuki case also confirms our more general point in this book that in-person discursive performances involving careful rhetoric and the display of *ethos* are the most potent weapon in the activist arsenal. Slick, high-definition presentation ("spectacle") counts for little. *Ethos* will find a way to rise to the top – even from Kim Seong Lee's abandoned YouTube account.

Young people can be powerful catalysts of civil repair. As Alexander (2006a, 347–58) shows in his analysis of the 1963 "children's crusade" in Birmingham, Alabama, asking children to confront the powers that be can dramatically change the moral balance of social conflict. There, civil rights leaders put children in the streets to be herded off to jail by the police, thus "throw[ing] into sharper relief the irrational, violent repression of southern officials" (353). This marked the crucial turning point in the Birmingham campaign. Media representations of terrified children being blasted with fire hoses, attacked by police dogs, and crammed into overflowing jail cells unleashed an outpouring of civil solidarity from previously disengaged northern observers, thus creating the required interpretative context for regulatory reform. As culturally coded embodiments of goodness and innocence, children are strong generators of collective shame and civil outrage.

Yet this capacity for civil repair is tempered by the great complexity of global environmental politics. For all its straightforward similarities to theatre, the climate conference is in fact an especially fraught and multilayered dramatic genre. Much of this has to do with the sheer number of actors involved. Among government negotiators, there are "insiders" and "outsiders," "players," "bigshots," "watchers," and "wannabes." There are lobbyists and industry representatives, some powerful, some ignored. There are NGOs and activists, representatives of civil society, some near and some far from the centers of power. Then there are delegations of concerned citizens, agitators, provocateurs. And, of course, there is the media. Within a tightly circumscribed space and time, all are struggling to shape the public narrative, a process that becomes increasingly reflexive with each step in the plot. There are performances, interpretations, counterperformances, and counterinterpretations, and all coming from different places and aimed in different directions – toward the treaty itself, toward other participants and observers, toward the wider public. Although there is only one sanctioned stage, there are multiple satellite stages and even stages within stages – back rooms, lobbies, restaurants, public squares. As *New York Times* journalist Andrew Revkin (2011) put it describing the Durban meeting, "some voices are quiet and hidden, like those of lobbyists for fossil fuels, wind turbines, nuclear power and other special interests always huddled in back corners in the meetings. Some are impassioned and public, like those of the students who gave voice to youth."

Youth activists represent a critical though highly contingent element of the drama: the prophetic intervention. If they are able to disrupt the conference's flow of mundane, bureaucratic time and elicit a pro-social, collective emotional response, they can help steer the conference in a romantic direction, if only temporarily. These reorienting events provide a sudden opportunity for ritualistically affirming basic moral stakes: the health and well-being of future generations, the need for preserving functional ecosystems, global economic justice. They open the door to climate *communitas*, as Turner might put it. After all, more than any other social or environmental problem, climate change raises questions of intergenerational justice (Gardiner 2011; Sagoff 2011). This is why youthful truth-tellers can play such an important role. They "speak for the future." Just as important, they speak *against* a profligate past. People in their twenties are the first generation to grow up with climate change as a social fact. For many, it is not an "issue" or "problem" but an unchanging, ominous backdrop to everyday life.

Yet youth activists also occupy a precarious position in the civil sphere. If they are perceived as merely "rabble-rousing," "acting out," or "making unreasonable demands," they can be easily excluded. The same goes for other marginalized groups, especially women and indigenous people. As performers, these groups face an exceptionally fickle audience. To activate what we might think of as the "David and Goliath effect," they must present themselves as *more* civilized, *more* reasonable, *more* democratically minded than the powers that be. When they succeed, the payoff can be tremendous. The first Earth Week, for example, was largely youth driven (Rome 2013). More than 20 million Americans participated, an astonishing number by today's standards. The event helped spark the largest of wave of environmental regulatory reform in American history. Yet even then students – just like the Woodstock crowds of a year before (Smith 2012) – had to walk the knife's edge of the civil-uncivil binary. Summing up CBS's special coverage of Earth Day, Walter Cronkite said, "The greatest disappointment today was the degree of non-participation across the country, and especially the absence of adults. And the young people that did participate were in a skylark mood which contrasted rudely with the messages of apocalypse" (Earthweek1970.org).

At Copenhagen, we showed this "skylark mood" shaded darkly into the anarchistic carnival of ill-disciplined and even violent protest. Too often, youths are seen as an anticivil force.

However, today there may be a more banal threat to youth climate activism: the cultural codes, expectations, and stereotyping activity of institutionalized civil society itself. As activists, and even the United Nations, grow increasingly desperate to sway intransigent governments, youths offer a convenient cultural tool for leveraging public outrage. Yet when it is apparent that young people are no longer autonomous, when they appear like puppets used by others, when they are read as an ersatz source of kitsch and *pathos* manipulated by powerful actors with anticivil motives, drama can quickly descend the genre scale. A related set of issues can be summed up with terms like *cooptation* and *cliché*. The *ethos* of the speaking young person comes from codings to naturalism and spontaneity. Once this is caged, it becomes fake, phony, and somehow less interesting – much as music genres such as punk are said to have declined once they became "commercial."

In this context the decision of the UN to hold a competition open to women aged under thirty to speak at the 2014 climate conference in New York was a risky play. It flirted with disenchanting the subject position of 'young woman telling truth' by making a form of cultural power that is "natural" visible as a stylized play and subsequently amenable to social reflexivity and emotional distancing (the sin of disclosure of which we too are guilty in this book). The UN sought the galvanizing effect that Malala Yousafzai – the teenaged Pakistani education activist and shooting victim – has engendered globally. Yet, even neutral commentary seemed discomforted. As the BBC (2014) noted, many entrants were looking less like true representatives of the Global South and more like cosmopolitan climate conference veterans with a well-rehearsed stump speech. Moreover, the decision to restrict the competition to young women appeared sexist, ageist, and arbitrary to some. It needed defending by the UN with reference to the "next generation" and the fact that 70 percent of the world's poor were women. The eventual choice of poet Kathy Jetnil-Kijiner from the Marshall Islands was a seemingly defensive response that shucked the risk of cooptation we have identified but at the same time did not reach for the prize. Pitched as 'the voice of civil society' (and not as 'the voice of youth'), Jetnil-Kijiner was a twenty-six-year-old mother. Her speech, and a following poem written for her baby, played upon and were spoken from the subject position of concerned motherhood. Poised and determined, she appeared neither as an innocent, nor as a puppet, but rather as a strong-willed person who would fight for what was right. The problem was that, at the end of the day, this looked like an experienced 'activist' speaking, not one of the truly disadvantaged, not a real victim. A disaster was averted, but an opportunity was lost. The speech gained no visibility in the mainstream media even if it reverberated briefly in the eco-left blogosphere.

The UN's decision not to pick a Malala clone is understandable. The failure of an initiative aimed at channeling youth-the-symbol can be humiliating. This is arguably what happened at the 2012 UN climate talks in Doha. There roughly one hundred members of the ten-week-old Arab Youth Climate Movement (AYCM) helped lead what was reported to be the first-ever public demonstration in modern Qatar. It was portrayed by numerous news outlets, especially in the Arab world, as a "watershed moment" for the oil-rich Arab state and a turning point for the Middle East. According to the *Guardian*'s John Vidal (2012), however, "this was no impromptu 'Arab spring' uprising, as much as a carefully and expensively orchestrated exercise by western-based NGOs and the Qatari government." Youth activists from sixteen countries were given free flights, put up in the five-star Crown Plaza hotel (normally five hundred dollars per night), asked to gather in the streets at 7:00 A.M., and issued official guidelines on how and what to protest. According to Vidal, the guidelines warned, "Qatar is an Islamic country so we need to be respectful of the culture: men and women should dress modestly...tops should cover the shoulders and upper arms, and skirts or shorts should fall to or below the knee. This march is for environmental issues only." The day before, Qatar had jailed for life the poet Muhammad Ibn al-Dheeb al-Ajami for penning "an Arab-spring-inspired verse that officials claim insults Qatar's emir and encourages the overthrow of the nation's ruling system" (Rebhy 2012). Later that week, two AYCM activists unfurled a banner at the conference reading, "Qatar, why host not lead." They were thrown out of the convention and, according to the magazine *Arabian Business*, summarily deported (Reuters 2012).

As was widely reported in the run-up to the meetings, Arab leaders – particularly leaders in the host country, which produces the largest per capita volume of greenhouse gases in the world – were anxious to use the Doha meetings to show the world that they are not, as many believe, climate obstructionists. Yet the end result was, from a dramatic perspective at least, less than convincing. Many had hoped that Qatar and its regional allies would pledge to reduce their emissions. Instead, the host country merely announced the foundation of a new climate research center.

Toward the end of the meetings, Britain's *Daily Telegraph* reported, anger toward Arab nations was rising among many attendees (Gray 2012). A few days after commending Qatar on Al Jazeera (2012), Ali Fakhry of the AYCM told the *Telegraph*, "We are starting to believe that hosting the meeting was green wash and PR" (Gray 2012). In the end, not a single new pledge by a major emitter to cut pollution was gained at Doha. "As thousands of delegates checked out of their air-conditioned hotel rooms in Doha to board their jets for home," reported Reuters, "some asked whether the U.N. system even made matters worse by providing cover for leaders to take no meaningful action" (Lewis and Doyle 2012). Indeed, the bitterness and disappointment that follows each UN conference seems to act as a kind of meaning-surfactant, dispersing symbols and tropes that might have coalesced into unifying patterns. Whether groups like the AYCM can learn to reverse this process remains to be seen.

Conclusion

Cancun was a rare moment of good news. The institutional odds are stacked against this eventuality. It is said that any publicity is better than none. Perhaps in the world of celebrity, this is the case. But when it comes to a matter like climate change, things are very different. What are needed are stories on the reality of the threat and, most of all, on the capacity of people to face up to the challenge. As we saw in an earlier chapter, this was the narrative that Al Gore propagated. Yet in our prior chapter, we saw that when climate change makes the news, the focus is overwhelmingly on human failure. Efforts to do something about climate change – whether science, politics, or civil society activism – become newsworthy generally when they involve deviance or expose deep social fault lines. The same rules apply for the climate conference. Cancun did well to be noticed. So have one or two speakers who seized the moment. The way these easily overlooked exemplars were narrated and propagated is something that should be closely studied. As Cicero put it, "omnium rerum principia parva sunt."

8

Local Dramas

The Places of Climate Change

For a philosopher who wrote brilliantly on the general concept of place (Casey 1997; Curry 1996), Aristotle had amazingly little to say about the fact that every story must happen "somewhere." The Greek tragedies and comedies that he studied were located in kingdoms, cities, islands, deserts, temples, and so forth. These settings might be expected to influence mood or audience interpretations due to their aesthetic properties or the background myths of place with which they are associated. Exploiting these is a common principle of contemporary staging in theatre, film, and opera. Regrettably Aristotle remains silent. His interest in the relationship of plot and character reigns supreme in the *Poetics*. As in our chapter on climate change art, we ask here whether his focused attention on these variables is analytically or pragmatically sufficient. Might not some attention to the settings of action pay some dividends? Might place have implications for the social drama of climate change with much the same force as character? We begin our chapter by mapping and justifying this theoretical possibility. We end it with some empirical investigations of the ways that settings are imbricated with plot and character in the telling of particular climate change dramas.

In their darker hours, environmentalists often say that apathetic members of affluent societies will only take climate change seriously when it starts to "hit home" – when they and their families and friends start to suffer from unmistakable, localized changes: wells running dry, neighborhoods lost to the sea, crops failing year after year. As long as she sees it as somebody else's problem, the argument goes, the average member of the middle class will find other issues to worry about. In more optimistic moments, the same environmentalists tell a different version of this story.

Individuals, they say, will band together to fight climate change when they feel they are fighting for home, when concrete, meaningful place – not abstract, global space – becomes the focus of their shared concern. The moral of this story is that "decarbonizing" and "building adaptive capacity" must begin at the local scale. They must begin *here*.

But where exactly *is* here? How local is local enough? What kind of place do people care about most: their neighborhood? their city? their state? their region? their planet? And why should observing climate change firsthand lead to political action in the first place? Despite their commonsense appeal, these stories rest on a number of problematic assumptions about the relationship between place, identity, and social change. Unpacking these assumptions fully would take a much longer book than ours. What interests us here is something few researchers have bothered to explore: the culture structures behind such talk about place. What are the narrative opportunities and challenges that come with drawing attention to the scenery rather than to the actors? How does the stage itself relate to genre and character in the social drama of climate change? Finally, does there seem to be any evidence that "making it local" is more effective as a strategy than some of the others we have reviewed in this book: identifying heroic individuals, demonstrating global unity in conferences, or trying to create powerful aesthetic forms?

In this chapter we begin by agreeing that activists need the concept of place to construct a social memory of climate change. In making this claim we look back to the influential writings of Durkheim's student Maurice Halbwachs (1992), who stressed society's need to anchor collective memory in totemic spatial representations – monuments, battlefields, plazas. Keenly aware of the social significance of place, Halbwachs used the term "topography" to describe "the symbolic mapping of places through the narration of group stories" (Till 2005, 135). As materialist scholars of so-called contentious politics have increasingly argued (Leitner, Sheppard, and Sziarto 2008; Martin and Miller 2003; Tilly 2000), this process of topographic narration can serve as a powerful fulcrum for social mobilization. For these scholars, however, place is instrumental; it is just another weapon in the representational arsenal. Yet as the more culturally attuned historian William Sewell (2001, 64) notes, "sometimes the normative meanings and uses of places *are themselves* a significant focus of social movement activity" (Sewell 2001, 64, our italics). Sewell points to the desegregation of public spaces by civil rights activists, Take Back the Night marches by feminists, and kiss-ins by gay rights activists. Such activities "sacralize" these spaces as "sites of transcendent significance," producing a kind of "spatial agency" that helps impel social change (65). These movements aim to remake place as much as they aim to remake society. And they do so, in part, by telling stories and performing dramas *about* good and bad places. In such contexts, place more so than Aristotle's beloved "character" becomes symbolically central as exemplar, totem, and myth engine. For example, during the French Revolution the Bastille was stormed. The identities of those taking over the fortress are forgotten, except to historians. What remains is the conquest of a symbol of evil and a consecrated place that continues to play a role in both the French national narrative and in ritual gatherings of protest (Smith 1999).

In the social drama of climate change, place matters in this dual sense. It is both a tool for shaping public memory and, as something to be saved from ecological catastrophe, a precious end in itself. The ways in which a shifting climate influences historical events (violent conflict over resources, for example) and people's everyday "sense of place" loom large in the script. Yet both the physical and social realities of climate change impose seemingly insurmountable burdens on those who would use these geographic themes to build a historical stage for climate change. Political revolutions provide the clearest contrast. Where is the Tahrir or Tiananmen Square of climate change? For environmentalists, there is no oppressive regime to battle at what Edward Shils (1975) called the "sacred center" of society, only an omnipresent and seemingly omnipotent carbon economy. There are no massacres or mass arrests to commemorate, only natural disasters linked in complex and often tenuous ways to greenhouse gas emissions. There are no democratic reforms to uphold, only a wholesale and almost inconceivably wrenching transformation of everyday life. In their efforts to construct a social memory of climate change – one that moves environmentalism from the margins to the center of the civil sphere – activists must transform mundane places into sacred *lieux de mémoire* (Nora 2001–2010). They must commit traumatic events to social-spatial memory. But what does it mean to remember something that might not have happened, or for that matter something that is happening everywhere, all of the time, but imperceptibly? Spatially and temporally, climate change seems to scramble all the relevant signals. At least this is the orthodoxy.

Yet if the global climate shift considered as a totality really is too vast, abstract, or complex to comprehend (we disagree), what else can be done other than to battle through the difficulties and to try to construct "local dramas"? These are not necessarily "local" in the sense that only some "local" people will care about or be impacted by them. Rather, these dramas are local in that they situate climate change primarily within a particular *chronotope*, to borrow a concept from Mikhail Bakhtin (1981). By this he means landscapes in space and time – or "space-time wholes" (Entrikin 1991, 139n23) – that structure thought by placing human agents within a defined or concrete environment for action. The meaningful landscape provides a context that makes actions meaningful within it. We stress that the turn from global dangers to local impacts is more than a simple reduction in spatial scale and a shift from the generic to the particular. Cognitive processing and emotional identification are made possible by an iconic process where there is a condensation of misty background representations onto a selection of visible symbols and narratives. In this sense, place and character are remarkably similar. A parallel exists in the way that charities foreground the experiences of specific, named individuals in some publicity campaigns rather than the suffering of thousands. Likewise the six million deaths of the Holocaust are barely comprehensible. The discovery and publication of the diaries of Anne Frank made the tragedy human. She stands at once as the generic and as the particular Holocaust victim. Scaled down in this way the barbarism becomes one that killed six million unique individuals, not the inconceivable horror of mass extermination on a continental scale. But if the chronotopic domains of climate change offer a dramatic resource for activists and a reality that we must study, just how to do so remains unclear. The work of Valerie Gunter and Steve Kroll-Smith (2007) suggests this is a promising path. In their study of environmental controversies they show how place histories, local social capital and knowledge, and situated perceptions of fairness offer mobilization potential for the specifically affected communities. Yet in contrast to the familiar geographically bounded disputes involving local communities and impacts that they study (such as toxic waste dumping, oil spills, industrial development, natural disasters, and ecosystem management), climate change seems to offer unique challenges. To understand just why, we must first lay some further theoretical groundwork.

Place, Drama, and Social Memory

Place, in its most basic geographic sense, is space made socially meaningful (Tuan 1977, 1996). But it is other things as well. It is a tool for pursuing moral, social, and political projects (Agnew 1987; Harvey 2000, 2009; Sack 1997); a process through which identities and institutions are formed (Pred 1984); and an idea with a complex cultural history that conditions its operation *as* both tool and process (Curry 1998, 2002; Entrikin 1991, 1999, 2002). Through symbolic and narrative process, the raw stuff of nature is brought into the cultural world as the carrier of value, myth, affect, and aesthetics. Particularity is born, and along with this human investment in geography becomes possible. These meanings coded into place come to provide imperatives that shape human actions – for example, to conserve or change, to visit or avoid. Precisely because places are coded in such meaningful ways, they might be expected to carry intensified anxieties over the climate change process. By the same token, they might be expected to carry intensified hopes. This is true not only of specific places but of the concept of place itself, which has become a symbolic bulwark not only against the perceived alienation and cultural homogeneity of modern life (Entrikin 1991, 60–83) but also against the imaginary of the paralyzing complexity of global environmental change. In a world where a new market for cheap fat to use in American candy bars and cosmetics (palm oil) can help turn the third largest island in the world (Borneo) from a net carbon sink into a net carbon source in a matter of years (Folke et al. 2011), is it any wonder that farmers' markets make people feel a bit more hopeful about their futures? Even the dimmest awareness of globalization and its environmental consequences can produce intense forms of what the geographer Yi-Fu Tuan (1974) called *topophilia*. For activists, the task is to translate these place-attachments into collective, *thymotic* action. It is to construct a moral geography – that is, to make place morally meaningful in the drama of climate change. Places, much like people, must become exemplary embodiments of good and evil.

Anyone who is familiar with the writings of Bill McKibben, America's most prominent climate activist, knows how strong the moral pull of place can be. McKibben, adapting to the theme of climate change a long tradition in American environmental writing, has built his career around the promise of place-based responses to ecological crisis, from local food systems (McKibben 2008) to decentralized government (McKibben 2010). He and other ecocommunitarians are far from alone in seeing "the local" as our last, best hope. An entire genre of social scientific research has grown up around testing this proposition, not to mention a substantial amount of environmental policy.[1] Although some of these researchers

---

[1] As mainstream climate change research takes tentative steps toward qualitative cultural analysis, the concept of place has naturally come to the fore (e.g., Agyeman et al 2009;

have relatively straightforward empirical interests in the localized effects of global change – how climate disruption effects mental and physical health, for example (Cunsolo Willox et al. 2012; Hess et al. 2008) – this focus on the "local" often has a strongly normative flavor. For many scholars and activists alike, place matters not simply because it represents the real but also because it represents the *good*. The clichéd exhortation to "think globally, act locally" has become something of a buried mantra in these academic circles (Devine-Wright 2013). The notion that we must "localize the problem" to "make people act," and that "local action" is somehow morally superior to "global action," and worse, patronizing telescopic philanthropy has become a kind of academic common sense.

Yet missing from most of this research is much sense of the "local" as a complex cultural construction in its own right, one with ambiguous and unpredictable links to democratic politics (Harvey 1996, 2000). Following a long and seemingly indestructible social scientific tradition (Agnew 1989), these researchers treat place as the organic home of "community," hence the natural terrain for social mobilization. This approach fits particularly well with the pragmatic strain of cultural theory, in which place fits neatly alongside nation, gender, and class in the cultural tool kit of a given social group. Unlike these rather slippery and frequently controversial cultural tools, however, place seems to possess a benign, uncontested, obvious, and seemingly uncomplicated materiality, something activists and researchers can grasp in their attempts to make climate change salient and real – firm ground to stand on, literally and metaphorically. It thus seems to offer a route toward a romantic resolution to the crisis of environmental apathy (e.g., Norgaard 2011, 207–209).

It is often difficult to disentangle this faith in "local solutions" from a more deeply rooted fascination with the geographic diversity of human-environment relations. Mike Hulme (2008, 2009, 2010), for example, has argued repeatedly for engaging with "the deeper and more intimate meanings of climate" that arise through our phenomenological embeddedness in place (Hulme 2008, 355). For this camp, cultural analysis

Devine-Wright 2013; Fresque-Baxter and Armitage 2012; Scannell and Gifford 2011; Smith et al. 2012). Environmental economist Neil Adger, lead author for the chapter on human security in the Fifth IPCC Assessment Report, has been one of the most prominent voices calling for closer attention to place as well as for more serious consideration of meaning and identity in climate change research (Adger et al. 2011, 2013). For Adger, focusing on local places corrects the global gaze of mainstream climate science, which "render[s] invisible human-scale patterns and loss" (Adger et al. 2011, 20).

serves to explain the "sense of place" that affects a local community's capacity to adapt to specific climatic changes or to explore the microscale linkages between place-based identities and vernacular climate knowledge (e.g., Geoghegan and Leyson 2012). For Hulme (2008, 9), the point is "repairing our idea of what climate means in different places and to different peoples and at different times." Others have asked more skeptically whether such attachments to place might exist at multiple scales and whether privileging the local might not foreclose possibilities for a more cosmopolitan climate politics (Devine-Wright 2013; Heise 2008; Jasanoff 2010a, 2011). Some of the best journalistic and ethnographic writing on climate change shows that the experience of place shapes people's knowledge about climate change in very complicated and even contradictory ways, even in places like the Arctic and the American Southwest, where the effects of climate change are starkest (DeBuys 2011; Ross 2011; Wohlforth 2005). As the ecocritic Rob Nixon (2011, 242) wisely warns, although emotional attachments to place can be "an invaluable resource for environmental mobilization.... such attachments do not possess any inherent politics: they can induce a conservative, bigoted environmental ethic or a progressive, inclusive one."

What many bioregionalists, urbanists, and other place-boosters tend to miss is that our experience of place is always symbolically mediated by systematically structured, widely circulating cultural forms and not just proximate, embodied personal experience in everyday life. Place is always narrativized. Moreover, such place myths and meanings are relevant for mobilizing not just local communities (see Gunter and Kroll-Smith 2007) but also distant spectators. They might have some emotional or cognitive investment in far-away places that may be known to them only through shared collective representations. Although it is certainly possible to notice that winters have gotten feebler and feebler in one's neighborhood, people might also be alerted to climate change through stories about other places. In social drama this is how things usually happen – somewhere distant but also known to us through circulating cultural mediations becomes the center of symbolic activity, not our own backyard. A warm winter elsewhere can become meaningful as a story *about* climate change when filtered through a set of broader cultural narratives about the meaning of winter as these relate to narratives about this or that place – say, the imagery of Robert Frost's New England or Jack London's Alaska. We need not be dependent on our family and community tellings about "the way it used to be" right here.

William Cronon (1992), in an influential essay on environmental historiography, gives us some important clues about how those narratives work. Using the example of the Dust Bowl, Cronon distinguishes between two types of environmental narrative: the progressive and declensionist/ tragic. Progressive narratives depict the Dust Bowl as a natural disaster overcome by courageous settlers, a character-building episode in the civilizing saga of the Plains. Declensionist narratives depict the Dust Bowl as nature's revenge on a hubristic and shortsighted capitalist society. In both, the place itself mirrors society's ascent and decline. Here Cronon (1354) invokes Kenneth Burke's notion of the "scene-act ratio," according to which "the succession of scenes both *realistically reflects* the course of the action and *symbolizes* it" (Burke 1945, 3). Depictions of place drive the moral trajectory of both narratives. Were the Plains a hostile, desolate place in need of human improvement, or were they a harmonious ecosystem whose fragile balance was destroyed by human greed?[2] Equally important here (though missed by Cronon) is Burke's concept of the "scene-agent ratio," where the "synecdochic relation is between person and place" and which correlates "the quality of the country and the quality of its inhabitants" (Burke 1945, 7–8). In environmental storytelling, place, event, and *ethos* are thus intimately connected. Transformative events like the Dust Bowl make places into historical actors whose characters and fortunes are thoroughly entangled with those of the human actors who shape them. At these moments, geography and history become practically indistinguishable.

This fusion of place and event in public memory is a performative achievement. For activists, the goal is to imbue place with a catalytic "event-ness" (Mast 2006), to fuse places and events into historical turning points and thus redraw the background map of collective representations that guide social action. In so doing, they create an irresistible, visceral sense not only that *this* event could *only* have happened here but that *this* event happened *because* it happened here. As a result, place is experienced

---

[2] Cronon explains further: "If the tale is of progress, then the closing landscape is a garden; if the tale is of crisis and decline, the closing landscape (whether located in the past or the future) is a wasteland. As an obvious but very important consequence of this narrative requirement, opening landscapes must be different from closing ones to make the plot work. A trackless waste must become a grassland civilization. Or: a fragile ecosystem must become a Dust Bowl. The difference between beginning and end gives us our chance to extract a moral from the rhetorical landscape. Our narratives take changes in the land and situate them in stories whose endings become the lessons we wish to draw from those changes" (1370).

as both arena and agent, as both material context and efficient cause. By staging dramatic clashes between sacred and profane forces, pure and impure actors, movements give historical agency to place itself. Yet unlike places of, say, national or ethnic trauma (Gettysburg, Ground Zero, Auschwitz) or, for that matter, places of national or ethnic triumph, *environmental* places of memory are extraordinarily difficult to construct. An industrial villain is usually needed to propel an antipastoral narrative of "Eden betrayed" (Buell 1998, 647) – Union Carbide at Bhopal, Hooker Chemical at Love Canal, Exxon in Prince William Sound. Such morally and physically polluted places play the leading role in most environmental dramas. Yet as Ted Nordhaus and Michael Shellenberger (2004) famously pointed out, climate change does not fit the "pollution paradigm." Who are the villains? Who are the victims? What is the crime? None of this is clear (Jamieson 2011). Attempts to dramatize place through melodrama are thus easily derailed.

As Entrikin notes, natural disasters – no matter how calamitous – rarely rise to the level of cultural trauma.[3] Perhaps four million people were killed by the 1931 China Floods, but even in China the historical significance of this event pales in comparison to less devastating, human-caused calamities. Robert Merton noted long ago that social disorganization caused by the actions of morally flawed individuals is far more likely to attract attention and lead to radical policy intervention that that arising from poor systemic coordination. Times are changing, and in the wake of Hurricane Katrina, it is likely that nature will be absolved of some responsibility in the future. Of course, in twenty years, we may all classify such floods as human-caused, "unnatural" disasters. But this etiology is far from universally accepted today. As more and more people accept that greenhouse gas emissions are "loading the climate dice," as James Hansen likes to say, the boundary between natural and unnatural disasters grows more and more fraught. Yet far from putting the question

---

[3] Echoing Douglas and Wildavsky (1983), Entrikin (2007, 164) draws attention to the "collective moral cartography of good and bad places" that structures modern responses to natural disasters, even when those disasters are "officially" explained in purely scientific terms. Narrating natural disasters not only makes them comprehensible (Erikson 1994); it also "map[s] relations of moral distance between the victims and other social groups" (Entrikin 2007, 164), thus determining the extent of restorative solidarity in both time and space. Put another way, the likelihood of widespread, sustained support for disaster-stricken places depends heavily on how that disaster is publicly narrated. And how that disaster is publicly narrated in turn depends heavily on how that place and its inhabitants are imagined. Levels of concern are never determined simply by spatial or social proximity, but by complex, historically inflected moral geographies.

of causality to rest, science *intensifies* conflict by raising questions of blame. Indeed, as we shall see with Superstorm Sandy, even when scientists are fairly certain that weather extremes are linked to climate change, it is extremely risky for activists and scientific communicators to pin those extremes to human activity, and not only because skeptics are so good at using the rhetoric of scientific uncertainty (they are). It is risky to say that climate change caused a hurricane or a devastating flood or a crippling drought because it sounds like you are blaming victims for their own misfortune – or, perhaps even worse, that you are blaming ordinary people for victimizing distant strangers, simply by participating in the fossil fuel economy. At the visceral register of climate politics, science and theology *sound* the same. Nature becomes a cruel "avenging angel" (Cronon 1996) as it executes a divine judgment for our ecological sins and then inflicts punishment on others selected with a seemingly random, malevolent caprice, as if from the casting of lots. Take Darfur.

Tragic Places: Themes of Descent

Broadly speaking, stories about climate change and place select from two realms of landscape possibility. One looks at distant others – a village in the Arctic, a camp in the Sahara, a South Pacific atoll. A second genre explores impacts for members of affluent populations in more temperate climes. As we will see, each kind has its own problems. Nevertheless, there are remarkable structural continuities in the kinds of narratives that must be presented. Consistent with the Aristotelian arguments we have been proposing throughout this book, *the chronotope – and by this we mean geographically bounded landscapes and places with their constituent people, ways of life, and ecosystems – must itself be situated within a tragic narrative as a "character."* It is subject to undeserved punishment at the hands of fate; it is the victim of cruel injustice; it must make tough choices, experience turning points, reversals of fortune, or learning and growth. Using themes of descent, climate change is generally depicted as the causal agent propelling the hapless chronotope from order to disorder, and the people within it from solidarity to failed sociability. Hence fragility, pollution, and risk will start to invade or occupy what was previously a domain of safety, purity, and predictability. Only when the agents embedded within the chronotope pull together – when the chronotope "learns" (*anagnorisis*) through some kind of recognition (*peripeteia*) – can a reversal of fortune take place and positive societal outcomes emerge. Because we live in a mass-mediated world, witnessing this process at a distance and learning through the observation of exemplary settings must also be considered as principal components of the spatial dramas of climate change.

The oft-quoted example of Darfur stands as a representative exhibit here for a wider storytelling pattern (e.g., Parenti 2012). Darfur is frequently said to be the first war "caused" by climate change. It is more cautiously used to leverage claims that widespread conflict will result from emerging resource tensions generated by climate change, especially in sub-Saharan Africa. Although the genocide in Darfur was initially attributed to primordial ethnic tensions, an increasingly popular alternative reading introduced climate change as the prime mover. The writings of Stephan Faris (2007, 2009) on the topic have been quoted by United Nations secretary general Ban Ki Moon (2007) and widely used as a prompt in op-eds on environmental issues. What is particularly interesting – if hardly surprising by now to readers of this book – is the structure of the storytelling. Writing in _Scientific American_, Faris (2008) conjures a "before and after" exemplary narrative. He begins:

Until the rains failed in Darfur, the region's pastoralists lived amicably with the settled farmers. The nomadic herders grazed their camels on the rocky hillsides between fertile plots and fed their animals on the leavings from the harvest.

Here there is a picture of symbiosis and stability, the oft-noted starting point of most environmental tragedies (Buell 1998; Cronon 1996; Merchant 2004). There is social and environmental harmony and even some resonance with biblical images of the desert-dwelling Israelites. It is a prelapsarian Eden that we might want to care about rather than a dusty, sunbaked hellhole we would rather ignore. Enter the themes of descent:

But with the land crippled by a decades-long drought, the region was no longer able to support both. Farmers began to fence off their fields and clashes broke out between sedentary and nomadic tribes... the camel-herding Arabs – those most envious of the farmers' land – became Khartoum's staunchest stalwarts.... The roots of the drying in Darfur lay in changes to the global climate.

As Faris (2007) explained in the _Atlantic Monthly_, next followed "ethnic cleansing targeting Darfur's blacks, the armed militia men raped women, burned houses, and tortured and killed men of fighting age. Through whole swaths of the region, they left only smoke curling into the sky."

Now we have a classic movement from unity to disunity and from harmony or balance to chaos and then evil. Net sociability decreases (farmers now fence their fields) and negative emotions start to drive human action (the camel herders have "envy"). Those who had been living a simple, traditional life make an alliance with a corrupt and fractious regime that turns a blind eye to atrocity. A land that had been a paradise of innocents becomes a paradise lost. Faris discussed nine other places in his *Scientific American* article. Online feedback suggests his effort to communicate climate change through local dramas failed. Discussion consisted of the inevitable flame war over the reality of climate change, more specifically whether we were simply experiencing one of the many warmings that the earth has had during human history. There was no discussion of the case studies. This might reflect lack of concern or information about distant places – always a problem with particularizing strategies. But this does not square with the tremendous interest in Darfur in America, especially among evangelical Christians (Eichler-Levine and Hicks 2007). Distance matters, but it can be overcome by care and curiosity.

Darfur remains the most frequently debated example of violent conflict generated by climate change. Broadly speaking, a reduction of rain since the 1980s has stressed arable land. The rain reduction is attributed to changes in the monsoon, these linked in turn to ocean surface temperatures generated by greenhouse gases. Few analysts draw direct causal arrows from climate change to conflict; however, just as few question that environmental degradation played a significant role. It is more a matter of emphasis (Mazo 2010, 85). According to the UN Environmental Programme's (2007, 8) postconflict environmental assessment:

there is a very strong link between land degradation, desertification and conflict in Darfur. Northern Darfur – where exponential population growth and related environmental stress have created the conditions for conflicts to be triggered and sustained by political, tribal or ethnic differences – can be considered a tragic example of the social breakdown that can result from ecological collapse.

Conversely, Darfur expert Alex de Waal (2007) warns against a "simplistic" linking of climate change to the Darfur crisis. "Climate change causes livelihood change," de Waal writes, "which in turn causes disputes. Social institutions can handle these conflicts and settle them in a nonviolent manner – it is mismanagement and militarization that cause war and massacre." More recent research by a team of Norwegian researchers (Benjaminsen et al. 2012) found little evidence that climate variability has driven conflict in the Sahel more generally.[4] Journalist Rob Crilly (2007),

---

[4] For detailed discussions of Darfur and related conflicts, see a recent special issue of the *Journal of Peace Research* (2012) on climate change and armed conflict.

author of a book on Darfur, goes so far as to accuse the UN of using climate change as an excuse for inaction. "It lets the UN off the hook for its failures in Darfur," Crilly writes, "... and pins the blame on the developed world and its carbon emissions. So with the guilt receptors nicely triggered, aid agencies and the UN can embark on a fresh round of fundraising in the West."

There is little new about the ideological contours of this debate. It revolves around a set of very old questions about nature's control over human history (Glacken 1967), not to mention the profound influence of Malthusian thinking on population growth and resource scarcity. Those who blame Darfur on climate change side with a long line of environmental determinists, represented today by authors such as Jared Diamond and Robert D. Kaplan. Those who dismiss such claims side with an equally long tradition of human exceptionalism. What *is* new about this debate, however, is the moral geography of blame. Faris (2007) puts it this way:

Among the implications arising from the ecological origin of the Darfur crisis, the most significant may be moral. If the region's collapse was in some part caused by the emissions from our factories, power plants, and automobiles, we bear some responsibility for the dying.

There is no question that industrialized nations are responsible for the vast majority of greenhouse gas emissions and little doubt that poor nations will suffer the most as a result. As the philosopher Dale Jamieson (2011, 45) puts it, "the rich countries of the North do most of the emitting, but the poor countries of the South do most of the dying." Yet drawing direct causal arrows from American SUVs to ethnic cleansing in Sudan stretches ordinary conceptions of moral responsibility to the breaking point. Perhaps more importantly, it sounds like a kind of reverse theodicy: *Darfur suffers because of our sins.* Though the physical linkages may be real, the narrative form flirts with hellfire and damnation. Pat Robertson lurks in the wings.

The case of Darfur used genocide in a remote location as the index of tragic impacts within a particular chronotope. We note that milder claims can be presented in contexts that might be more familiar to affluent Western citizens. For example, the Union of Concerned Scientists (Kling et al. 2003) makes an argument pivoting around the concept of "loss" in a report discussing changes to the Great Lakes region. We know from social psychology experiments on pricing that most people overvalue what they have. Somewhat irrationally, they also fear potential loss more than they hope for an equivalent potential gain. Probably informed by this research, the brief item by the Union of Concerned Scientists repeats the words "loss" and "losing" nine times – a technique that can be now found in books introducing the techniques of salesmanship ("You don't want to lose out on this deal"). Drawing, as we do, on the work of Yi-Fu Tuan, the report suggests that a warming climate will erode a sense of place that has been embodied in cultural activities and everyday life alike within the chronotope:

> Our songs, our art, our literature include winter as a strong element. We like to ice fish; we hunt deer with snow on the ground; we like cross-country skiing during the winter holiday, or to skate and have sleigh rides; we have fun traveling by snowmobile; and we even have dog sledding. For those providing services in support of these activities, the loss of winter (as we know it) has direct economic consequences.

The "social" is here too, albeit in an implicit and nostalgic ice-picket-fences way. Potentially solitary and contemplative activities are framed as collective ones that are part of a shared culture that binds people through locality. By implication, the loss of these winter activities and winter-themed cultural products will involve the attrition of community too. The problem with such little dramas about the "loss" of cherished local attributes is that with a little imagination, people can also see things that they would "gain" from climate change. "Loss" might have more currency than "gain" in the wiring of the human brain, but net receipts can still be somewhat equalized by attending to the other side of the equation.

This is especially the case for colder climates such as in the Great Lakes region. For much of northern Europe, to take another, the shift from a temperate to a Mediterranean climate would offer guaranteed summers and snow-free winters. This would translate into improved lifestyle as most residents would currently define this. There could also be economic benefits. For example, in 2005, the U.K. Climate Impacts Programme (UKCIP) reported on likely climate change outcomes for agriculture. Of course, more water would need to be stored in future to cover summer drought. Yet the overall picture was reported as quite attractive. According to the Farmer's Guardian (2005), there would be a longer growing season. Crops like grapes, sunflowers, and new potatoes would become possible. The future offered hope of a competitive advantage over Spanish farmers. The report was couched in economic terms, but the sense of England becoming more like Spain or the South of France can also be seen in lifestyle magazines looking at gardening, fishing, and home decor.

Challenging this vision of improving quality of life requires rescripting the drama and locating nonobvious dangers that are cunningly masked by immediate gains. Writing in the *Guardian*, the noted and ubiquitous British environmentalist politician George Monbiot (2009) concedes that a Mediterranean climate would be a wonderful thing for the United Kingdom's chilly seaside resorts. However, he would be unable to rejoice. This would actually be a sign that civilization was on the verge of collapse. As the United Kingdom becomes Mediterranean, other parts of the world would become overheated dust bowls and the global food supply would collapse. He goes on to conjure the apocalyptic scenario we have seen elsewhere in this book:

dozens of other nations will hit the wall; unable to feed their people, without sufficient water supplies, poleaxed by devastating drought just as the global population reaches its peak. The consequences are too horrible to contemplate. They have belonged, until now, to the realm of science fiction. Now they belong to the realm of science.

Monbiot suggests it would be immoral for the United Kingdom to have the romantic upside while others suffer in an apocalyptic Armageddon. What looks like a gain is in fact a net loss for the planet considered as a whole. Monbiot's cosmopolitan geouniversalism is just one possible narrative move here. Another more selfish one is to find local downsides lurking behind that upgrade to a Mediterranean climate. A provider of renewable energy in Cornwall points to freak weather events that would push up house insurance costs and lead to the loss (that word again) of "much loved Cornish plants like daffodils, crocuses and snowdrops," the erosion of beaches, and the emergence of new pests like termites and malarial mosquitoes (Cornwall Switch 2005). Here, as in the case of the Great Lakes region, we see the strategy of talking about beloved things that are gone, but this time accompanied by a discourse of nasty alien threats and invaders. Cornwall Switch did not mention that heating bills would likely go down in a warmer climate or that new gardening opportunities would present themselves. However the BBC's horticultural webpages challenge any complacency on the latter front:

Longer summer and warmer weather might sound like a dream come true, but the effects of climate change are not all good and could have far reaching consequences for our gardens.

It goes on to predict tough times for traditional English features such as lawns, yew hedges and cottage gardens. New Mediterranean species might sound like attractive replacements, but they would be vulnerable to winter "waterlogging." There would also be a plague of pests such as "lily beetle, rosemary beetle, berberis sawfly, red spider mite and new vine weevil species" (BBC 2013).

Let's be clear: such representations of minor irritations for English gardeners and Great Lakes ice fishermen do little to persuade that radical actions are needed. There are bad consequences, but we can live with them, as they impact only on lifestyle choices and local traditions. New opportunities will replace them. What of the alternative? We have already seen that distant places face challenges. Darfur was too far away and the causal line too muddled to be a convincing call to action. Even places like Arctic Alaska where global climate change appears to be driving rapid socioecological change seem immune to widespread, thymotic sympathy from afar. One option that might work is to tie climate change action more clearly to the opportunity for magnifying and improving existing locality rather than the arrival of external threats and the loss of tradition. For example, the local carbon budget of the English Lake District might be associated with place- and lifestyle-enhancing shifts toward locally sourced Cumbrian beer and food, improved rail connections, and land management. It can also be associated with local autonomy and pride as decisions about policy are devolved to stakeholders (see Willis 2013). Yet such upside outcomes probably seem too trivial to engender radical changes in sensibility. Hence activists have long suggested that a major disaster in a place of undisputed global economic and symbolic centrality might offer the best opportunity to leverage the reality of climate change against a geographic fulcrum. There need to be witnessable negative impacts right at the sacred centers of the developed world. In 2012, Superstorm Sandy was to finally provide this long-awaited opportunity. Would it be enough?

Pivots of History? The Traumatic Turning Point

In their tragic guise, hurricane stories – like many climate change stories about place – draw on dystopian narratives. They point to the futility of human action in the face of fate; of mismanagement and of the evils of human nature that are revealed as the social order breaks down. This was the tale of Hurricane Katrina. Yet at the same time, disasters invoke romantic and even utopian themes of renewal and civil solidarity: ordinary people rolling up their shirt-sleeves and getting down to the business of sustainable place-making (e.g., Solnit 2009). In the aftermath of

Superstorm (formerly Hurricane) Sandy, which struck the New York–New Jersey metropolitan area in October 2012, we can see these declensionist and progressive narratives vying for dominance in the public sphere. What made Sandy especially interesting was the overt tension between these two genres in the performative interventions of "carrier groups": activists, commentators, politicians. Within minutes of the storm's landfall, a battle ensued to direct the mise-en-scène of this terrifying "Frankenstorm," a battle that continued in the weeks and months after it transfixed the country with images of flattened neighborhoods and flooded subway stations. What kind of chronotope would Sandy create? What kind of emotions would it inspire? Would it change the way Americans think about climate change? If so, how? From the start, these questions were part of the story itself, making Sandy one of the first fully reflexive episodes in the social drama of climate change (e.g., Battistoni 2012; Hertsgaard 2012). With Sandy, Americans watched themselves watching themselves reacting to the disaster, openly asking if this is what it would take to make them come to grips with the problem. Not surprisingly, they did so through the discourse of civil society. What would constitute a civil response to this tragedy? Who would embody that response?

As noted earlier, there are important structural relationships between place, event, and *ethos* in most environmental dramas, captured in part by Burke's interrelated concepts of the scene-act and scene-agent ratios. Our understanding of these relationships is deepened when we bring in Max Weber's theory of charisma. As Smith (2000, 102) notes, "a defining strand of Weber's original formulation is that charisma relates to the sacred qualities of an individual and the sense of mission and duty that defines the relationship between the individual leader and his or her followers." These leaders are framed within a salvation narrative built around strong binary oppositions between good and evil. Charisma is salvific and involves a project. It emerges in opposition to profane, polluting forces that threaten to overwhelm society (Smith 2000). Climate change would thus seem to offer the perfect milieu for the cultivation of charisma; indeed, "the eco-apocalypse seems made for charismatic persons in Weber's sense," writes the German environmental historian (and Weber biographer) Joachim Radkau (2012, 500). Yet as we have seen repeatedly in our case studies, this has not happened. Why not? The aftermath of Sandy provides important clues, especially when we consider attempts by political leaders to narrate the event and the form their narrations took.

Even as the death toll mounted on October 30 and the full extent of the storm's devastation began to enter public consciousness, environmental activists sought to frame the event not only as a man-made disaster but as an act of aggression. An e-mail sent out by 350.org (2012), penned by McKibben, struck an extremely combative tone, declaring that Sandy's "real name" should be "Hurricane Chevron" or "Hurricane Exxon." "Right now, the most important thing we can do is come together as a community and support the relief efforts that are already underway," McKibben wrote:

But we're not going to simply mourn our losses. The images coming out of the Atlantic seaboard, and from the refugee camps in Haiti, made us not just sad but angry.... These fossil fuel corporations are driving the climate crisis and spending millions to block solutions. Instead of buying climate silence, the fossil fuel industry should be funding climate relief.

McKibben (2012b) repeated these themes in an op-ed for the *New York Daily News* that same day, this time opening with the more politic, "As gutsy New Yorkers begin the task of drying out the city..." The attack on "Big Oil" was nothing new. It has been part of a deliberate strategy by climate activists to infuse the problem with anticorporate populism (e.g., Klein 2011). But the conceit of naming storms after corporations seemed contrived: it did not seem to break out of the so-called echo chamber of the environmentalist blogosphere. What did seem to break out was an increasing openness to nonscientific framings of the crisis, to explicitly moralistic pictures of evil forces, charismatic leaders, and victimized citizens. In the climate change blogosphere, a parallel debate about causation emerged between skeptics and true believers, alongside a more complex debate about risk perception and public opinion. *Grist*'s arch–climate hawk David Roberts battled with the *New York Times*'s arch-realist Andrew Revkin over the meaning of Sandy. Revkin (2012), standing for "sound science," warned against pointing the finger at climate change. Roberts (2012), sounding as if he had experienced a sudden conversion to Mary Douglas–style Cultural Theory (see Chapter 2), wrote:

Most of the public doesn't have a clue about climate science and never will, any more than they understand health science or biological evolution.... What the public wants and needs is a sense of what climate change *means*, how it fits into their worldview, what values and feelings to associate with it.... A storm like Sandy provides an opportunity for those who understand climate change to help construct that context. It provides a set of experiences – a set of images, sounds, smells, feelings, experiences – that can inscribe climate change with the cultural resonance it lacks. That's what persuades and motivates people: not the clinical language of science, but experiences and emotions and associations.

On his blog, Al Gore (2012) did his best to frame Sandy as just such an emotional turning point, or what we would call a *chronotopic anagnorisis*. Recalling the unprecedented flooding in his hometown, Nashville, two years earlier, he wrote that "Hurricane Sandy may prove to be a similar event: a time when the climate crisis – which is often sequestered to the far reaches of our everyday awareness became a reality." Shifting from the folksy to the prophetic mode we identified in Chapter 4, he continued, "Hurricane Sandy is a disturbing sign of things to come. We must heed this warning and act quickly to solve the climate crisis. Dirty energy makes dirty weather." Like McKibben, Gore sought to name an enemy, a source of both symbolic and physical pollution: "dirty energy." Unlike McKibben, however, he defined that enemy in a diffuse, impersonal way, drawing more on the language of disease and defilement than of greed and exploitation. Speaking at a campaign rally for Barack Obama, Bill Clinton was more pointed when he reminded the audience that Mitt Romney, in a presidential debate, had "ridiculed the president for his efforts to fight global warming in economically beneficial ways."

None of these leaders could speak "for New York," however. That was for Mayor Michael Bloomberg and Governor Andrew Cuomo. With consummate rhetorical skill, Cuomo in particular seized on Sandy to frame climate change in a new and potentially transformative way. At a press conference on October 29, the day of the storm, Cuomo told the cameras:

I'm hopeful that not only will we rebuild this city and metropolitan area but use this as an opportunity to build it back smarter. There have been a series of extreme weather events. That is not a political statement; that is a factual statement. Anyone who says there is not a change in weather patterns is denying reality. (Vielkind 2012a)

The next day, Cuomo was interviewed by ABC's Diane Sawyer at the site of the World Trade Center memorial, spectacular images of which were appearing everywhere showing it being deluged by storm surge. Sawyer asked Cuomo about Al Gore's statement and whether Sandy represented "the future of New York." Gravely, Cuomo said Gore was right, adding, "It's undeniable but that we have a higher frequency of these extreme weather situations, and we're going to have to deal with it." Then came the critical symbolic move toward the sacred place of collective memory: Cuomo compared Sandy to September 11, calling the memorial a twofold "monument to New York resilience."

Over the coming days and weeks, this narrative of pragmatic solidarity would be tested by reports of social disintegration, government neglect, and near-riots at gas stations (reports that triggered long-standing fears about postdisaster urban chaos, often revolving around race; Nye 2010). But Cuomo had tapped a rich symbolic vein at what seemed to be a liminal moment. In the coming days, President Obama would tour the wreckage with the Republican governor of New Jersey, Chris Christie, and speculation was rampant that this show of bipartisan cooperation would swing the election in Obama's favor. Christie praised Obama effusively for his response to the disaster, infuriating his own political party. Bloomberg, a moderate republican, endorsed Obama, citing the president's willingness to confront climate change as the deciding factor. These politicians may have also been emboldened by the New York media, which was unequivocal about blaming climate change. The magazine *Bloomberg Business Week* (2012) ran a cover with a photograph of a lone figure wading down a flooded street in Lower Manhattan under a headline in giant black letters against a red background: "It's Global Warming, Stupid." Polls showed that two-thirds of New Yorkers made the same connection (Siena Research Institute 2012). At a press conference on October 31, Cuomo used the term "climate change" for the first time and introduced a new sound bite, one that would become the core of his framing of Sandy: "the new normal." "It's a longer conversation," Cuomo said, "but I think part of learning from this is the recognition that climate change is a reality, extreme weather is a reality, it is a reality that we are vulnerable.... There's only so long you can say, 'this is once in a lifetime and it's not going to happen again'" (Vielkind 2012b).

In a short amount of time, Cuomo became the primary carrier of an increasingly dominant script, one built around three primary claims. First, New Yorkers are tough-minded realists who know a problem when they see it. Those who deny the existence of climate change are simply "playing politics," or worse. Second, Sandy, like 9/11, was a body blow to the city, but like a champion prizefighter, the city will rise up stronger than before. Third, there are practical solutions to the problem: build better infrastructure, plan smarter, reduce emissions. But running beneath these themes was a constant undercurrent of meta-commentary – *will this be enough to make us take climate change seriously?* When asked, for example, by the left-wing commentator Rachel Maddow why

Sandy seemed to be a "wake-up call" for many Americans, Cuomo said:

I think the reason you felt the receptivity on the [part of the] audience is sometimes you have a thought or a feeling that's percolating, but not actualized. And I think people have been sensing there is something going on with the weather and forget the politics of it – they just know from their own life experience something is going on. I said right in the midst of [the storm]: This is climate change. And it's not a political concept; it's a practical concept. It's not debatable and not ideological or philosophical; it is reality-based. Changing weather patterns create real, practical issues for the world. Let's build an awareness, a consensus, and let's educate and mobilize the body politic around it. When do politicians succeed in bringing change? When the people are ready. (Maddow 2013)

Through a series of carefully staged performances, Cuomo aligned his audience ("the people") with the sacred-civil side of a series of core symbolic binaries: rational/irrational, practical/political, realistic/foolish. To this he added believer/skeptic. He did not need to name Exxon or Mitt Romney or anyone else. The Uncivil Other was simply out there in America, "playing politics" and threatening our future.

Cuomo derived ethical authority not just by uniting his audience against reality deniers but also by aligning them with images of the civil center. Although a self-identified liberal democrat, Cuomo was careful to distance himself from environmental "extremists" as well as "deniers." In a November 15 editorial in the *New York Daily News* – titled "We Will Lead on Climate Change" and accompanied by the now de rigueur apocalyptic photograph of Breezy Point, Queens, a neighborhood anni-hilated by fires during the storm – Cuomo condensed this script into an easily transposable formula:

Extreme weather is the new normal. In the past two years, we have had two storms, each with the odds of a 100-year occurrence. Debating why does not lead to solutions – it leads to gridlock. The denial and deliberation from extremists on both sides about the causes of climate change are distracting us from addressing its inarguable effects. Recent events demand that we get serious once and for all.
    We need to act, not simply react (Cuomo 2012).

A list of practical solutions follows, laced with key signifiers of pro-social progress: "rebuild," "reduce energy consumption" (not by decarbonizing but by "changing building codes"), "relocate infrastructure," "diversify transit options," help "first responders," "strengthen communications systems." The cumulative message of these proposals is clear: we can take control of this terrifying situation by rolling up our sleeves and working together.

Finally, Cuomo drew on a deep well of place-specific myths to inspire hope. We can do this, he said, because of *who* we are and *where* we live. In his editorial, Cuomo concludes:

New York has a natural advantage in this seemingly daunting task. We begin with an extraordinary enterprising spirit, unparalleled resiliency and a long history of engineering the impossible.

We are the state that built the Erie Canal, opening up commerce to the West. We built a subway system so extensive that its 800 miles of track could run from New York all the way to Chicago.

Time and again, we pushed boundaries and broke records. We have been tested before, and we have always risen to the challenge. We will not allow the national paralysis over climate change to stop us from pursuing the necessary path for the future.

As the national sacralization of firemen and other first responders after September 11 showed, it is not just New Yorkers who respond to these mythic tropes of innovation and resilience. But for New Yorkers most of all, their emotional pull is powerful. Aristotle believed that "without membership in a *polis*, one cannot have a properly developed *thymos*" (Garver 1994, 113). He also believed that *thymos* was unevenly distributed. Just as Greece occupied the climatic and thus civilizational center of the world (or so the ancients believed), Greeks possessed the perfect balance of spiritedness and reason and thus were most the most capable of governing themselves and others (Garver 1994). Cuomo – who speaks with a broad Queens accent and plays up his image as a shrewd urbanite – understood perfectly that appealing to New York's *thymos*, its sense of itself as the center of the world, would open the door to themes of ascent. He deploys the scene-act and scene-agent ratios with aplomb, shifting genre from tragedy to low mimesis and onward toward romance. "One of the things that comedy and romance as a whole are about, clearly, is the unending, irrational, absurd persistence of the human impulse to struggle, survive, and where possible escape," writes Frye (1976, 136). By wrapping the idea of environmental resilience in the mantle of New York mythology – a mythology he could convincingly personify – Cuomo appeared to have nudged the drama toward climate change *communitas*. Whether he and others can continue to do so remains to be seen.

Conclusion

In an important sense, Cuomo and those in his carrier group seem to have tentatively confirmed the hypothesis that local, place-based dramas can be effective in changing sensibilities and priorities. Yet they also showed that not just any place will do. For a drama to be successful, action and *ethos* must be aligned with the correct geographical narratives. Character and action must suit the stage. In Arizona or Oklahoma, a different genius loci would need to be conjured – perhaps one that activates the progressive mythos of frontiersmanship and conquest that Cronon and other environmental historians have so long decried.

Had Sandy missed Manhattan, would it have been discussed as a "wake-up call" or "turning point" in quite the same way? Would it have been imbued with quite the same "event-ness"? We doubt it. New York has special meanings as a center of finance, as a melting pot, as a symbol of America, and as the so-called capital of the world. Yet at the same time, its place-myth was constraining even as it enabled climate change activism. This was a city of can-do, no-nonsense people. Cuomo's position suggested there could be pragmatic fixes that would toughen up New York. By tinkering with building codes and seawalls, the worst of the damage could be mitigated in the future. Sensible local decisions would lead to target hardening. Meanwhile newscasts documented the community spirit of individuals helping each other rebuild their lives. Things seemed to be getting back to normal very quickly. Unlike Katrina, Sandy had produced a romantic narrative that quickly tended toward the low mimetic. The kind of fundamental genre shift that might have led to radical new carbon policies and political will to make sacrifices to lifestyle and endorse global treaties could not emerge. By the end of 2012, the tendencies implicit in the early rhetorical response to Sandy began, like charisma in Weber's account, to be routinized and institutionalized. A conference entitled "Rebuilding a Resilient New Jersey," held on December 7, featured speakers outlining the "new normal" and "opportunities for state and regional action to enhance resilience." This event was about digging in at a local level and solving problems locally, not changing carbon lifestyles or global solidarity (New Jersey Future 2012). Likewise, the Department of Housing and Urban Development, in association with other high-profile institutions such as New York University's Institute for Public Knowledge, launched its Rebuild by Design (2013) competition. Looking through the contestants, we find the idea of "resilience" taking center stage, this assisted by thesaurus buddies such as "resist," "mitigation," "protect," and "adapt." The competition entries seem attractive and environmentally sensitive, but they remain nevertheless local, defensive responses to the "new normal" that is now deemed inevitable.

What would it take to break this pattern of circling wagons and make such local drama more universal and more ambitious? Clues can be found in the history of environmentalism. The most famous place-narrative in American environmental literature (after *Walden*) is Rachel Carson's ([1962] 2002) "Fable for Tomorrow," the opening chapter of *Silent Spring*. In it, Carson tells of how "a town in the heart of America where all life seemed to live in harmony with its surroundings" is afflicted by an "evil spell" that leaves a silent trail of death in its wake. "No witchcraft, no enemy action had silenced the rebirth of new life in this stricken world," Carson wrote. "The people had done it themselves" (3). But as *Silent Spring* went on to demonstrate as it converted middle-class suburbanites to the cause of environmentalism, people did *not* blame themselves, nor did Carson. They blamed the chemical companies, the scientists, and the government regulators who had released this "strange blight" into American domestic space. Without this moral geography, Carson's fable would have failed. Similar narrative strategies have proven transformative in bottom-up struggles for environmental justice. Take the Kenyan environmental activist and Nobel laureate Wangari Maathai, whose Greenbelt Movement used tree planting to enact a moral confrontation between Kenya's rural poor and its urban kleptocracy. This "theater of the tree," as ecocritic Rob Nixon (2011, 136–137) correctly terms it, "staged a showdown between the forces of incremental violence [i.e., deforestation] and the forces of incremental peace; in so doing [it] gave a symbolic and dramatic shape to public discontent over the official culture of plunder." By simultaneously "naming the agents of destruction" (136) and articulating a hopeful, thymotic vision of sustainable place-making, Maathai wrote just the kind of chronotopic script that we believe climate change has lacked.

Of course, climate change *is* a fundamentally different kind of problem. As Ulrich Beck (1992, 33) argued in *Risk Society*, "everyone is cause *and* effect, and thus *non-cause*," and this brutal fact produces a pervasive condition of "general complicity" matched by a "general lack of responsibility." Because global ecological risks like climate change are produced by "the system," Beck noted, we can abdicate responsibility and continue to act "physically, without acting morally or politically" (33). This is what Kari Norgaard (2011) calls "the absurdity of the double life." For environmental rhetoric to succeed, we suggest, this absurdity must be overcome by civil discourse channeled through ethical, charismatic authority. There must be heroes and heroines (like Carson and Maathai) to defend civil society against dangerous enemies – even if that enemy is in fact itself.

As Cuomo demonstrated after Sandy, would-be leaders must mobilize utopian narratives of social progress and renewal, and they must do so by invoking places, real or imagined, that inspire both hope and pride. Blame alone does not construct ethical authority.

9

Conclusion

The Show Must Go On

> It may be said that every individual man and all men in common aim at a
> certain end which determines what they choose and what they avoid. This
> end, to sum it up briefly, is happiness.
>
>   – Aristotle, *Rhetoric*, 1.5.1360b4–6

> To argue on the basis of reason alone is a character flaw, a failure of ēthos,
> and therefore a failure to persuade.
>
>   – Eugene Garver (1994, 183)

Can climate change make us happy? The question might seem glib, but we
ask it in earnest. Happiness, for Aristotle, was the goal of all deliberation.
Without showing that he cared first and foremost about the happiness of
his audience, a speaker was sunk. Deliberation over climate change is no
different. And climate science cannot tell us how to be happy.

Others have made the same point, but they have tended to conceive of
happiness in restrictive ways: ethical, psychological, economic.[1] We conceive of happiness in more inclusive sociological terms. It is about more
than feelings of security or the promise of prosperity. In the Aristotelian
tradition, happiness (*eudemonia*) is not simply pleasure or contentment
but "is something like flourishing human living, a kind of living that is

---

[1] Mike Hulme, for example, argues for reframing climate change in postmillennialist terms
such as "Jubilee" – "an opportunity to create new potency behind movements for social
and environmental justice" (2009, 354). Others, most prominently Ted Nordhaus and
Michael Shellenberger (2007), have tried to reframe climate change as a catalyst for
economic growth and technological innovation. We can even see evidence of this emphasis
on happiness in seemingly sterile policy debates about "cap-and-trade" versus "cap-and-
dividend" – a scheme for funneling proceeds from emissions permits directly to consumers
(e.g., Skocpol 2012).

active, inclusive of all that has intrinsic value, and complete" (Nussbaum 2012, 342). In American civil discourse, something like this view of flourishing has echoes in talk of "community" or even "freedom" in the way that they capture the societal actualization of latent possibility. From the perspective of cultural sociology, happiness is, above all, socially integrative. As Durkheim (1965) argued in the *Elementary Forms*, it arises in the form of solidarity from a complex mixture of shared memories, shared emotions, shared ends, shared activity, and shared symbolic systems.

It also arises from shared *beliefs*, which, in Aristotle's view (and Durkheim's), are closely linked to shared emotions, including fear.[2] Consensus matters. As Martha Nussbaum (2012, 345) puts it, "a necessary and sufficient condition of an emotion's being truly positive – in the sense of making a positive contribution toward a flourishing life – is that it be based on true beliefs, both about value and about what events have occurred. This is as true of good-feeling as of bad-feeling emotion." Fear of climate chaos is fully compatible with happiness, much as terror at an encounter with the sacred, as Durkheim showed, can be a source of renewal. Aristotelian *eudemonia* encompasses "positive pain, that is, the grief that expresses love, the fear that expresses a true sense of a threat directed at something or someone one loves, the compassion that shares the pain of a suffering person, the anger that says, 'This is deeply wrong and I will try to right it'" (Nussbaum 2012, 345). Hence the happiness of climate change may be traumatic. The notion of a "just war" might be the closest analogue. There must be light at the end of the tunnel. But it need not be the rosy, artificial light of simple optimism.

We know that many people feel this existential urgency about climate change. But they have largely failed to translate this urgency into a compelling vision or representation of collective, solidaristic, actualizing happiness.[3] Although many activists claim that fighting climate change will lead to a better society, that message is not getting through – even to

---

[2] Much of this is elaborated in his *Nichomachean Ethics*. "In Aristotle's view, emotions are not blind animal forces, but intelligent and discriminating parts of the personality, closely related to beliefs of a certain sort, and therefore responsive to cognitive modification. He calls for cultivation of many emotions as valuable and necessary parts of virtuous agency" (Nussbaum 1996, 303).

[3] On the substantive nature of environmental happiness, we are agnostic. In sociology (as in a number of fields), there is growing interest in Aristotelian virtue ethics and in the essential nature of human flourishing (e.g., Gorski 2012; Sayer 2011). Our interest is rather different. It concerns the formal, rhetorical attributes of a successful *appeal* to happiness.

some of those who share their fears about the state of the planet. Why not? One powerful but ultimately simplistic answer is that these people cannot escape the grip of apocalyptic, moralistic, antimodern pessimism. As Bruno Latour (2012) puts it with unusual clarity:

> In the name of indisputable facts portraying a bleak future for the human race, green politics has succeeded in leaving citizens nothing but a gloomy asceticism, a terror of trespassing Nature, and a diffidence toward industry, innovation, technology, and science. No wonder that, while political ecology [i.e., environmentalism] claims to embody the political power of the future, it is reduced everywhere to a tiny portion of electoral strap-hangers.... Set in contrast to the modernist narrative, this idea of political ecology could not possibly succeed. There is beauty and strength in the modernist story of emancipation. Its picture of the future is so attractive, especially when put against such a repellent past, that it makes one wish to run forward to break all the shackles of ancient existence.... To succeed, an ecological politics must manage to be at least as powerful as the modernizing story of emancipation without imagining that we are emancipating ourselves from Nature.

Others have taken the same argument in more pragmatic directions. Take the Hartwell Paper, an attempt by a group of prominent policy experts "to reframe the climate issue around matters of human dignity. Not just because that is noble or nice or necessary . . . but because it is likely to be more effective than the approach of framing around human sinfulness – which has just failed" (Prins et al. 2010, 35). Grasping at Latour's emancipation narrative, these authors assert that "securing access to low-cost energy for all, including the very poor, is truly and literally liberating. Building resilience to surprise and to extremes of weather is a practical expression of true global solidarity. Improving the quality of the air that people breathe is an undeniable public good" (35–36).

Fair enough. But "public goods" are notoriously difficult to express in the abstract languages of both theory and policy. If comparative anthropology teaches us anything, it is that dignity means different things in different places. So perhaps the answer is to train our ethnographic eye on cultural particularities. In America, for example, many have asked whether religious leaders – particularly leaders of the country's large and hugely influential evangelical constituency – might be able to turn the tide of public opinion by reframing environmentalism as "care for creation" or even as an intergenerational expression of "family values." This question is guided by the assumption that the communication strategies of liberal environmental elites are rife with moral choices and ideological biases that nonenvironmentalists find off-putting – agrarian aesthetics, ascetic spirituality, antimodern nostalgia, and various clubby appeals to radical chic – or that they are simply smug and sanctimonious.

There is something to this critique, too. Environmentalism's elite origins are well documented, and despite becoming a much more inclusive movement in recent decades, these roots still show. Even among ordinary citizens who are deeply worried about climate change, support for a radical greening of society is unlikely to materialize any time soon. As hard as it may be for some environmentalists to accept, knitting your own muesli on a biodynamic farm in a countercultural corner of Vermont or bartering for fair-trade, organic edamame at the Park Slope Food Coop in hipsterville Brooklyn does not sound like "the good life" to a great many Americans. But this kind of explanation, as the prior sentence demonstrates, quickly and all too easily shades into facile ideological caricature. The cultural polarization that marks contemporary environmental politics may in fact be fragile and historically evanescent. It is worth remembering that the first Earth Day in 1970 – an event suffused with apocalyptic rhetoric – was the largest demonstration in American history, drawing millions upon millions of ordinary people into the streets (Rome 2013). That same year, the fundamentalist theologian Francis Schaeffer – an architect of the Christian Right and arch–culture warrior – published a fierce call for environmental action titled *Pollution and the Death of Man*. In it he wrote:

The hippies of the 1960s did understand something. They were right in fighting the plastic culture, and the church should have been fighting it too. . . . More than this, they were right in the fact that the plastic culture – modern man, the mechanistic worldview in university textbooks and in practice, the total threat of the machine, the establishment technology, the bourgeois upper middle class – is poor in its sensitivity to nature.

Schaeffer, who did more than anyone to conjure "secular humanism" as the *bête noire du jour* of the American conservative, would have had much to mourn with the liberal Bill McKibben, himself a Methodist Sunday school teacher, about that plasticity of modern culture. The history of environmentalism contains more strange bedfellows and ideological ambiguities than we might expect, including a tradition of right-wing activism (Drake 2013). We believe that skilled social dramatists can navigate such shifting and deceptive subcultural sands.

But how do we find the elusive path to some climate change *eudemonia* where emotions, reason, and the collective will line up and form a virtuous and rewarding societal response to risk? We are not the first scholars to consider this issue, and we do not think we have all, even many, answers (see, e.g., Hulme 2014). Nor do we underestimate the basic difficulty of the task. As John Urry (2011, 99) rightly notes, "protesting against high carbon forms of life and their resultant carbon emissions is historically unusual and hugely difficult to realize. Most politics historically has been *against* the income, wealth and power of other social groups, against their 'goods.'" Climate politics, as most honest analysts recognize, is fundamentally different: "Unlike almost all other politics in world history, it is a politics for lower consumption of goods and services for one's own social group" (100). With reflexive modernization come new structural conditions for environmental mobilization, and no amount of cultural maneuvering can change that structural reality. But we do believe our turn to the perspectives of both contemporary cultural sociology and Aristotelian cultural theory offered fresh ways of reflecting on these familiar difficulties. Our starting point was to realize that climate change is not just a natural process. As we showed at the outset of our book, it is also something distinctly nonmaterial. It is a signifier within a discursive field that is made up of codes and narratives, characters and plots, performances and settings whose totality is captured in the concept of the social drama.

To use the word "drama" to capture this complex collective act of representation and interpretation is not to suggest falsehood, deception, or irrationality. It is to imply that in reaching toward rationality, we, as a civil society or as a public sphere, "reason" in surprisingly nonrational ways. Our means are not narrowly circumscribed by data, logic, experimental findings, mathematics, or even any ethics of procedure. It is also through aesthetic and generic forms, as well as through codes of civility and the narrative actions of shared representation, that the environment becomes culturally relevant or "known" in the public sphere. And this is not the end of it. There is also a meta-narrative concerning those acts of narration and representation themselves. Storytellers and stories are themselves subject to evaluation, explanation, coding, and commentary. We have suggested that in exactly this way climate change comes to be a "social drama" – a vast, layered, ongoing saga of gestures, initiatives, trajectories, characters, and critiques that is visible as such.

To use an expression from Lévi-Strauss, through this social drama, nature is "cooked" and invisible risk made amenable to practical human actions (*phronesis*). This performative and hermeneutic approach goes well beyond the dominant account of risk that was provided by the social thinker Ulrich Beck (1992). To recap one more time from Chapter 2, for Beck modernity has generated risks as externalities of economic and technological development. In the Beckian vision, proliferating risks have implanted themselves into the social and political lives of our culture in a more or less hypodermic way. The risk exists, we pay attention on account of its danger, we form a collective response. That response is characterized by Beck as "reflexive modernity" – a sort of critical engagement with ideas of progress that is informed by egalitarian and green politics. This involves an awareness of a shared human destiny, the impossibility of outsourcing risk to poor people or poor nations due to "boomerang effects," and intense popular pressures for restrictions on pollution. Not altogether unlike Marxism in its logic, Beck's argument stresses objective and material contradictions that come with time to undermine the conditions of their own existence. For Marx the growth of capitalism changed objective social relations. The progressing immiseration of the proletariat and their spatial concentration in cities and workplaces led to working-class consciousness and political mobilization. For Beck, it is the manufacture of unavoidable pollutions and industrial dangers that leads to blowback. Although in his final years he belatedly emphasized that these dangers must be "staged" to enter the attention space (see also Chapter 2), Beck treats such cultural performance as an afterthought. His hoped-for cosmopolitan consciousness would seem to emerge organically from the inner workings of reflexive modernization.

Such theories about stages of social development offer attractive ironies but have loose ends. For the most part, full-blown industrial capitalism did not lead to revolution, as Marx expected, but rather to political incorporation. To the contrary, it was the laggards and peasant economies that defected to socialism. Cultural variables have often been used to explain this result, including by Marxists themselves. Much the same could be said for the risk society thesis. Were the world changing in the way that Beck described, the problem of climate change would have been adequately addressed by now. The objective but simultaneously unquantifiable dangers of escalating CO_2 would have triggered alarm and a mass green democratic mobilization; this would have made Kyoto a transformative event. Game over.

Alas, as Beck himself came to realize, things are a little more complex. There is a huge, sometimes even boundless elasticity between risk and representation, and then again between representation and action – an elasticity that is to a large degree captured by the conceptual resource of the social drama. Although peak political and scientific bodies have marked out climate change as a problem of the first order for some time, the risk consciousness that has developed is strictly minor league. Importantly, this is not simply a question of net sensitivity to environmental issues but is also one of uneven attachment. Consistent with the risk society hypothesis, our world has indeed become far more reflexive about the ecological costs of modernity. Yet climate change does not seem to be a magnet issue within this wider sensibility. Ideas about stewardship might be somewhat decoupled from existential risk. For example, in 2013, one in ten people in the United Kingdom was a member or donor to conservation or environmental groups such as Greenpeace, Oxfam, or the National Trust. Yet of the billion or so pounds raised by such groups, less than 10 percent went to deal with climate change. Issues such as conservation, biodiversity, land management, and water quality tended to get the lion's share of funding, as did regional and local initiatives (Vidal 2013). Even in a country as green as the United Kingdom, "saving the whales" still seems more pressing, attractive, or achievable than curbing planetary emissions of carbon dioxide, which could kill the oceans altogether.

What is to be done? Fatalism has attractions for the professional ironist. So one option is to throw up one's hands as a cultural analyst and to declare that "nothing works." This perspective is, we believe, an untenable abdication of responsibility. A good deal of evidence points in the other direction. For example, we might take heart from the fact that comparatively lightweight threats like Y2K, SARS, and mad cow disease were able to punch well above their weight, sometimes for weeks on end. Take bird flu. As the media researchers Tammy Boyce and Justin Lewis (2009, 11) show, in 2006, this disease (which was already an old story) earned almost twice the media coverage in the United Kingdom as did climate change (22 percent vs. 13 percent), and this was an exceptionally good year for climate coverage! Why do we call threats like bird flu, SARS, and the rest lightweight? Although people really died, at the end of the day none of these did much harm, at least not compared to the harms already inflicted by climate change. Even if worse case scenarios had eventuated, none had the capacity to destroy the entire biosphere for centuries. Each would have had severe but temporary impacts, and mostly for just the human population of this planet. Rather than complaining that climate change has been left behind by such usurpers, we might gain hope from them. They dominated headlines and gripped the popular imagination without seeming to require expensive marketing campaigns or even much by way of documented witnessable harm. On the basis of speculations about future catastrophic possibilities they generated decisive policy changes by governments and led to rapid shifts in individual behavior within everyday life.

Turning to the specifics of Y2K, SARS, and mad cow disease, some properties stand out. There was a vivid imagery of creeping invisible proliferation, this tied in turn to ideas of infection, dread, and catastrophe. In these cases an apocalyptic imagery of diabolical threats fell into place, at least for a while. Low-mimetic alternatives were all but invisible. Perhaps more important, discussions on these problems avoided distracting digression. They stayed for the most part on point. Warnings from authority – notably for our perspective from the United Nations – were taken seriously. The discursive field widened out to become more reflexive and critical only after the danger had passed. The overamplification of dangers by scientific bodies, for example, was a low-priority theme of feature articles, opinion pages, and cartoons – and even then only once the event had been proven to be a bust. Put another way, for a while, these problems were taken literally and seriously and without much derailing and irony. As social dramas, they were elementary and took a form closer to that of the moral panic. This contrasts with the cultural systems of climate change. This seems to have generated a far more convoluted series of dramatic forms. We have shown throughout this book that these look to actors and their motivations, identify hypocrisy, decode abstruse imagery, and diagnose the failures of advertising campaigns. The problem here seems to be too much irony, too much dialogue, and too much distraction. There is a continual derailing of debate in unproductive directions, an inability to stay on point.

Is this such a bad thing? If frustrating to activists, the more elaborated communicative exchanges of the climate change field are in many ways ethically attractive. They conform closely to pluralist ideals of deliberation advocated by normative political theorists like Jürgen Habermas and his interlocutors. There is a healthy suspicion of authority and a very well defined capacity to widen out technical and administrative debates to the concerns of the lifeworld. We also find the use of multiple codes of discourse: the personal and contextual, and the general and universal; the scientific and the aesthetic; the visual and the narrative. This offers not only multiple avenues for persuasion but also a capacity for a sedimented, thicker, denser, more layered and polyvalent bedrock of meanings. We are optimistic that this deposit can withstand the truly seismic shake-up that will test social ties and solidarities to the limit once a risk awareness of climate change becomes tectonically active. In the long run, this is the competitive advantage of the complex social drama over the simpler moral panic.

But how is this drama to be best formed? We cannot give all the answers, and we are certainly not offering a complete recipe for staging a successful social movement. Although it seems increasingly inevitable that such a movement will emerge, who knows what form it will take? What symbolic weapons will it wield? What dramatic tools will it use? Will it follow the emancipatory model of civil rights, as so many environmental activists hope? Will it take the form of anticorporate populism? Will it have totalitarian overtones, as radical critics on the Right and Left worry? We cannot say. We sit in the audience. But that said, as informed critics, we can offer some summary diagnostics.

The first elements to think about are *plot and genre*. For Aristotle, getting the plot right such that it met the artistic potentials of tragedy or comedy was the single most important challenge for dramaturgy. Our analysis in Chapter 3 suggested that a different and analytically prior problem faced climate change – there was no consensus on genre. It was ambivalent by virtue of inhabiting contending locations on the genre gamut that allocates danger to uncertainty. We showed that, over time and in various contexts, it has shifted up and down the scale, and when it does settle, it comes to rest as an ironic melodrama, where the audience goes "to hiss the villain with an air of condescension," as Frye put it. This is probably good for no one. Public opinion research is a notoriously clumsy tool for investigating the kind of subtle interpretative processes we are describing here, but if the increasingly frustrated pronouncements of opinion leaders can be taken as indicators of underlying trends, the moral polarization of climate politics has backfired. As the rise of various "postenvironmentalist" agendas suggests – from the grassroots environmental justice movement to the "green modernism" and "ecopragmatism" of intellectuals in the mold of Latour (Kloor 2012) – there are more and more Americans and Europeans, including many environmentalists, and even quite a few scientists, who are fed up with the preachy scientism of traditional green politics. They are sick of being told that their profligate, greedy, and meaningless lifestyle is destroying the planet. They are weary of being force-fed data and statistics. They are tired of being admonished to drive less, to eat healthier food, to stop watching so much television, to "listen to the experts." At the same time, there appear to be many Americans – as the growing evangelical climate movement suggests (Wilkinson 2012) – who are fed up with the know-nothing skepticism and obstructionism of antienvironmental rhetoric. They are sick of being told that climate change is a hoax or a natural cycle. They are weary of being force-fed smug appeals to common sense and economic prudence. They are tired of being admonished to care more about jobs, to trust in the resiliency of nature, to stop being hysterical. It is safe to say that in much of the public eye, climate change has become a melodramatic conflict between these two ideological extremes. The plots and characters are too thin and predictable. And melodrama, as we have shown elsewhere in this book, has a natural tendency to shade into prurient metadrama. Like an episode of *American Idol* or a lackluster presidential election, the audience finds itself watching itself watching two equally unappealing actors duke it out on the stage. The focus shifts from substantives to an evaluation of the effectiveness of this or that rhetorical punching strategy. The inevitable end point seems to be the detached, hopeless stance of tragic irony. It is a kind of postmodern *Punch and Judy* show.

How to shift from melodrama to romance, from anomie and irony to civil solidarity? We have argued that this, not the accurate communication of yet more scientific facts, is the biggest question facing climate activism today. Every other genre seems to have its own carrier group, its own troupe of wandering players. There is still a large contingent of low-mimetic technocrats, led by "luke-warmists" like Lomborg. They argue that innovations like cold fusion, geothermal power, or genetically engineered carbon sinks will probably save the day and allow lifestyles to go on much as before. An insurgent comic contingent has emerged on the pro-growth, modernist Left. This faction urges Americans to "think big" and treat climate change as an opportunity to revolutionize energy production, even to advance social justice. They see life getting better if we just grasp the nettle. By contrast, there are the old-school tragedians, hunkering down in their coastal enclaves, scanning the skies for signs of the End. Committed ironists are few and far between, haunting some history departments, advertising agencies, and corporate offices, getting on with the absurdity of life. Then there are those – perhaps a majority of citizens – who cannot decide which camp to join because there are too many genres to choose from.

To their credit, green actors are finally facing up to this reality of failed emplotment and genre confusion. They recognize that without a broad-based, mainstream social movement organized around a realistic, inclusive, romantic plotline, nothing meaningful can be accomplished. Hence, in a highly reflexive article about flawed narrative structures and green strategy, the British environmentalist George Marshall (2013) suggests that the time has come to move on from simplistic efforts to find an enemy such as oil companies, the Koch brothers, or furtive peddlers of denial. These simply generate counterclaims and confusion. For example, in the U.K. case he discusses, arguments about overcharging by unethical big energy led to a pushback in which green taxes on energy were blamed for high electricity prices. Politicians attempted to capitalize on all this by making themselves the heroes who would save the day. Marshall asserts that the time has come to be more reflexive and to avoid the "partisan game." There should be more recognition that "we are all responsible" and a stronger focus given to the "common concerns and aspirations of all people."

Likewise in the widely read article in *Rolling Stone* we also cited in the previous chapter, Bill McKibben (2012a) spoke of the need for the middle classes to come to terms with their own role in a more mature way. Often panned by the Left for privileging local action and personal morality (e.g., White 2012), he candidly assessed the need to stage a ubiquitous social drama, one that shifts emphasis from the sinful consumerism of ordinary Americans to their shared interest in a sustainable future. For McKibben, as for many other environmental strategists, this has involved nudging the audience into a new subject position: the well-intentioned but morally conflicted middle-class citizen, worried about climate change but overwhelmed by the scale of the problem. Thus he writes:

[Environmentalists'] record of failure means we know a lot about what strategies *don't* work. Green groups, for instance, have spent a lot of time trying to change individual lifestyles: the iconic twisty light bulb has been installed by the millions, but so have a new generation of energy-sucking flatscreen TVs. Most of us are fundamentally ambivalent about going green: We like cheap flights to warm places, and we're certainly not going to give them up if everyone else is still taking them. Since all of us are in some way the beneficiaries of cheap fossil fuel, tackling climate change has been like trying to build a movement against yourself – it's as if the gay-rights movement had to be constructed entirely from evangelical preachers, or the abolition movement from slaveholders.

You might think we are a bunch of holier-than-thou elites, McKibben tells his audience, *but really we are just like you.* Yet at the end of the day, even a highly reflexive cultural performer like McKibben cannot seem to find a way to separate romance from melodrama, as George Marshall would wish. Clearly these genres have elective affinities. So in his writing we see yet again the fiercely binary logic of the apocalyptic genre bubbling to the surface – the language of heroes and villains, the saved and the damned. Even as he calls for a social movement to face up to the messy realities of decarbonization, McKibben argues, "A rapid, transformative change would require building a movement, and movements require enemies. As John F. Kennedy put it, 'The civil rights movement should thank God for Bull Connor. He's helped it as much as Abraham Lincoln.' And enemies are what climate change has lacked." To fill that gap, McKibben proposes the fossil fuel industry: "It has become a rogue industry, reckless like no other force on Earth. It is Public Enemy Number One to the survival of our planetary civilization."

Among loyalists, McKibben's article struck a nerve, and it was widely shared and reposted. As of August 2014, almost fourteen thousand comments had been posted on the *Rolling Stone* website. Whether this moral confrontation with an Uncivil Other will mobilize nonenvironmentalists, making them actors rather than yet more distant spectators of the tawdry metadrama that George Marshall identifies remains to be seen. As the sociologists Jeff Goodwin and James Jasper (2006, 624) explain, infusing emotion into a social cause through demonization can force difficult trade-offs. "In the days of Aristotle and face-to-face communication," they write,

the orator had to think about his audience as a whole, largely ignoring individual differences. This is still a challenge, but one matched by differences among entire groups. Thanks to modern communications, words, gestures, and bodily expressed emotions can go to friends, foes, authorities, and bystanders all at once. Telling your group that your opponents are incorrigibly evil may strengthen your group, but it will not help you deal with those you have demonized once they find out.

For climate activists, this is a perilous trade-off indeed. On one hand, surveys show widespread distrust of fossil fuel companies. But on the other, demonizing Big Oil can have unintended consequences, as campus activists for fossil fuel divestment have recently discovered. By pressuring colleges and universities to shun the carbon industries, they effectively force the leaders of those institutions – many of whom are deeply concerned about climate change – to "pick sides." When the target was the racist and repressive government of South Africa, the choice was much clearer. But perhaps this moral gamble will pay off. As this book neared publication, the divestment movement appeared to be gaining steam. Either way, it confirms our argument that an understanding of the cultural logics of social drama will be fundamental to environmentalist *phronesis*, to use Aristotle's term for practical knowledge, from this moment forward.

The subtitle to our chapter is "The Show Must Go On." We intend this to be read as both a normative and a factual statement. If the dangers of climate change are as catastrophic as the scientific community maintains, then our social drama *needs* to grow more compelling and pervasive. Because the drama of climate change is already compelling and pervasive, is already a fact of life in the public sphere, the show *will* go on. We cannot predict the exact content of future episodes of the saga, but we have excavated some theoretical tools for thinking about those yet-to-be-written chapters. We have also provided some case studies. These illustrate the modes of representation, themes, and the communicative forms through which the drama will likely play out. At various points in our book, we were drawn to the centrality of *ethos*. By focusing on performance and the self, we might easily be read as attacking the character and capabilities of environmental actors. Nothing could be further from the truth. *Ethos* is about social relations of trust. It is a sine qua non of deliberative rationality. It is about more than "image" or identity or spin management. By exposing or even ignoring the failed logocentrism of some environmental actors – for example, their faith in "reports" and "scientific consensus" – we do not mean to imply that they should simply replace evidentiary argument with feel-good appeals to the lowbrow center. We are not suggesting that Tom Hanks, Captain America, or Garth Brooks become the face of climate change. Nor are we suggesting that activists should engage in activities that garner attention but risk trivializing the issues at stake through inappropriate genre choices.

Aristotle said that we must speak seriously of serious things: stunts probably don't help. For example, when actor Billy Talen, dressed as a preacher and accompanied by actors in toad helmets, invaded a JP Morgan Chase bank in New York, the result was simply chaotic, with the toads "jumping on the bank's furniture, running about the bank, and screaming loudly at others." Some customers and staff were upset as they thought a robbery was in progress. Notwithstanding – or perhaps partly because of – the Reverend Billy's Baptist-style sermon on the evils of Chase's financing of fossil fuel projects, any possibility for *ethos* was lost (*Guardian* 2013). Only a little less problematic is a spoof video suggesting major storms be named after climate change–denying politicians (Climate Name Change 2013). Although the video was amusing to activists and attracted more than 2.5 million hits in just a few months, comments on YouTube were characterized by an unusual degree of incivility. Comedic irony garnered attention but did not lead to productive dialogue. Likewise, we have reservations about the work of the Yes Men (see http://www.theyesmen.org). Much admired in the culture-jamming world, their techniques include spoof press releases and the impersonation of business leaders. These can easily be read, on one hand, as dishonest and as exploiting the credence and hospitality of others and, on the other, as the behavior of entitled frat boys. Words like "prank," "hoax," "impostor," and "fake" invariably accompany accounts of their actions. Such terms do not line up easily with those Aristotelian theory predicts are more helpful, such as "trust," "transparency," and "goodwill," and in fact might be antithetical to these. As Canada's *Globe and Mail* (2010) put it in an editorial, such actions "threaten the believability of all forms of communications" and so could "eventually undermine the very kinds of positive achievements the activists claim to demand."

As Aristotle pointed out long ago, character stands out as a pivotal variable whenever political oratory is at hand. Within the public sphere, the discourse of civil society sets the standard for a character evaluation of claims makers and the allocation of *ethos*. The "sacred" side of the code demands that actors are rational, autonomous, and motivated by ideals rather than irrational, dependent, and materialistic. Al Gore became unexpectedly persuasive once he was shown to be a person of substance who was prepared to crusade on behalf of a losing cause. He was depicted suffering, learning, and growing. Once a self-centered and achievement-oriented boffin, Gore became a humble person who was able to communicate in a level-headed manner. The young people who spoke up at climate conferences were understood as trustworthy and plain-speaking innocents. By contrast, the people behind the 10:10 "No Pressure" advertising campaign appeared to have lost touch with reality, confusing humor with violence, patronizing their audience. Critics sneered that the artist Antony Gormley was raking in money, not acting for the good of the planet, when he pitched for environmental art and environmentally sensitive art production. The Climategate scientists were not as honorable as we had hoped – they were taken to be petty, defensive, and sneaky. They had let down the ideals of science by avoiding transparency and not sharing their data. Unsubstantiated sleaze allegations tainted a later version of Al Gore. Such negative character attributes – real or simply "attributed" as a component of public discourse – drag the narrative of climate change back down the genre ramp. The players now seem inferior to "us," readers and viewers. Ironic, fatalistic, and cynical attitudes fall into place that are rewarding only if we assume the subject position of the amused or indignant spectator.

Plot, genre, and *ethos* need to be better coordinated so as to maximize communicative impact. As Aristotle noted, effective drama and effective public speaking involve the careful alignment of such variables around a single communicative enterprise. Getting the ducks in a row is a tall order, even in the controlled environment of the theatre. Be those difficulties as they may, we feel that much climate change activism can be indicted as failing at this task of coordination due to narcissism, parasitic behaviors, and a general unconcern for the anonymous other. We saw this most acutely in online threads relating to climate change art. At CoolClimate, posters asked administrative questions, complained about the judging in the climate change art competition they themselves had freely chosen to enter, and pestered artists with technical queries about art production. How many onlookers would have been inspired by this? Blogs on the Copenhagen art exhibit broke down into incoherence, with the free-riding contributors neglecting to signal that they were responding to a string of discourse. There was no evident solidarity. In other contexts questions and prompts received no replies. Protestors at the Copenhagen conference who seemed prepared for violence had helped sour the mood of the week. We feel they might have drawn attention to environmental problems in a more appropriate way, thereby generating interpretative synergies with the artistic, spiritual, and social movement actors who were also campaigning there. Apologies after the 10:10 "No Pressure" debacle were not responsive to the reception of the advertisements. They apologized for the most part to other activists and sponsors and seemed to put public disgust down to defective interpretation.

We can do better that that. The delegates at Cancun engaged in collective bodily signs of mutual appreciation and respect as they voted on their significant final resolution. In Al Gore's *An Inconvenient Truth*, sometimes applauding, sometimes laughing, sometimes silent audiences function in much the same way. This sort of overseen choreography is associated with Frye's Themes of Ascent, which speak of a net increase in sociability in romantic narratives. In contrast to the chaos of "*Schlechten Krieg*", to be organized is to be social. Aristotle understood this too when he spoke of the relations between characters and the chorus as pivotal to the cathartic possibilities of drama. These points relating to emotional responses all confirm the centrality of *pathos*. This sense of nonrational identification with heroic agents or distant suffering is crucial to the emergence of *thymos* or collective will. Our book has shown that, all too often, the climate community has made mistakes that have soured its own reputation. They have damaged its credibility or *ethos* and prevented solidarities from emerging by projecting selfish and incivil motivations; by appearing to hate enemies, mock critics, or patronize the public.

Even if our research documents such successes and failures for climate activists, it is important to step back and engage in auto-critique. First we must consider the dangers for and of this book. Like all arguments pointing to the role of symbolic construction in shaping human action and belief, our argument is vulnerable to a cartoonish misreading by critics. This would have it that we argue reality is "all in the mind," that "truth is relative" and that climate change is just a "game of contending representations." An equally false reading is possible by enthusiasts. This would see us as arguing radical changes can come about simply through society learning to think in creative and new ways. We must crush this nonsense here and now. Drawing on the vocabulary of critical realism (Bhaskar 1975), we can state that nature is "intransitive." This means that there are real causal mechanisms at work and that the climate has an objective reality that has consequences regardless of how we choose to think about it. Islands will go under water, houses will be destroyed, people will get sick, and economies will suffer regardless of the symbolic constructions we or others put upon them. Human symbolic constructions and forms of knowledge can impact this reality only if and when they come to shape action and policy. So our perspective, like that of critical realism, is that reality bites. In the context of climate change we see both natural science and social science as pragmatic and imperfect ("transitive") attempts to imagine the complex "laminated systems" (Bhaskar 2010) and interdependences that tether the intransitive ways of nature to reflexive and contingently produced social structures, actions, and ways of life (Forsyth 2001). Within this wider picture that necessarily requires interdisciplinary cooperation (Bhaskar 2010), our endeavor has simply been to clarify some of the symbolically mediated modes through which society represents nature to itself, itself within nature, and itself to itself. Unfortunately these representations can impact on the intransitive reality that is climate change only indirectly and, given the lags involved in reducing atmospheric carbon dioxide levels, slowly. This does not mean, however, that we should give up on the attempt.

A second danger of this book is that it will inform activist praxis in a naive way. True enough, we show that visibility and performance matter. Yet – as we discussed earlier – we are emphatically not calling for more stunts, humor, or desperate attempts to gain visibility, nor are we calling for cynical attempts to manufacture *pathos* by blaming disasters on carbon-spewing evildoers. Generally speaking, when these strategies have become visible to the news cycle, they have also been a liability for the environmentalist community. Our findings, to the contrary, have consistently pointed to the need for a considered effort at balanced communication that respects the dignity of both speakers and audience and recognizes the serious nature of the issue at hand. Paradoxically, there is an urgent need to slow down – and think.

Those are the dangers. And what of the limitations to this book? Most obviously our method has consisted of the hermeneutic reconstruction of systems of meaning relating to the first- (nature), second- (actors and acts), and third- (strategies and impacts) order narration of the drama of climate change. We have disciplined and documented our reading through the use of quotation and citation from exemplary cases. Nevertheless, questions can be asked concerning the extent to which our "expert" interpretations are shared by "ordinary" people; the extent to which the drama in the United States or United Kingdom matches that of other countries; whether the case studies we select are representative of the total universe of public expression, and so forth. These are matters of validity and generalizability that are common to all qualitative historical and textual research, including that of giant figures in the social sciences and humanities. Geertz, for example, was taken to task for reading too much into the Balinese cockfight (Crapanzano 1986); Foucault for packaging the details of prison history too neatly (Perrot 1980). We followed modestly in their footsteps: although we have invested thousands of hours engaging with primary materials, we chose not to pursue a systematic, positivist sampling strategy. We preferred instead to pragmatically identify fruitful avenues for theoretical and empirical activity or for public exposition with an eye to generating scholarly debate. Much as a literary critic identifies key passages in a novel for study and accounting, this is an activity involving judgment and, with readers, trust in our competence. With such reservations in mind, we propose our research be seen as a provocation and invitation to future scholarship. As much as we have set out to provide answers, we have also set out to offer new ways of seeing. We hope others will take up the baton and, if necessary, challenge our core claims through, for example, audience ethnography, comparative media sociology, and survey research into public reputations, climate belief, and technical knowledge.

A second limitation involves issues of scope. We have established the validity of a particular perspective through theory construction and case study analysis. This has required us to put to one side a number of issues that are of burning concern to many in the field. We do not consider the social transmission of scientific information in any narrow sense, so we cannot say what kinds of new facts about climate change will impact public opinion. We do not evaluate the accuracy of any particular claims about climate change but prefer instead simply to explore the nature of representations. Nor did we explore how inequities in power allow some groups to exert disproportional weight in the scripting of our drama. We did not unpack how cultural bias and psychological processing load the dice of opinion formation. We did none of these things because, as we showed in Chapter 2, we believe others are already doing them very well. However, we concede that a useful next step in the research process would be to connect social drama process with these literatures. For example, which kinds of dramatic interventions allow scientific facts to be effectively communicated? To what extent do inequities in representational power allow for narrative closure? How might cultural bias create engagement or disengagement with particular dramatic personae? Finally, we did not consider how ongoing social change might facilitate or hinder public engagement with the drama of climate change. This last point brings us to the issue of reflexive modernization.

As we explained in Chapter 2 and also earlier in this one, for Ulrich Beck and his followers, modernity has generated reflexivity and complexity. The production of environmental harms and the emergence of postindustrial economic affluence have provided fertile soil for the emergence of environmentalist sensibilities. There can be little doubt something of this nature has been going on in affluent economies of northern Europe. Places like Denmark, Sweden, and Germany seem to be enthusiastic early adopters of environmental initiatives. Tracing how such societal reflexivity maps onto dramatic engagement is beyond the scope of our book, but we do feel that this might be a fruitful path for future inquiry. At the same time, we would stress, with Norgaard (2011), that the results can often be paradoxical. In affluent Norway, the finger is pointed elsewhere so as to justify current lifestyles, however sheepishly. Moreover, we are concerned that belief in the redemptive power of an unfolding modernity can lead to fatalism and ethical apathy, a point underlined in another context by thinkers as ideologically diverse as Antonio Gramsci (1992) and Karl Popper (1971). Much as early-twentieth-century European Communists sat back and waited for the right objective conditions for revolution to fall into place, so might environmentalists take cheer in the knowledge that change is on its way. From our perspective the question to ask here is, Which will come first, environmentally ethical behavior or irreversible global crisis? The evidence to date is not encouraging on this score. Beck's landmark analysis of *Risk Society* was published in 1992. Given that such social theory shoots at a moving target, we have now had three, four, or perhaps five decades of reflexive modernity. Even if environmental concern has been mainstreamed, few would argue that our lifestyles have become less carbon hungry over this period.

To sum up, our research suggests that there needs to be a consistency on genre that ends genre confusion yet does not result in the melodrama that shades to metadrama. Furthermore, more needs to be done to locate speakers who embody *ethos* and can do so reliably rather than episodically. When *thymos* is generated, this needs to be public and visible, operating as a sign to onlooking publics that romance is possible. The search for iconic representations of climate change might perhaps be dialed back, with greater emphasis given to effective personal and local narratives that serve as telling examples of *anagnorisis* (learning) in action and that are visibly encoded as such. The result might perhaps be some provisional *eudemonia* that emerges from shared moods, understandings of reality, and hopeful sacrifices. It seems inevitable that the experience and idea of place, of small-scale struggles to adapt, will play a central role in this process.

We believe there is a real possibility for climate change to emerge as a truly compelling social drama – a cultural form that will change history for *us* before climate-change-the-natural-event changes it radically *for* us. This, of course, is not very surprising to any optimist. What is surprising has been the inability of climate activism to understand – or perhaps merely enact – some simple communicative formulas. Al Gore got it right. Once. For some people. With an assist from an unprecedented weather system, Mayor Cuomo managed to catalyze New York. But briefly. At various conferences, noted individuals have stepped up and spoken from the heart. Coherently. And with impact. Learning from such positive examples, as well as from disasters, debacles, and scandals, and thinking about them with the tools of social drama theory might provide a way forward. At least, we would like to think it is a productive possibility.

References

350.org. 2012. "Sandy's Real Name." E-mail to mailing list, October 30. On file with authors.

Adger, W. Neil, Jon Barnett, F. S. Chapin, and Heidi Ellemor. 2011. "This Must Be the Place: Underrepresentation of Identity and Meaning in Climate Change Decision-Making." *Global Environmental Politics* 11(2):1–25.

Adger, W. Neil, Jon Barnett, Katrina Brown, Nadine Marshall, and Karen O'Brien. 2013. "Cultural Dimensions of Climate Change Impacts and Adaptation." *Nature Climate Change* 3:112–117.

Agnew, John. 1987. *Place and Politics: The Geographical Mediation of State and Society*. Boston: Allen and Unwin.

Agnew, John. 1989. "The Devaluation of Place in Social Science." Pp. 9–29 in *The Power of Place: Bringing Together Geographical and Sociological Imaginations*. London: Unwin Hyman.

Agyeman, J., P. Devine-Wright, and J. Prange. 2009. "Close to the Edge, Down by the River? Joining Up Managed Retreat and Place Attachment in a Climate Changed World." *Environment and Planning A* 41(3):509–513.

Alexander, Jeffrey C. 2004. "Cultural Pragmatics: Social Performance between Ritual and Strategy." *Sociological Theory* 22(4):527–573.

Alexander, Jeffrey C. 2006a. *The Civil Sphere*. New York: Oxford University Press.

Alexander, Jeffrey C. 2006b. "Performance and Counter-Power: The Civil Rights Movement and the Civil Sphere." *Culture* 20(2):1–3.

Alexander, Jeffrey C., and P. Smith. 1993. "The Discourse of American Civil Society: A New Proposal for Cultural Studies." *Theory and Society* 22(2):151–207.

Alexander, Jeffrey C., and Philip Smith. 1996. "Social Science and Salvation: Risk Society as Mythical Discourse." *Zeitschrift für Soziologie* 25(4):251–262.

Alexander, Jeffrey C., Dominik Bartmanski, and Bernhard Giesen, eds. 2012. *Iconic Power: Materiality and Meaning in Social Life*. New York: Palgrave Macmillan.

Alexander, Jeffrey C., Ronald Jacobs, and Philip Smith. 2012. *The Oxford Handbook of Cultural Sociology*. New York. Oxford University Press.

Al Jazeera. 2012. "Protest in Qatar Calls for Climate Action." December 1. http://www.aljazeera.com/video/middleeast/2012/12/2012121152948774513.html.

Althusser, Louis. 1971. *Lenin and Philosophy and Other Essays*. New York: Monthly Review Press.

Anderson, Alison. 2011. "Sources, Media, and Modes of Climate Change Communication: The Role of Celebrities." *Wiley Interdisciplinary Reviews: Climate Change* 2(4):535–546.

Aristotle. 1954. *Rhetoric*. New York: Modern Library.

Aristotle. 1998. *Poetics*. Translated by S. H. Butcher. New York: Hill and Wang.

Aristotle. 2007. *On Rhetoric: A Theory of Civic Discourse*. 2nd ed. New York: Oxford University Press.

Art Newspaper. 2010. "Exhibition and Museum Attendance Figures 2010." 223:23–30.

Associated Press. 2009. "Protests Erupt at Deadlocked Climate Conference." *USA Today*, December 16. http://usatoday30.usatoday.com/weather/climate/globalwarming/2009-12-16-climate-conference-wednesday_N.htm.

Baker, Stephanie. 2014. *Social Tragedy*. New York: Palgrave Macmillan.

Bakhtin, M. Mikhail. 1981. *The Dialogic Imagination: Four Essays*. Austin: University of Texas Press.

Barkun, Michael. 2003. *A Culture of Conspiracy: Apocalyptic Visions in Contemporary America*. Berkeley: University of California Press.

Barthes, Roland. 1972. *Mythologies*. New York: Farrar, Straus, and Giroux.

Barthes, Roland. 1975. *The Pleasures of the Text*. New York: Hill and Wang.

Battistoni, Alyssa. 2012. "Will 2013 Be the Year We Finally Address Climate Change?" *Salon.com*, December 31. http://www.salon.com/2012/12/31/will_2013_be_the_year_we_finally_address_climate_change.

Bazin, André. 1967. *What Is Cinema?* Berkeley: University of California Press.

BBC. 2009. "Climate Activists Condemn Copenhagen Police Tactics." *BBC News*, December 13. http://news.bbc.co.uk/2/hi/8410414.stm.

BBC. 2013. "BBC – Gardening – Gardening Guides: Basics – Climate Warming." http://www.bbc.co.uk/gardening/basics/weather_climatewarming.shtml#top.

BBC. 2014. "UN Seeks 'Malala' on Climate Change." *BBC News*, August 29. http://www.bbc.com/news/science-environment-28958227.

Beck, Ulrich. 1992. *Risk Society: Towards a New Modernity*. London: Sage.

Beck, Ulrich. 2009. *World at Risk*. English ed. Cambridge: Polity.

Beck, Ulrich. 2010. "Climate for Change, or How to Create a Green Modernity?" *Theory, Culture, and Society* 27(2–3):254–266.

Beck, Ulrich, Anthony Giddens, and Scott Lash. 1994. *Reflexive Modernization*. Stanford, CA: Stanford University Press.

Becker, Howard S. 1967. "Whose Side Are We On?" *Social Problems* 14(3):239–247.

Behringer, Wolfgang. 2010. *A Cultural History of Climate*. Cambridge: Polity.

Bellah, Robert. 1979. *Beyond Belief*. New York: Harper and Row.

Benjaminsen, Tor A., Koffi Alinon, Halvard Buhaug, and Jill Tove Buseth. 2012. "Does Climate Change Drive Land-Use Conflicts in the Sahel?" *Journal of Peace Research* 49(1):97–111.

Besa, Glen. 2010. "Litigation Ignores Science and the Law." *Richmond Times Dispatch (Virginia)*, February 14, A-9.

Bhaskar, Roy. 1975. *A Realist Theory of Science*. London: Verso.

Bhaskar, Roy. 2010. "Interdisciplinarity and Climate Change." Pp. 1–24 in *Transforming Knowledge and Practice for Our Global Future (Ontological Explorations)*, edited by R. Bhaskar, C. Frank, K. G. Hoyer, P. Naess, and J. Parker. London: Routledge.

Biernacki, Richard. 2012. *Reinventing Evidence in Social Inquiry*. New York: Palgrave Macmillan.

Block, Ben. 2008. "A Look Back at James Hansen's Seminal Testimony on Climate, Part Two." *Grist*, June 18. http://grist.org/article/a-climate-hero-the-testimony/.

Bloomberg Business Week. 2012. "It's Global Warming, Stupid." November 1.

Bocking, Stephen. 2004. *Nature's Experts Science, Politics and the Environment*. Piscataway, NJ: Rutgers University Press.

Boia, Lucian. 2005. *The Weather in the Imagination*. London: Reaktion Books.

Bojanowski, Axel. 2011. "Naked Bodies and a New Messiah: Green Groups Try to Sex Up Climate Change." *Spiegel Online*, January 3. http://www.spiegel.de/international/world/naked-bodies-and-a-new-messiah-green-groups-try-to-sex-up-climate-change-a-737451.html.

Booth, William. 2006. "Al Gore, Sundance's Leading Man." *Washington Post*, January 26. http://www.washingtonpost.com/wp-dyn/content/article/2006/01/25/AR2006012502230.html.

Bourdieu, Pierre. 1993. *The Field of Cultural Production*. Cambridge: Polity Press.

Boyce, Tammy, and Justin Lewis, eds. 2009. *Climate Change and the Media*. New York: Peter Lang.

Boyer, Paul S. 1992. *When Time Shall Be No More: Prophecy Belief in Modern American Culture*. Cambridge, MA: Belknap Press of Harvard University Press.

Boykoff, Maxwell T. 2011. *Who Speaks for the Climate? Making Sense of Media Reporting on Climate Change*. New York: Cambridge University Press.

Boykoff, Maxwell T. and Jules M. Boykoff. 2004. "Balance as bias: global warming and the U.S. prestige press." *Global Environmental Change*, 15(2):125–36.

Boykoff, Maxwell T., and Jules M. Boykoff. 2007. "Climate Change and Journalistic Norms: A Case-Study of US Mass-Media Coverage." *Geoforum* 38(6):1190–1204.

Brechin, Steven R. 2010. "Public Opinion: A Cross-National View." Pp. 179–209 in *Routledge Handbook of Climate Change and Society*, edited by Constance Lever-Tracy. New York: Routledge.

Brechin, Steven R., and Medani Bhandari. 2011. "Perceptions of Climate Change Worldwide." *Wiley Interdisciplinary Reviews: Climate Change* 2(6):871–885.

Brighenti, Andrea. 2010. *Visibility in Social Theory and Social Research*. New York: Palgrave Macmillan.

Broad, William J. 2007. "From a Rapt Audience, a Call to Cool the Hype." *New York Times*, March 13. http://www.nytimes.com/2007/03/13/science/13gore.html.

Broder, John M. 2011. "U.S. Climate Envoy Seems to Shift Stance on Timetable for New Talks." *New York Times*, December 8. http://www.nytimes.com/2011/12/09/science/earth/us-climate-envoy-seems-to-shift-position-on-time table-for-new-international-talks.html?_r=0.

Brown, Nicolas, dir. 2006. *Global Warming: What You Need to Know*. United States: Discovery Channel.

Buckland, David. 2007. "About Cape Farewell – Cape Farewell – The Cultural Response to Climate Change." http://www.capefarewell.com/about.html.

Buell, Frederick. 2003. *From Apocalypse to Way of Life: Environmental Crisis in the American Century*. New York: Routledge.

Buell, Lawrence. 1995. *The Environmental Imagination: Thoreau, Nature Writing, and the Formation of American Culture*. Cambridge, MA: Belknap Press of Harvard University Press.

Buell, Lawrence. 1998. "Toxic Discourse." *Critical Inquiry* 24(3):639–665.

Buell, Lawrence. 2001. *Writing for an Endangered World: Literature, Culture, and Environment in the U.S. and Beyond*. Cambridge, MA: Belknap Press of Harvard University Press.

Bunting, Madeleine. 2009. "The Rise of Climate-Change Art." *The Guardian*, December 2. http://www.guardian.co.uk/artanddesign/2009/dec/02/climate-change-art-earth-rethink.

Burke, Kenneth. 1945. *A Grammar of Motives*. New York: Prentice Hall.

Burke, Kenneth. 1950. *Rhetoric of Motives*. Berkeley: University of California Press.

Burke, Kenneth. 1984. *Attitudes toward History*. Berkeley: University of California Press.

Burnett, H. Sterling. 2010. "Congress Must Seek Real Science and Real Answers on Climate Issue." *Augusta Chronicle*, February 12, A11.

Butler, Catherine, and Nick Pidgeon. 2009. "Media Communications and Public Understanding of Climate Change: Reporting Scientific Consensus on Anthropogenic Warming." Pp. 43–58 in *Climate Change and the Media*, edited by Justin Lewis and Tammy Boyce. New York: Peter Lang.

Canberra Times. 1997. "Don't Panic on Warming Report, PM Says." November 19, A6.

Canning, Doyle. 2010. "Reclaiming Power: On Copenhagen and Climate Justice | Left Turn – Notes from the Global Intifada." http://www.leftturn.org/Copenhagen-Climate-Justice.

Carey, Mark. 2012. "Climate and History: A Critical Review of Historical Climatology and Climate Change Historiography." *Wiley Interdisciplinary Reviews: Climate Change* 3(3):233–249.

Carrington, Damian. 2010. "There Will Be Blood – Watch Exclusive of 10:10 Campaign's 'No Pressure' Film." *The Guardian*, September 30. http://www.guardian.co.uk/environment/blog/2010/sep/30/10-10-no-pressure-film.

Carson, Rachel. (1962) 2002. *Silent Spring*. Boston: Houghton Mifflin.

Carvalho, Anabela, and Jacquelin Burgess. 2005. "Cultural Circuits of Climate Change in U.K. Broadsheet Newspapers, 1985–2003." *Risk Analysis* 25(6):1457–1469.

Casey, Edward S. 1997. *The Fate of Place: A Philosophical History*. Berkeley: University of California Press.

Chakrabarty, Dipesh. 2009. "The Climate of History: Four Theses." *Critical Inquiry* 35(2):197–222.

Chemnick, Jean, and Lisa Friedman. 2010. "Deal in Cancun Restores Faith in UN Climate Process: But Many Questions Remain." *New York Times*, December 13. http://www.nytimes.com/gwire/2010/12/13/13greenwire-deal-in-cancun-restores-faith-in-un-climate-pro-7267.html?partner=rss&em.

Christian Science Monitor. 1977. "Stem the Global Warming Trend." September 23.

Climate Name Change. 2013. "Climate Name Change." http://www.youtube.com/watch?v=efAUCG9oTb8#t=39.

Collett-White, Mike. 2010. "Japan Dominates Art Newspaper Exhibition Ranking." Reuters, March 31. http://uk.reuters.com/article/2010/03/31/uk-finearts-exhibitions-ranking-idUKTRE62U23F20100331.

Collins, Randall. 2004. *Interaction Ritual Chains.* Princeton, NJ: Princeton University Press.

Cook, Greg. 2007. "Burning Issues." *Boston Phoenix*, June 20. http://thephoenix.com/boston/arts/42125-burning-issues/.

Coolclimate Art Competition. 2010. "Winners Announced." http://www.coolclimate.deviantart.com.

Cornwall Switch. 2005. "Turn on to Energy That Doesn't Cost the Earth." http://www.cornwall-switch.org/why-switch/impact-of-global-warming-on-cornwall.htm.

Cosgrove, Denis E. 1994. "Contested Global Visions: One-World, Whole-Earth, and the Apollo Space Photographs." *Annals of the Association of American Geographers* 84(2):270–294.

Cosgrove, Denis E. 2008. "Images and Imagination in 20th-Century Environmentalism: From the Sierras to the Poles." *Environment and Planning A* 40(8):1862–1880.

Cotgrove, Stephen S. 1982. *Catastrophe or Cornucopia: The Environment, Politics and the Future.* New York. John Wiley.

Cottle, Simon. 1998. "Ulrich Beck, Risk Society and the Media: A Catastrophic View?" *European Journal of Communication* 13(1):5–32.

Cottle, Simon. 2004. *The Racist Murder of Stephen Lawrence: Media Performance and Public Transformation.* Westport, CT: Praeger.

Cottle, Simon. 2008. "Social Drama in Mediated World: The Racist Murder of Stephen Lawrence." Pp. 108–124 in Graham St. John, ed., *Victor Turner and Contemporary Cultural Performance.* New York: Berghahn.

Cottle, Simon. 2013. "Mediatized Disasters in the Global Age: On the Ritualization of Catastrophe." Pp. 259–286 in *The Oxford Handbook of Cultural Sociology*, edited by Jeffery Alexander, Ronald N. Jacobs, and Philip Smith. Oxford: Oxford University Press.

Cox, Robert. 2013. "Climate Change, Media Convergence and Public Uncertainty." Pp. 231–243 in *Environmental Conflict and the Media*, edited by Libby Lester and Brett Hutchins. New York: Peter Lang.

Crate, Susan A. 2011. "Climate and Culture: Anthropology in the Era of Contemporary Climate Change." *Annual Review of Anthropology* 40(1):175–194.

Crate, Susan A., and Mark Nuttall. 2009. *Anthropology and Climate Change: From Encounters to Actions.* Walnut Creek, CA: Left Coast Press.

Cresswell, Tim. 2004. *Place: A Short Introduction*. Malden, MA: Blackwell.

Crilly, Rob. 2007. "A Convenient Excuse." *South of West*. https://robcrilly .wordpress.com/2007/10/15/a-convenient-excuse/.

Cronon, William. 1992. "A Place for Stories: Nature, History, and Narrative." *The Journal of American History* 78(4):1347–76.

Cronon, William. 1996. "In Search of Nature." Pp. 23–52 in *Uncommon Ground: Rethinking the Human Place in Nature*. New York: W. W. Norton.

Cunsolo Willox, Ashlee, et al. 2012. "'From This Place and of This Place': Climate Change, Sense of Place, and Health in Nunatsiavut, Canada." *Social Science and Medicine* 75(3):538–547.

Cuomo, Andrew. 2012. "We Will Lead on Climate Change." *NY Daily News.com*, November 15. http://www.nydailynews.com/opinion/lead-climate-change-article-1.1202221.

Curry, Michael. 1996. "On Space and Spatial Practice in Contemporary Geography." Pp. 3–32 in *Concepts in Human Geography*, edited by Carville Earle, Kent Mathewson, and Martin S Kenzer. Lanham, MD: Rowman and Littlefield.

Curry, Michael. 1998. *Digital Places: Living with Geographic Information Technologies*. New York: Routledge.

Curry, Michael. 2002. "Discursive Displacement and the Seminal Ambiguity of Space and Place." Pp. 502–517 in *The Handbook of New Media*, edited by Leah Lievrouw and Sonia Livingstone. London: Sage.

Daily Telegraph. 2010. "Cancun Climate Conference: What It All Means." December 11. http://www.telegraph.co.uk/earth/environment/climatechange/8196246/Cancun-Climate-Conference-what-it-all-means.html.

Dallas Morning News. 2009. "Our Q and A with Sen. James Inhofe." December 4.

Dauvergne, Peter, and Kate J. Neville. 2011. "Mindbombs of Right and Wrong: Cycles of Contention in the Activist Campaign to Stop Canada's Seal Hunt." *Environmental Politics* 20(2):192–209.

DeBuys, William Eno. 2011. *A Great Aridness: Climate Change and the Future of the American Southwest*. New York: Oxford University Press.

Delingpole, James. 2010. "Eco-fascism Jumps the Shark: Massive, Epic Fail!" *News – Telegraph Blogs*, October 1. http://blogs.telegraph.co.uk/news/jamesdelingpole/100056586/eco-fascism-jumps-the-shark-massive-epic-fail/.

Demeritt, David. 2001. "The Construction of Global Warming and the Politics of Science." *Annals of the Association of American Geographers* 91(2):307–337.

Democracy Now. 2011. "I'm Scared for My Future: Student Disrupts Speech by US Climate Envoy Todd Stern in Durban." December 8. http://www .democracynow.org/2011/12/8/im_scared_for_my_future_student.

Denby, David. 2014. "Man Overboard." *New Yorker*, March 31. http://www .newyorker.com/magazine/2014/04/07/man-overboard.

Dershowitz, Alan. 2001. *Supreme Injustice: How the High Court Hijacked Election 2000*. New York. Oxford University Press.

Deviant Art. 2010a. CoolClimate Homepage and Comments Thread. http://www .coolclimate.deviantart.com/?offset=5#comments.

Deviant Art. 2010b. "*No Pollution Please*." Winning image and thread of responses. http://coolclimate.deviantart.com/art/No-pollution-please-171587779.

Devine-Wright, Patrick. 2013. "Think Global, Act Local? The Relevance of Place Attachments and Place Identities in a Climate Changed World." *Global Environmental Change* 23(1):61–69.

De Waal, Alex. 2007. "Is Climate Change the Culprit for Darfur?" *African Arguments.* http://africanarguments.org/2007/06/25/is-climate-change-the-culprit-for-darfur/.

Dimitrov, Radoslav S. 2010. "Inside Copenhagen: The State of Climate Governance." *Global Environmental Politics* 10(2):18–24.

Dispensa, Jaclyn Marisa, and Robert J. Brulle. 2003. "Media's Social Construction of Environmental Issues: Focus on Global Warming – a Comparative Study." *International Journal of Sociology and Social Policy* 23(10):74–105.

Douglas, Mary. 1994. *Risk and Blame: Essays in Cultural Theory.* London: Routledge.

Douglas, Mary, and Aaron Wildavsky. 1983. *Risk and Culture: An Essay on the Selection of Technical and Environmental Dangers.* Berkeley: University of California Press.

Downing, Phil, and Joe Ballantyne. 2007. *Tipping Point or Turning Point? Social Marketing and Climate Change.* London: Ipsos-Mori.

Doyle, Julie. 2011. *Mediating Climate Change.* Farnham, UK: Ashgate.

Drake, Brian Allen. 2013. *Loving Nature, Fearing the State: Environmentalism and Antigovernment Politics before Reagan.* Weyerhaeuser Environmental Books. Seattle: University of Washington Press.

Dunaway, Finis. 2005. *Natural Visions: The Power of Images in American Environmental Reform.* Chicago: University of Chicago Press.

Dunaway, Finis. 2008. "Gas Masks, Pogo, and the Ecological Indian: Earth Day and the Visual Politics of American Environmentalism." *American Quarterly* 60(1):67–99.

Dunaway, Finis. 2009. "Seeing Global Warming: Contemporary Art and the Fate of the Planet." *Environmental History* 14(1):9–31.

Dunier, Mitchell. 2000. *Sidewalk.* New York: Farrar, Strauss, and Giroux.

Dunlap, Riley, and William Catton. 1994. "Struggling with Human Exemptionalism: The Rise, Decline and Revitalization of Environmental Sociology." *The American Sociologist* 25(1):5–30.

Durkheim, Emile. 1965. *The Elementary Forms of Religious Life.* New York: Free Press.

Durkin, Martin. 2007. *The Great Global Warming Swindle.* London: Channel Four Films.

Duxbury, Lesley. 2010. "A Change in the Climate: New Interpretations and Perceptions of Climate Change through Artistic Interventions and Representations." *Weather, Climate, and Society* 2(4):294–299.

Earthweek1970.org. 1970. "Earth Day 1970: CBS News Special Report with Walter Cronkite." http://earthweek1970.org/videos/.

Economist. 1977. "Changing the Climate." June 4, 88.

Economist. 1979. "From Icebox to Greenhouse." March 17, 96.

EdMass. 2011. "Cop 17 – Speaking Truth to Power – Todd Stern Gets Shellacked." *The Daily Kos,* December 9. http://www.dailykos.com/story/2011/12/09/1043728/-COP-17-Speaking-truth-to-power-Todd-Stern-gets-shellacked.

Edwards, Paul N. 2010. *A Vast Machine: Computer Models, Climate Data, and the Politics of Global Warming*. Cambridge, MA: MIT Press.

Eichler-Levine, Jodi, and Rosemary Hicks. 2007. "'As Americans' against 'Genocide': The Crisis in Darfur and Interreligious Political Activism." *American Quarterly* 59(3):711–735.

Eide, Elisabeth, Risto Kunelius, and Ville Kumpu. 2010. *Global Climate, Local Journalisms: A Transnational Study of How Media Make Sense of Climate Summits*. Bochum: Projectverlag.

Eilperin, Juliet. 2006. "Censorship Is Alleged at NOAA." *Washington Post*, February 11. http://www.washingtonpost.com/wp-dyn/content/article/2006/02/10/AR2006021001766.html.

Entrikin, J. Nicholas. 1991. *The Betweenness of Place*. Baltimore: The Johns Hopkins University Press.

Entrikin, J. N. 1999. "Political Community, Identity and Cosmopolitan Place." *International Sociology* 14(3):269–82

Entrikin, J. Nicholas. 2002. "Democratic Place-Making and Multiculturalism." *Geografiska Annaler. Series B, Human Geography* 84(1):19–25.

Entrikin, J. Nicholas. 2007. "Place Destruction and Cultural Trauma." Pp. 163–179 in *Culture, Society, and Democracy: The Interpretive Approach*, edited by Jeffrey Alexander and Isaac Reed. Boulder, CO: Paradigm Press.

Ereaut, Gill, and Nat Segnit. 2006. *Warm Words: How Are We Telling the Climate Story and Can We Tell It Better?* London: Institute for Public Policy Research.

Erikson, Kai T. 1994. *A New Species of Trouble: Explorations in Disaster, Trauma, and Community*. New York: W. W. Norton.

Ethington, P. J. 2007. "Placing the Past: 'Groundwork' for a Spatial Theory of History." *Rethinking History* 11(4):465–493.

Eyerman, Ron. 2008. *The Assassination of Theo Van Gogh: From Social Drama to Cultural Trauma*. Durham, NC: Duke University Press.

Faris, Stephan. 2007. "The Real Roots of Darfur." *The Atlantic*, April. http://www.theatlantic.com/magazine/archive/2007/04/the-real-roots-of-darfur/305701/.

Faris, Stephan. 2008. "Top 10 Places Already Affected by Climate Change: Scientific American." *Scientific American*, December 23. http://www.scientificamerican.com/article.cfm?id=top-10-places-already-affected-by-climate-change.

Faris, Stephan. 2009. *Forecast: The Consequences of Climate Change, from the Amazon to the Arctic, from Darfur to Napa Valley*. New York: Henry Holt.

Farmer's Guardian. 2005. "Climate Change Offers Opportunities for a Greater Range of Crops." January 7.

Finley, Nolan. 2009. "'Climategate' Puts Warming in Question." *Detroit News*, November 26, B1.

Fleming, James Rodger. 1998. *Historical Perspectives on Climate Change*. New York: Oxford University Press.

Fleming, James Rodger. 2007. *The Callendar Effect: The Life and Times of Guy Stewart Callendar (1898–1964), the Scientist Who Established the Carbon*

Dioxide Theory of Climate Change. Boston: American Meteorological Society. http://link.springer.com/openurl?genre=book&isbn=978-1-878220-76-9.

Folke, Carl, et al. 2011. "Reconnecting to the Biosphere." *AMBIO* 40:719–738.

Forsyth, Tim. 2001. "Critical Realism and Political Ecology." Pp. 146–154 in *After Postmodernism: Critical Realism?*, edited by A. Stainer and G. Lopez. London: Athlone Press.

Foucault, Michel. 1983. *Discourse and Truth: The Problematization of Parrhēsia (Six Lectures Given by Foucault at Berkeley, 1983)*. http://www.naturalthinker.net/trl/texts/Foucault,Michel/Foucault%20-%20Discourse%20and%20truth.pdf.

Foust, Christina R., and William O'Shannon Murphy. 2009. "Revealing and Reframing Apocalyptic Tragedy in Global Warming Discourse." *Environmental Communication: A Journal of Nature and Culture* 3(2):151–167.

Fox News. 2009. "Copenhagen 'Circus' Turning into Feel-Good Jamboree, Critics Say." December 8. http://www.foxnews.com/story/02933579734,00.html.

Fox News. 2010. "Fox Coverage of 10:10 Global Warming Shock Video." http://www.youtube.com/watch?v=jqTdog48ZY4.

Fresque-Baxter, Jennifer A., and Derek Armitage. 2012. "Place Identity and Climate Change Adaptation: A Synthesis and Framework for Understanding." *Wiley Interdisciplinary Reviews: Climate Change* 3(3):251–266.

Friedman, Lisa, and Jean Chemnick. 2010. "Usual Frenzy Is Gone from Climate Talks, but Results Still Seem Distant." *New York Times*, December 6. http://www.nytimes.com/cwire/2010/12/06/06climatewire-usual-frenzy-is-gone-from-climate-talks-but-21843.html.

Friend, Tad. 2014. "Heavy Weather." *New Yorker*, March 10. http://www.newyorker.com/magazine/2014/03/17/heavy-weather-2.

Frumhoff, Peter. 2009. "Contrarians Using Hacked E-mails to Attack Climate Science." http://www.ucsusa.org/news/press_release/hacked-climate-e-mails-0306.html.

Frye, Northrop. 1957. *Anatomy of Criticism; Four Essays*. Princeton, NJ: Princeton University Press.

Frye, Northrop. 1976. *The Secular Scripture: A Study of the Structure of Romance*. Cambridge, MA: Harvard University Press.

Fukuyama, Francis. 1992. *The End of History and the Last Man*. New York: Free Press.

Gamson, William A., and Andre Modigliani. 1989. "Media Discourse and Public Opinion on Nuclear Power: A Constructionist Approach." *American Journal of Sociology* 95(1):1–37.

Gardiner, Stephen M. 2011. *A Perfect Moral Storm: The Ethical Tragedy of Climate Change*. New York: Oxford University Press.

Garrard, Greg. 2001. "Environmentalism and the Apocalyptic Tradition." *Green Letters* 3(1):27–68.

Garrard, Greg. 2011. *Ecocriticism*. 2nd ed. London: Routledge.

Garver, Eugene. 1994. *Aristotle's Rhetoric: An Art of Character*. Chicago: University of Chicago Press.

Geertz, Clifford. 1983. "Local Knowledge: Fact and Law in Comparative Perspective." Pp. 167–234 in *Local Knowledge: Further Essays in Interpretive Anthropology*. New York: Basic Books.

Geoghegan, Hilary, and Catherine Leyson. 2012. "On Climate Change and Cultural Geography: Farming on the Lizard Peninsula, Cornwall, UK." *Climatic Change* 113(1):55–66.

Giannachi, Gabriella. 2012. "Representing, Performing and Mitigating Climate Change in Contemporary Art Practice." *Leonardo* 45(2):124–131.

Giddens, Anthony. 2009. *The Politics of Climate Change*. Cambridge: Polity.

Gieryn, Thomas F. 1999. *Cultural Boundaries of Science: Credibility on the Line*. Chicago: University of Chicago Press.

Gillespie, Ed. 2009. "Plane Stupid's Shock Ads Linking Flights with Polar Bear Deaths Could Fall Flat." *The Guardian*, November 20. http://www.guardian .co.uk/environment/blog/2009/nov/20/polar-bears-plane-stupid.

Glacken, Clarence J. 1967. *Traces on the Rhodian Shore; Nature and Culture in Western Thought from Ancient Times to the End of the Eighteenth Century*. Berkeley: University of California Press.

Globe and Mail. 2010. "Say No to the Jaded Worldview of the Yes Men." May 23. http://www.theglobeandmail.com/globe-debate/editorials/say-no-to-the-jaded-world-view-of-the-yes-men/article4320156/.

Glover, Michael. 2009. "Earth – Art of a Changing World, Royal Academy of Arts, London." *The Independent*, December 9. http://www.independent.co .uk/arts-entertainment/art/reviews/earth-ndash-art-of-a-changing-world-royal-academy-of-arts-london-1835286.html.

Goffman, Erving. 1959. *The Presentation of Self in Everyday Life*. New York: Doubleday.

Goodwin, Jeff, and James M. Jasper. 2006. "Emotions and Social Movements." Pp. 610–631 in *Handbook of the Sociology of Emotions*, edited by Jan E. Stets and Jonathan H. Turner. New York: Springer.

Gore, Al. 2012. "Statement on Hurricane Sandy." *Al Gore* (blog), October 30. http://blog.algore.com/2012/10/statement_on_hurricane_sandy.html.

Gormley, Antony. 2010. "Art's Lost Subject." *The Guardian*, February 12. http://www.guardian.co.uk/artanddesign/2010/feb/13/antony-gormley-climate-change-art.

Gorski, Philip S. 2012. "Recovered Goods: Durkheimian Sociology as Virtue Ethics." Pp. 77–104 in Philip Gorski, David Kyuman Kim, John Torpey, and Jonathan VanAntwerpen, eds., *The Post-secular in Question: Religion in Contemporary Society*. New York: Social Science Research Council and New York University Press.

Graham, Stephen. 2011. *Cities Under Siege*. London: Verso.

Gramsci, Antonio. 1992. *Prison Notebooks Volume 1*. New York: Columbia University Press.

Gray, Louise. 2012. "Doha: Talks on Brink of Collapse as Anger Rises against Qatari Hosts." *Daily Telegraph*, December 6. http://www.telegraph.co.uk/ earth/environment/9727685/Doha-Talks-on-brink-of-collapse-as-anger-rises-against-Qatari-hosts.htm.

Great Britain. 2006. *The Economics of Climate Change: Stern Review on the Economics of Climate Change*. England: HM Treasury.

Grove, Richard. 1995. *Green Imperialism: Colonial Expansion, Tropical Island Edens, and the Origins of Environmentalism, 1600–1860*. Cambridge: Cambridge University Press.

Grundmann, Reiner. 2012a. "'Climategate' and the Scientific Ethos." *SSRN e-Library*. http://papers.ssrn.com/sol3/papers.cfm?abstract_id=2047403.

Grundmann, Reiner. 2012b. "The Legacy of Climategate: Revitalizing or Under-mining Climate Science and Policy?" *Wiley Interdisciplinary Reviews: Climate Change* 3(3):281–288.

Guardian. 2013. "Reverend Billy faces year in prison for JP Morgan Chase Toad Protest." November 25. http://www.theguardian.com/environment/2013/nov/25/reverend-billy-jpmorgan-chase-toad-protest-talen?CMP=twt_fd&CMP=SOCxx2I2.

Guggenheim, Davis, dir. 2006. *An Inconvenient Truth*. United States: Paramount Pictures Corporation.

Gunter, Valerie, and Steve Kroll-Smith. 2007. *Volatile Places: A Sociology of Communities and Environmental Controversies*. Thousand Oaks, CA.: Pine Forge Press.

Guydenning. 2006. Online response to Hubbard 2006. http://www.newstatesman.com/200612040038.

Halbwachs, Maurice. 1992. *On Collective Memory*. Edited by Lewis A. Coser. Chicago: University of Chicago Press.

Hall, Stuart. 1973. "The Determinations of News Photographs." Pp. 176–190 in *The Manufacture of News: Deviance, Social Problems and the Mass Media*, edited by S. Cohen and J. Young. London: Constable.

Hamblyn, Richard. 2009. "The Whistleblower and the Canary: Rhetorical Con-structions of Climate Change." *Journal of Historical Geography* 35(2):223–236.

Hardin, Garrett. 1968. "The Tragedy of the Commons." *Science* 162(3859):1243–1248.

Harris, Richard. 2011. "At Climate Talks, Frustration and Interruptions." *NPR.org*. December 8. http://www.npr.org/2011/12/08/143379789/at-climate-talks-frustration-and-interruptions.

Harvey, David. 1996. *Justice, Nature and the Geography of Difference*. Oxford: Blackwell.

Harvey, David. 2000. *Spaces of Hope*. Berkeley: University of California Press.

Harvey, David. 2009. "Places, Regions, Territories." Pp. 166–201 in *Cosmopoli-tanism and the Geographies of Freedom*. New York: Columbia University Press.

Harvey, Eugenie. 2010. "Statement from 10:10 UK Director." http://www.1010global.org/uk/2010/10/statement-1010-uk-director.

Hass, Kristin Ann. 1998. *Carried to the Wall: American Memory and the Vietnam Veterans Memorial*. Berkeley: University of California Press.

Hegel, Georg Wilhelm Friedrich. 1975. *Aesthetics/Lectures on Fine Art, Volume Two*. Translated by T. M. Knox. Oxford: Oxford University Press.

Heinlein, Kurt Gerard. 2007. *Green Theatre: Promoting Ecological Preservation and Advancing the Sustainability of Humanity and Nature*. Saarbrucken: VDM Verlag.

Heise, Ursula K. 2008. *Sense of Place and Sense of Planet: The Environmental Imagination of the Global*. New York: Oxford University Press.

Henig, Jess. 2009. "Climategate." *FactCheck.org*. http://www.factcheck.org/2009/12/climategate/.

Henry, Holly, and Amanda Taylor. 2009. "Re-thinking Apollo: Envisioning Environmentalism in Space." *Sociological Review* 57:190–203.

Hertsgaard, Mark. 2012. "Hurricane Sandy as Greek Tragedy." *The Nation.com*, October 30. http://www.thenation.com/article/170918/hurricane-sandy-greek-tragedy.

Hess, Jeremy J., Josephine N. Malilay, and Alan J. Parkinson. 2008. "Climate Change: The Importance of Place." *American Journal of Preventive Medicine* 35(5):468–478.

Heymann, Matthias. 2010. "The Evolution of Climate Ideas and Knowledge." *Wiley Interdisciplinary Reviews: Climate Change* 1(4):581–597.

Hilgartner, Stephen. 2000. *Science on Stage: Expert Advice as Public Drama*. Stanford, CA: Stanford University Press.

Hinkle, A. Barton. 2010. "Hinkle: First They Came for the Climatologists . . ." *Richmond Times-Dispatch*, May 11.

Hogan, Trevor, Divya Anand, and Kirsten Henderson. 2010. "Environment and Culture." Pp. 337–346 in *Handbook of Cultural Sociology*, edited by John R. Hall, Laura Grindstaff, and Ming-cheng Lo. Hoboken, NJ: Routledge.

Houser, Heather. 2014. *Ecosickness in Contemporary U.S. Fiction: Environment and Affect*. New York: Columbia University Press.

Howe, Joshua P. 2012. "The Stories We Tell." *Historical Studies in the Natural Sciences* 42(3):244–254.

Howe, Joshua P. 2014. *Behind the Curve: Science and the Politics of Global Warming*. Seattle: University of Washington Press.

Hubbard, Sue. 2006. "The New Romantics." *New Statesman*, December 4.

Hulme, Mike. 2008. "Geographical Work at the Boundaries of Climate Change." *Transactions of the Institute of British Geographers* 33(1):5–11.

Hulme, Mike. 2009. *Why We Disagree about Climate Change: Understanding Controversy, Inaction and Opportunity*. Cambridge: Cambridge University Press.

Hulme, Mike. 2010. "Problems with Making and Governing Global Kinds of Knowledge" *Global Environmental Change* 20:558–564.

Hulme, Mike. 2014. "Climate Change and Virtue: An Apologetic." *Humanities* 3(3):299–312.

Hulme, Mike, and Jerome Ravetz. 2009. "'Show Your Working': What 'Climate-Gate' means." *BBC*, December 1. http://news.bbc.co.uk/2/hi/8388485.stm.

Ignatow, Gabriel. 2007. *Transnational Identity Politics and the Environment*. Lanham, MD: Lexington Books.

Intergovernmental Panel on Climate Change (IPCC). 1995. *Summary for Policymakers: The Economic and Social Dimensions of Climate Change – IPCC*

Working Group III. http://www.ipcc.ch/publications_and_data/publications_and_data_reports.shtml#1.

Intergovernmental Panel on Climate Change (IPCC). 2014. *Fifth Assessment Report (AR5).* http://www.ipcc.ch/.

Jacobs, Ronald N. 2000. *Race, Media, and the Crisis of Civil Society: From Watts to Rodney King.* New York: Cambridge University Press.

Jacobs, Ronald N., and Philip Smith. 1997. "Romance, Irony, and Solidarity." *Sociological Theory* 15(1):60–80.

Jacobs, Ronald N., and Eleanor Townsley. 2011. *The Space of Opinion: Media Intellectuals and the Public Sphere.* New York: Oxford University Press.

Jacques, Peter J. 2009. *Environmental Skepticism.* Farnham, UK: Ashgate.

Jacques, Peter, R. E. Dunlap, and M. Freeman. 2008. "The Organisation of Denial: Conservative Think Tanks and Environmental Skepticism." *Environmental Politics* 17(3):349–385.

Jameson, Fredric. 1984. "Postmodernism, or The Cultural Logic of Late Capitalism." *New Left Review* 46:53–92.

Jamieson, Dale. 2011. "The Nature of the Problem." Pp. 38–54 in *The Oxford Handbook of Climate Change and Society*, edited by John S. Dryzek, Richard B. Norgaard, and David Schlosberg. New York: Oxford University Press.

Jamieson, Dale. 2014. *Reason in a Dark Time: Why the Struggle against Climate Change Failed – and What It Means for Our Future.* New York: Oxford University Press.

Jasanoff, Sheila. 2001. "Image and Imagination: The Formation of Global Environmental Consciousness." Pp. 309–337 in *Changing the Atmosphere: Expert Knowledge and Environmental Governance*, edited by Clark Miller and Paul Edwards. Cambridge, MA: MIT Press.

Jasanoff, Sheila. 2010a. "A New Climate for Society." *Theory, Culture, and Society* 27(2–3):233–253.

Jasanoff, Sheila. 2010b. "Testing Time for Climate Science." *Science* 328(5979):695–696.

Jasanoff, Sheila. 2011. "Cosmopolitan Knowledge: Climate Science and Global Civic Epistemology." Pp. 129–143 in *The Oxford Handbook of Climate Change and Society*, edited by John S. Dryzek, Richard B. Norgaard, and David Schlosberg. Oxford: Oxford University Press.

Jasanoff, Sheila. 2012. *Science and Public Reason.* New York: Routledge.

Jasanoff, Sheila, and Brian Wynne. 1998. "Science and Decisionmaking." Pp. 1–87 in *Human Choice and Climate Change*, edited by Steve Rayner and Elizabeth L. Malone. Columbus, OH: Battelle Press.

Jerusalem Post. 1997. "Planet Health Warning." December 7, 8.

Jervey, Ben. 2011. "COP16 Cancún Climate Talks: Everything You Need to Know." *GOOD.* http://www.good.is/posts/cancun-climate-talks-give-us-something-to-feel-good-about-for-a-little-while.

Johnson, Brad. 2011. "Durban Climate Hero Abigail Borah: I Am Speaking on Behalf of the United States of America Because My Negotiators Cannot." *Climate Progress*, December 8. http://thinkprogress.org/climate/2011/12/08/385820/durban-climate-hero-abigail-borah-i-am-speaking-on-behalf-of-the-united-states-of-america-because-my-negotiators-cannot/?mobile=nc.

Kador, John. 2013. "Why Lance Armstrong's Apology Was Just Plain Sorry." *Wall Street Journal*, January 18. http://blogs.wsj.com/speakeasy/2013/01/18/why-lance-armstrongs-apology-was-just-plain-sorry/.

Kahan, Dan. 2010. "Fixing the Communications Failure." *Nature* 463(7279): 296–297.

Kahan, Dan. 2012a. "Why We Are Poles Apart on Climate Change." *Nature* 488(7411):255.

Kahan, Dan. 2012b. "Cultural Cognition as a Conception of the Cultural Theory of Risk." Pp. 725–759 in *Handbook of Risk Theory*, edited by Sabine Roeser, Rafaela Hillerbrand, Per Sandin, and Martin Peterson. Amsterdam: Springer.

Kahan, Dan M., Hank Jenkins-Smith, and Donald Braman. 2011. "Cultural Cognition of Scientific Consensus." *Journal of Risk Research* 14(2):147–174.

Kaufman, Leslie. 2010. "Climate Video Gets a Thumbs Down from Critics." *Green Blog*. http://green.blogs.nytimes.com/2010/10/04/climate-video-gets-a-thumbs-down-from-critics/.

Kearns, Laurel. 2011. "The Role of Religions in Activism." Pp. 414–430 in *The Oxford Handbook of Climate Change and Society*, edited by John S. Dryzek, Kari Marie Norgaard, and David Schlosberg. Oxford: Oxford University Press.

Keenlyside, N. S., Mojib Latif, J. Jungclaus, L. Kornblueh, and E. Roeckner. 2008. "Advancing Decadal-Scale Climate Prediction in the North Atlantic Sector." *Nature* 453(7191):84–88.

Kelsey, Colleen. 2013. "MoMa PS1's Current Climate." *Namac/Engage Interview Art Magazine*, May. http://engagenamac.tumblr.com/post/48895311441/momaps1-interview-magazine-art-moma-ps1s.

Kennedy, George Alexander. 1984. *New Testament Interpretation through Rhetorical Criticism*. Chapel Hill: University of North Carolina Press.

Kennedy, Maev. 2001. "Art's Old Masters Draw the Queues." *The Guardian*, February 9. http://www.guardian.co.uk/culture/2001/feb/10/artsfeatures2.

Killingsworth, M. J., and J. S. Palmer. 1996. "Millennial Ecology: The Apocalyptic Narrative from Silent Spring to Global Warming." *Green Culture: Environmental Rhetoric in Contemporary America* 21–45.

Klein, Ezra. 2006. "The New New Gore." *The American Prospect*, March 21. http://prospect.org/article/new-new-gore-0.

Klein, Naomi. 2011. "Capitalism vs. the Climate." *The Nation*, November 9. http://www.thenation.com/article/164497/capitalism-vs-climate.

Kling, George, et al. 2003. *Confronting Climate Change in the Great Lakes Region*. Cambridge, MA: Union of Concerned Scientists. http://go.ucsusa.org/greatlakes/glchallengereport.html.

Kloor, Keith. 2012. "The Great Schism in the Environmental Movement." *Slate*, December 12. http://www.slate.com/articles/health_and_science/science/2012/12/modern_green_movement_eco_pragmatists_are_challenging_traditional_environmentalists.html.

Krosnick, Jon A., and Bo MacInnis. 2013. "Does the American Public Support Legislation to Reduce Greenhouse Gas Emissions?" *Daedalus* 142(1):26–39.

Krugman, Paul. 2011. "William Cronon and the American Thought Police." *New York Times*, March 27.

Kuhner, Jeffrey T. 2009. "A Convenient Lie; Radical Environmentalists Seek Secular Utopia." *Washington Times*, December 13. http://www.washingtontimes.com/news/2009/dec/13/a-convenient-lie/?page=all.

LaBarre, Suzanne. 2013. "Why We're Shutting Off Our Comments." *Popular Science*, September 24. http://www.popsci.com/science/article/2013-09/why-were-shutting-our-comments.

Lahsen, Myanna. 2008. "Experiences of Modernity in the Greenhouse: A Cultural Analysis of a Physicist 'Trio' Supporting the Backlash against Global Warming." *Global Environmental Change* 18(1):204–219.

Landsberg, Michele. 1992. "12-Year-Old Urges Leaders to Stop Poisoning World." *The Toronto Star*, July 21, B1.

Langer, Susanne. 1957. *Problems of Art: Ten Philosophical Lectures*. New York: Scribner.

Latour, Bruno. 2012. "Love Your Monsters – Why We Must Care for Our Technologies As We Do Our Children." *The Breakthrough Journal*, Winter. http://thebreakthrough.org/index.php/journal/past-issues/issue-2/love-your-monsters/.

Lawson, Nigel. 2008. *An Appeal to Reason: A Cool Look at Global Warming*. New York: Overlook Duckworth.

Lean, Geoffrey. 2010. "Cancun Climate Change Summit: Back from the Brink." *Daily Telegraph*, December 13. http://www.telegraph.co.uk/earth/earthcomment/geoffrey-lean/8198215/Cancun-climate-change-summit-Back-from-the-brink.html.

Leiserowitz, Anthony. 2006. "Climate Change Risk Perception and Policy Preferences: The Role of Affect, Imagery, and Values." *Climatic Change* 77(1):45–72.

Leiserowitz, Anthony, Edward Maibach, Connie Roser-Renouf, Geoff Feinberg, and Peter Howe. 2013. *Global Warming's Six Americas, September 2012*. New Haven, CT: Yale University and George Mason University, Yale Project on Climate Change Communication. http://environment.yale.edu/climate/publications/Six-Americas-September-2012.

Leitner, H., E. Sheppard, and K. M. Sziarto. 2008. "The Spatialities of Contentious Politics." *Transactions of the Institute of British Geographers* 33(2):157–172.

Lester, Libby, and Brett Hutchins, eds. 2013. *Environmental Conflict and the Media*. New York: Peter Lang.

Lewis, Barbara, and Alister Doyle. 2012. "Despair after Climate Conference: But UN Still Offers Hope." *Reuters*, December 9. http://www.reuters.com/article/2012/12/09/climate-talks-process-idUSL5E8N7BQV20121209.

Lewis, Justin, and Tammy Boyce. 2009. "Climate Change and the Media: The Scale of the Challenge." Pp. 4–16 in *Climate Change and the Media*, edited by Justin Lewis and Tammy Boyce. New York: Peter Lang.

Lindzen, Richard. 2006. "Climate of Fear." *Wall Street Journal*, April 12, A14.

Lipschutz, Ronnie, and Corina McKendry. 2011. "Social Movements and Global Civil Society." Pp. 369–383 in *The Oxford Handbook of Climate Change and Society*, edited by John S. Dryzek, Richard B. Norgaard, and David Schlosberg. Oxford: Oxford University Press.

Lomborg, Bjørn. 2006. "Stern Review." *Wall Street Journal, Eastern edition*, November 2, A12.

Lomborg, Bjørn. 2009. "Disastrous Strategy Won't Ease Global Warming." *Providence Journal*, December 18, 10.

Lorenzoni, Irene, and Nick F. Pidgeon. 2006. "Public Views on Climate Change: European and USA Perspectives." *Climatic Change* 77(1–2):73–95.

Lowell Sun. 2009. "All the President's Climategate Deniers." December 5, Opinions Section.

Luhmann, Niklas. 1989. *Ecological Communication*. Chicago: University of Chicago Press.

Luke, Timothy W. 2011. "Environmentality." Pp. 96–109 in *The Oxford Handbook of Climate Change and Society*, edited by John S. Dryzek, Richard B. Norgaard, and David Schlosberg. New York: Oxford University Press.

Maddow, Rachel. 2013. "Exclusive: Governor Cuomo on the Wrath of Superstorm Sandy." *Gotham Magazine*, January 15. http://gotham-magazine.com/personalities/articles/exclusive-rachel-maddow-interviews-governor-andrew-cuomo-on-superstorm-sandy.

Maher, Neil. 2004. "Neil Maher on Shooting the Moon." *Environmental History* 9(3):526–531.

Maibach, E., et al. 2012. "The Legacy of Climategate: Undermining or Revitalizing Climate Science and Policy?" *Wiley Interdisciplinary Reviews: Climate Change* 3(3):289–95.

Maibach, Edward, et al. 2013. *A National Survey of Republicans and Republican-Leaning Independents on Energy and Climate Change*. George Mason Center for Climate Change Communication and Yale Project on Climate Change Communication. http://climatechangecommunication.org/report/national-survey-republicans-and-republican-leaning-independents-energy-and-climate-change.

Malone, Elizabeth L. 2009. *Debating Climate Change: Pathways through Argument to Agreement*. Sterling, VA: Earthscan.

Marshall, George. 2013. "Climate Change Activists Are Playing a Dangerous Game with Their Enemy Narrative." *The Guardian*, November 16. http://www.theguardian.com/commentisfree/2013/nov/16/climate-change-dangerous-game-enemy-narrative.

Martin, Colin. 2006. "Science in Culture: Artists on a Mission." *Nature* 441(7093):578–578.

Martin, Colin. 2009. "Artistic Dispatches on Climate." *Nature* 462 (7275):852.

Martin, D. G., and B. Miller. 2003. "Space and Contentious Politics." *Mobilization: An International Quarterly* 8(2):143–156.

Mast, Jason L. 2006. "The Cultural Pragmatics of Event-ness: The Clinton/Lewinsky Affair." Pp. 115–145 in *Social Performance: Symbolic Action, Cultural Pragmatics, and Ritual*, edited by Jeffrey C Alexander, Bernhard Giesen, and Jason L. Mast. New York: Cambridge University Press.

Mast, Jason L. 2012. *The Performative Presidency: Crisis and Resurrection during the Clinton Years*. Cambridge: Cambridge University Press.

Mazo, Jeffrey. 2010. *Climate Conflict: How Global Warming Threatens Security and What to Do about It*. New York: Routledge and the International Institute for Strategic Studies.

McCammack, Brian. 2007. "Hot Damned America: Evangelicalism and the Climate Change Policy Debate." *American Quarterly* 59(3):645–668.

McCormick, Lisa. 2009. "Higher, Faster, Louder: Representations of the International Music Competition." *Cultural Sociology* 3(1):5–30.

McCright, Aaron M., and Riley E. Dunlap. 2000. "Challenging Global Warming as a Social Problem: An Analysis of the Conservative Movement's Counter-Claims." *Social Problems* 47(4):499–522.

McCright, Aaron M., and Riley E. Dunlap. 2003. "Defeating Kyoto: The Conservative Movement's Impact on U.S. Climate Change Policy." *Social Problems* 50(3):348–373.

McCright, Aaron M., and Riley E. Dunlap. 2010. "Anti-Reflexivity: The American Conservative Movement's Success in Undermining Climate Science and Policy." *Theory, Culture, and Society* 27(2–3):100–133.

McCright, Aaron M., and Riley E. Dunlap. 2011. "The Politicization of Climate Change and Polarization in the American Public's Views of Global Warming, 2001–2010." *Sociological Quarterly* 52(2):155–194.

McEwan, Ian. 2010. *Solar: A Novel*. New York: Doubleday.

McFarland, Daniel A. 2004. "Resistance as a Social Drama: A Study of Change-Oriented Encounters." *American Journal of Sociology* 109(6):1249–1318.

McIlroy, Anne. 2003. "Don't Call Her an Environmentalist." *Globe and Mail*, February 1.

McKibben, Bill. 2005. "What the Warming World Needs Now Is Art, Sweet Art." *Grist*, April 22. http://grist.org/living/mckibben-imagine/.

McKibben, Bill. 2008. *Deep Economy: The Wealth of Communities and the Durable Future*. Later printing. New York: Holt Paperbacks.

McKibben, Bill. 2009. "Four Years after My Pleading Essay, Climate Art is Hot." *Grist*. August 6. http://grist.org/article/2009-08-05-essay-climate-art-update-bill-mckibben/.

McKibben, Bill. 2010. *Eaarth: Making a Life on a Tough New Planet*. New York: Time Books.

McKibben, Bill. 2012a. "Global Warming's Terrifying New Math." *Rollingstone.com*, July 19. http://www.rollingstone.com/politics/news/global-warmings-terrifying-new-math-20120719.

McKibben, Bill. 2012b. "Name Storms after Oil Companies – They're the Ones Most Responsible for Climate Change." *New York Daily News*. http://www.nydailynews.com/blogs/the_rumble/2012/10/name-storms-after-oil-companies-theyre-the-ones-most-responsible-for-climate-chan.

McNeill, J. R. 2008. "Can History Help Us with Global Warming?" Pp. 26–48 in *Climatic Cataclysm: The Foreign Policy and National Security Implications of Climate Change*, edited by Kurt M. Campbell. Washington, DC: Brookings Institution Press.

McVeigh, Tracy. 2010. "Backlash over Richard Curtis's 10:10 Climate Film." *The Guardian*, October 2. http://www.guardian.co.uk/environment/2010/oct/02/1010-richard-curtis-climate-change.

Merchant, Carolyn. 2004. *Reinventing Eden: The Fate of Nature in Western Culture*. London: Routledge.

Merinda, Kevin. 1999. "Gore and the Bore Effect." *Washington Post*, June 7, CO1.

Merton, Robert K. 1973. *The Sociology of Science: Theoretical and Empirical Investigations*. Chicago: University of Chicago Press.

Michaels, Patrick. 2008. "Global-Warming Myth." Washington Times, May 16. http://www.washingtontimes.com/news/2008/may/16/global-warming-myth/.

Michaels, Patrick J. 2009. "How to Manufacture a Climate Consensus." *Wall Street Journal*, December 17.

Miles, Malcolm. 2010. "Representing Nature: Art and Climate Change." *Cultural Geographies* 17(1):19–35.

Miller, Carolyn R. 2003. "The Presumptions of Expertise: The Role of Ethos in Risk Analysis." *Configurations* 11(2):163–202.

Monbiot, George. 2009. "Why the Mediterranean Climate Message Is All Wrong." *The Guardian*, June 18. http://www.guardian.co.uk/environment/georgemonbiot/2009/jun/18/monbiot-climate-impacts.

Moon, Ban Ki. 2007. "A Climate Culprit in Darfur." *Washington Post*, June 16. http://www.washingtonpost.com/wp-dyn/content/article/2007/06/15/AR2007061501857.html.

Morse, Kathryn. 2012. "There Will Be Birds: Images of Oil Disasters in the Nineteenth and Twentieth Centuries." *Journal of American History* 99(1):124–134.

Moser, Susanne C. 2010. "Communicating Climate Change: History, Challenges, Process and Future Directions." *Wiley Interdisciplinary Reviews: Climate Change* 1(1):31–53.

Moser, Susanne C., and Lisa Dilling, eds. 2007. *Creating a Climate for Change: Communicating Climate Change and Facilitating Social Change*. Cambridge: Cambridge University Press.

Müller, Benito. 2011. *UNFCCC – the Future of the Process: Remedial Action on Process Ownership and Political Guidance*. Oxford: Climate Strategies. http://www.oxfordclimatepolicy.org/publications/documents/UNFCCC-TheFutureoftheProcess.pdf.

Nature. 2010. "Science Subpoenaed." May 13, 135–136.

Nerlich, Brigitte. 2010. "'Climategate': Paradoxical Metaphors and Political Paralysis." *Environmental Values* 19(4):419–442.

New Jersey Future. 2012. "Rebuilding a Resilient New Jersey Shore." http://www.njfuture.org/cevents/special-events/rebuilding-the-shore/.

Newman, Melanie. 2008. "Debate Is an Endangered Species, Says Climate Critic." *Times Higher Education*. http://www.timeshighereducation.co.uk/news/debate-is-an-endangered-species-says-climate-critic/403382.article.

New York Times. 1969. "Physical Scientist . . ." December 21, 46.

New York Times. 1983. "Excerpts from Climate Report." October 21, B5.

New York Times. 1986. "Scientists Warn of Effects of Human Activity in Atmosphere." January 13, 11.

New York Times. 2003. "Censorship on Global Warming." June 20. http://www.nytimes.com/2003/06/20/opinion/censorship-on-global-warming.html.

New York Times. 2009. "That Climate Change E-mail." December 6. http://www.nytimes.com/2009/12/06/opinion/06sun3.html?_r=0.

Nietzsche, Friedrich Wilhelm. 2000. *The Birth of Tragedy*. Oxford: Oxford University Press.

Nisbet, Matthew C., and Teresa Myers. 2007. "The Polls – Trends Twenty Years of Public Opinion about Global Warming." *Public Opinion Quarterly* 71(3):444–470.

Nixon, Rob. 2011. *Slow Violence and the Environmentalism of the Poor*. Cambridge, MA: Harvard University Press.

Nora, Pierre. 2001–2010. *Les lieux de mémoire*. Chicago: University of Chicago Press.

Nordhaus, Ted, and Michael Shellenberger. 2004. *The Death of Environmentalism: Global Warming Politics in a Post-environmental World*. http://www.thebreakthrough.org/images/Death_of_Environmentalism.pdf.

Nordhaus, Ted, and Michael Shellenberger. 2007. *Break Through: From the Death of Environmentalism to the Politics of Possibility*. Boston: Houghton Mifflin.

Norgaard, Kari Marie. 2011. *Living in Denial: Climate Change, Emotions, and Everyday Life*. Cambridge, MA: MIT Press.

Norris, Scott. 2009. "Contemporary Art and Climate Change: Rethink Opens in Copenhagen." *ArtCulture*, October 24. http://artculture.com/art-news/contemporary-art-and-climate-change.

Nussbaum, Martha C. 1996. "Aristotle on Emotions and Rational Persuasion." Pp. 303–323 in *Essays on Aristotle's Rhetoric*, edited by Amélie Oksenberg Rorty. Berkeley: University of California Press.

Nussbaum, Martha C. 2012. "Who Is the Happy Warrior? Philosophy, Happiness Research, and Public Policy." *International Review of Economics* 59(4):335–361.

Nye, David E. 2010. *When the Lights Went Out: A History of Blackouts in America*. Cambridge, MA: MIT Press.

O'Hanlon, Eilis. 2007. "Don't Put Your Faith in the Evils of Global Warming." *Sunday Independent*, December 30. http://www.independent.ie/irish-news/dont-put-your-faith-in-the-evils-of-global-warming-26341598.html.

O'Leary, Stephen D. 1994. *Arguing the Apocalypse: A Theory of Millennial Rhetoric*. New York: Oxford University Press.

Olmsted, Wendy. 2006. *Rhetoric: An Historical Introduction*. Malden, MA: Blackwell.

Oreskes, Naomi, and Erik M. Conway. 2010. *Merchants of Doubt: How a Handful of Scientists Obscured the Truth on Issues from Tobacco Smoke to Global Warming*. New York: Bloomsbury Press.

Palmlund, Ingar. 1992. "Social Drama and Risk Perception." Pp. 197–212 in *Social Theories of Risk*, edited by Sheldon Krimsky and Dominic Golding. Westport, CT: Praeger.

Paradi, David. 2009. "Presentation Lessons from 'An Inconvenient Truth.'" http://www.thinkoutsidetheslide.com/articles/inconvenienttruth.html.

Parenti, Christian. 2012. *Tropic of Chaos: Climate Change and the New Geography of Violence*. New York. Nation Books.

Pearce, Fred. 2010. *The Climate Files: The Battle for the Truth about Global Warming*. London: Random House.

Pearce, Fred, and Catherine Brahic. 2009. "Copenhagen Diaries: Capitalist Gods and Socialist Tantrums." *New Scientist*, December 18. http://www .newscientist.com/article/dn18306-copenhagen-diaries-capitalist-gods-and-socialist-tantrums.html.

Perrot, Michele. 1980. *L'Impossible Prison*. Paris: Editions du Seuil.

Pielke, Roger, Jr. 2009. "The 'Trick' in Context." *Rober Pielke Jr.'s Blog*. http://rogerpielkejr.blogspot.com/2009/12/trick-in-context.html.

Pittman, Joanna. 2009. "Earth: Art of a Changing World at the Royal Academy." *The Times (London)*, December 2. http://www.thetimes.co.uk/tto/arts/visualarts/article2423563.ece.

Plotz, David. 2014. "Noah's Environmental Views Are a Disaster." *Slate*, March 29. http://www.slate.com/blogs/browbeat/2014/03/29/noah_environmental_message_darren_aronofsky_s_movie_is_wrong_about_the_environment.html.

Popper, Karl. 1971. *The Open Society and Its Enemies, Volume Two: Hegel, Marx and the Aftermath*. Princeton, NJ: Princeton University Press.

Potter, Emily. 2012. "Environmental Art and the Production of Publics: Responding to Environmental Change." *International Journal of the Arts in Society* 3:1–6.

Pred, Allan. 1984. "Place as Historically Contingent Process: Structuration and the Time-Geography of Becoming Places." *Annals of the Association of American Geographers* 74(2):279–297.

Prins, Gwyn, et al. 2010. *The Hartwell Paper*. Institute for Science, Innovation and Society, University of Oxford and LSE Mackinder Programme for the Study of Long Wave Events. http://www2.lse.ac.uk/researchAndExpertise/units/mackinder/theHartwellPaper/Home.aspx.

Quinn, Michelle. 2008. "Duarte Design Helps Other Firms Make a Point." *Los Angeles Times*, September 15, Small Business Section.

Radkau, Joachim. 2012. "Religion and Environmentalism." Pp. 493–512 in *A Companion to Global Environmental History*, edited by J. R. McNeill and Erin Stewart Mauldin. Malden, MA: Wiley-Blackwell.

Rayner, Steve. 2009. "Foreword." Pp. xxi–xxiv in *Why We Disagree about Climate Change: Understanding Controversy, Inaction and Opportunity*. Cambridge: Cambridge University Press.

Rayner, Steve, and Michael Thompson. 1998. "Cultural Discourses." Pp. 265–343 in *Human Choice and Climate Change*, edited by Elizabeth L. Malone and Steve Rayner. Columbus, OH: Battelle Press.

Rebhy, Abdullah. 2012. "Lawyer: Qatari Poet Gets Life after Insulting Emir." *Associated Press*, November 29. http://bigstory.ap.org/article/lawyer-qatari-poet-gets-life-insulting-emir.

Rebuild by Design. 2013. "Rebuild by Design: Innovating by Design: Innovating Together to Create a Resilient Region." http://rebuildbydesign.org/.

Reuters. 2012. "Activists Deported after Doha Climate Protest." *Arabian-Business.com*, December 7. http://www.arabianbusiness.com/activists-deported-after-doha-climate-protest-482029.html.

Revkin, Andrew. 2011. "Young Voices Reverberate at Indeterminate Climate Talks." *New York Times*, December 10. http://dotearth.blogs.nytimes.com/2011/12/10/young-voices-at-deadlocked-durban-climate-talks/?_r=0.

Revkin, Andrew C. 2012. "On 'Frankenstorms,' Climate Science and 'Reverse Tribalism.'" *New York Times, Dot Earth Blog*, October 29. http://dotearth .blogs.nytimes.com/2012/10/29/on-frankenstorms-climate-science-and-reverse-tribalism/.

Revoir, Paul. 2009. "Climate Change Advert Featuring Drowning Puppies Is Probed by Watchdog after 350 Complaints." *Mail Online*, October 21. http://www.dailymail.co.uk/news/article-1221916/Climate-change-advert-featuring-drowning-puppies-dying-rabbits-probed-watchdog-350-complaints. html.

Richmond Times-Dispatch. 2010. "Global Warming: Unhealthy Climate." October 15, Commentary Section.

Ringmar, Erik. 2006. "Inter-Textual Relations: The Quarrel over the Iraq War as a Conflict between Narrative Types." *Cooperation and Conflict* 41(4):403–421.

Roach, David. 2008. "Gore Cites Political Will, Claims Scriptural Mandate on Environmental Issues." *Baptist Press*, January 31. http://www.bpnews.net/ bpnews.asp?ID=27293.

Roald, Vebjørn, and Linda Sangolt. 2012. *Deliberation, Rhetoric, and Emotion in the Discourse on Climate Change in the European Parliament*. Delft, Netherlands: Eburon Academic.

Roanoke Times, May 9, 2010 Sunday Metro Edition. "The commonwealth's inquisitor general." Editorial; Pg. 2.

Roberts, David. 2006. "An Interview with Accidental Movie Star Al Gore." *Grist*, May 10. http://grist.org/article/roberts2/.

Roberts, David. 2012. "Hawks vs. Scolds: How 'Reverse Tribalism' Affects Climate Communication." *Grist*, October 20. http://grist.org/climate-energy/ hawks-vs-scolds-how-reverse-tribalism-affects-climate-communication/.

Rohloff, Amanda. 2011. "Extending the Concept of Moral Panic: Elias, Climate Change and Civilization." *Sociology* 45(4):634–649.

Rome, Adam. 2013. *The Genius of Earth Day: How a 1970 Teach-in Unexpectedly Made the First Green Generation*. New York: Hill and Wang.

Ross, Andrew. 2011. *Bird on Fire: Lessons from the World's Least Sustainable City*. New York: Oxford University Press.

Rossellini, Roberto, dir. 1945. *Rome, Open City*. Rome, Italy: Excelsa Film.

Sack, Robert David. 1997. *Homo Geographicus: A Framework for Action, Awareness and Moral Concern*. Baltimore: The Johns Hopkins University Press.

Sagoff, Mark. 2011. "The Poverty of Climate Economics." Pp. 55–66 in *The Oxford Handbook of Climate Change and Society*, edited by John S. Dryzek, Richard B. Norgaard, and David Schlosberg. New York: Oxford University Press.

Sancton, Thomas A. 1989. "What on EARTH Are We Doing?" *Time*, January 2, 24.

San Jose Mercury News. 2009. "Editorial: What Americans Can Learn from Climategate." December 4.

Sayer, R. Andrew. 2011. *Why Things Matter to People: Social Science, Values and Ethical Life*. Cambridge: Cambridge University Press.

Scannell, Leila, and Robert Gifford. 2013. "Personally Relevant Climate Change: The Role of Place Attachment and Local versus Global Message Framing in Engagement." *Environment and Behavior* 45(1):60–85.

Schaeffer, Francis A. 1992. *Pollution and the Death of Man*. Edited by Udo W. Middelmann. Wheaton, IL: Good News.

Schechner, Richard. 2003. *Performance Theory*. New York: Routledge.

Schick, Yvonne. 2009. Various moderator posts at Rethinkclimate.org. Accessed October 14, 2010. (Website appears to no longer be operative.)

Schmidt, Gavin. 2006. "Art and Climate." *RealClimate*, March 8. http://www.realclimate.org/index.php/archives/2006/03/art-and-climate/.

Schudson, Michael. 2007. "The Anarchy of Events and the Anxiety of Story Telling." *Political Communication* 24(3):253–257.

Schwägerl, Christian. 2011. "Young Activists in Durban: Rebelling against the Climate Change Dinosaurs." *Spiegel Online*, December 9. http://www.spiegel.de/international/world/young-activists-in-durban-rebelling-against-the-climate-change-dinosaurs-a-802748.html.

Schwarze, Steven. 2006. "Environmental Melodrama." *Quarterly Journal of Speech* 92(3):239–261.

Sewell, William H., Jr. 2001. "Space in Contentious Politics." Pp. 51–88 in *Silence and Voice in the Study of Contentious Politics*, edited by R. Aminzade et al. Cambridge: Cambridge University Press.

Shabecoff, Philip. 1983. "Haste of Global Warming Trend Opposed." *New York Times*, October 21, 3.

Shapin, Steven. 1994. *A Social History of Truth: Civility and Science in Seventeenth-Century England*. Chicago: University of Chicago Press.

Shapin, Steven. 1995. "Cordelia's Love: Credibility and the Social Studies of Science." http://dash.harvard.edu/handle/1/3293019.

Shapin, Steven. 2004. "The Way We Trust Now: The Authority of Science and the Character of the Scientists." Pp. 42–62 in *Trust Me, I'm a Scientist*. London: British Council.

Shapiro, Ben. 2008. *Project President: Bad Hair and Botox on the Road to the White House*. Nashville, TN: Thomas Nelson.

Shear, Michael D. 2011. "Perry's Book Gives Rivals Ammunition." *The Caucus*. http://thecaucus.blogs.nytimes.com/2011/09/02/perrys-book-gives-rivals-ammunition/.

Shils, Edward. 1975. *Center and Periphery: Essays in Macrosociology*. Chicago: University of Chicago Press.

Siena Research Institute. 2012. "Voters: Cuomo, Obama, Bloomberg, MTA & FEMA Do Good Job Dealing with Sandy; ConEd Mixed Review; LIPA Panned Two-Thirds of Voters Say Recent Storms Demonstrate Climate Change Half of NYers Contribute to Storm Relief; One-Quarter Volunteer Time." http://www.siena.edu/uploadedfiles/home/sri/SNY%20December%203%202012%20Poll%20Release%20-%20FINAL.pdf.

Skocpol, Theda. 2013. "Naming the Problem: What It Will Take to Counter Extremism and Engage Americans in the Fight against Global Warming." Report prepared for the symposium "The Politics of America's Fight against Global Warming," cosponsored by the Columbia School of Journalism and the

Scholars Strategy Network, February 14, Harvard University. http://www
.scholarsstrategynetwork.org/content/politics-americas-fight-against-global-
warming-o.

Skrimshire, Stefan, ed. 2010. *Future Ethics Climate Change and Apocalyptic
Imagination.* New York: Continuum.

Smith, Jordan W., Dorothy H. Anderson, and Roger L. Moore. 2012. "Social
Capital, Place Meanings, and Perceived Resilience to Climate Change." *Rural
Sociology* 77(3):380–407.

Smith, Philip. 1999. "The Elementary Forms of Place and Their Transformations:
A Durkheimian Model." *Qualitative Sociology* 22(1):13–36.

Smith, Philip. 2000. "Culture and Charisma: Outline of a Theory." *Acta Socio-
logica* 43(2):101–111.

Smith, Philip. 2005. *Why War?* Chicago: University of Chicago Press.

Smith, Philip. 2008. *Punishment and Culture.* Chicago: University of Chicago
Press.

Smith, Philip. 2012. "Becoming Iconic: The Cases of Woodstock and Bayreuth."
Pp. 171–183 in *Iconic Power: Materiality and Meaning in Social Life*,
ed. J. Alexander, D. Bartmanski, and B. Giesen. New York: Palgrave
Macmillan.

Solnit, Rebecca. 2009. *A Paradise Built in Hell: The Extraordinary Communities
That Arise in Disasters.* New York: Viking.

South China Morning Post. 1997. "Earth Robbed in Kyoto." December 14.

Spaid, Sue. 2013. "Dark Optimism May 12–September 2, MoMA PS1."
Ecoartspaceblog, July 27. http://ecoartspace.blogspot.com/2013/07/sue-spaid-
reviews-expo-1-new-york-dark.html.

Speth, James Gustave. 2012. "America the Possible: A Manifesto, Part
II." *Orion Magazine*, March/April. http://www.orionmagazine.org/index.php/
articles/article/6681/.

Spillman, Lyn. 2012. *Solidarity in Strategy: Making Business Meaningful in American Trade Associations.* Chicago: University of Chicago Press.

St. John, Graham, ed. 2008. *Victor Turner and Contemporary Cultural Performance.* New York: Berghahn Books.

St. Louis Post-Dispatch. 2009a. "Hacked Climate E-mails Offer Some Flash, but
No Smoking Gun." November 24.

St. Louis Post-Dispatch. 2009b. "Open Secrets Our View – Hacked Climate
E-mails Offer Some Flash, but No Smoking Gun." November 24. http://www
.stltoday.com/news/opinion/editorial/open-secrets-our-view-hacked-climate-
e-mails-offer-some/article_49afd187-f013-5539-9d1e-54b6cfa94d0b.html.

Stark, Alex. 2010. "Optimism No Longer Cautious in Cancun." *Adopt a
Negotiator Project*, December 11. http://adoptanegotiator.org/2010/12/11/
optimism-no-longer-cautious-in-cancun/.

Stavins, Robert. 2011. "Why Cancun Trumped Copenhagen: Warmer Relations
on Rising Temperatures." *Grist*, January 3. http://grist.org/article/2011-01-
03-cancun-trumped-copenhagen-warmer-relations-rising-temperatures/.

Steel, Duncan. 2002. "Global Warming Is Good for You." *The Guardian*,
December 4. http://www.guardian.co.uk/environment/2002/dec/05/comment
.climatechange.

Steffen, Alex. 2006. "Interview: Davis Guggenheim and An Inconvenient Truth." Posted at *Worldchanging.com*, May 4. http://www.worldchanging .com/archives/004388.html.

Steig, Eric. 2006. "Al Gore's Movie." *RealClimate*, May 10. http://www .realclimate.org/index.php/archives/2006/05/al-gores-movie/.

Stephens, Bret. 2009. "Climategate: Follow the Money." *Wall Street Journal*, December 1. http://online.wsj.com/article/SB10001424052748703939404574 566124250205490.html

Stoll, Mark. 1997. *Protestantism, Capitalism, and Nature in America*. Albuquerque: University of New Mexico Press.

Strauss, Sarah, and Benjamin S. Orlove, eds. 2003. *Weather, Climate, Culture*. New York: Berg.

Swidler, Ann. 1986. "Culture in Action: Symbols and Strategies." *American Sociological Review* 51(2):273–286.

Swyngedouw, Erik. 2010. "Apocalypse Forever? Post-Political Populism and the Spectre of Climate Change." *Theory, Culture, and Society* 27:213–232.

Sydney Morning Herald. 1997. "Europe Attacks Australia's Deal." December 19: 10.

Szasz, Andrew. 2009. *Shopping Our Way to Safety: How We Changed from Protecting the Environment to Protecting Ourselves*. Minneapolis: University of Minnesota Press.

Sztompka, Piotr. 2007. "Trust in Science: Robert K. Merton's Inspirations." *Journal of Classical Sociology* 7(2):211–220.

Taylor, Bron, and Robin Globus. 2011. "Environmental Millennialism." Pp. 628–648 in *The Oxford Handbook of Millenialism*, edited by Catherine Wessinger. New York: Oxford University Press.

Thomas, W. I., and D. S. Thomas. 1928. *The Child in America*. New York: Knopff.

Thompson, Michael, Richard Ellis, and Aaron Wildavsky. 1990. *Cultural Theory*. Boulder, CO: Westview Press.

Till, Karen E. 2005. *The New Berlin: Memory, Politics, Place*. Minneapolis: University of Minnesota Press.

Tilly, Charles. 2000. "Spaces of Contention." *Mobilization: An International Quarterly* 5(2):135–159.

Tilly, Charles. 2003. "Contention over Space and Place." *Mobilization: An International Quarterly* 8(2):221–225.

Timoner, Ondi, dir. 2010. *Cool It*. Pasadena, CA: Interloper Films.

Townsley, Eleanor. 2001. "'The Sixties' Trope." *Theory, Culture, and Society* 18(6):99–123.

Tuan, Yi-fu. 1974. *Topophilia: A Study of Environmental Perception, Attitudes, and Values*. Englewood Cliffs, NJ: Prentice Hall.

Tuan, Yi-fu. 1977. *Space and Place: The Perspective of Experience*. Minneapolis: University of Minnesota Press.

Tuan, Yi-fu. 1996. *Cosmos and Hearth: A Cosmopolite's Viewpoint*. Minneapolis: University of Minnesota Press.

Turner, Victor Witter. 1968. *Schism and Continuity in an African Society: A Study of Ndembu Village Life*. Manchester, UK: Manchester University Press.

Turner, Victor Witter. 1974. *Dramas, Fields, and Metaphors: Symbolic Action in Human Society*. Ithaca, NY: Cornell University Press.

Turner, Victor. 1980. "Social Dramas and Stories about Them." *Critical Inquiry* 7(1):141–168.

Turner, Victor Witter. 1988. *The Anthropology of Performance*. New York: PAJ.

Turner, Victor. 1990. "Are There Universals of Performance in Myth, Ritual, and Drama?" Pp. 8–18 in *By Means of Performance*, edited by Richard Schechner and Willa Appel. New York: Cambridge University Press.

Ungar, Sheldon. 2000. "Knowledge, Ignorance and the Popular Culture: Climate Change versus the Ozone Hole." *Public Understanding of Science* 9(3):297–312.

Urry, John. 2011. *Climate Change and Society*. London: Polity.

USA Today. 1989. "Radical Lifestyle Changes Needed." June 13, 10.

USA Today. 2009. "'Climategate' Gives Ammo to Global Warming Skeptics." December 9. http://usatoday30.usatoday.com/printedition/news/20091210/editorial10_st.arto.htm

Van der Zee, Bibi. 2009. "Activists Reveal Tactics Used by Police to 'Decapitate' Copenhagen Climate Protests." *The Guardian*, December 17. http://www.guardian.co.uk/environment/2009/dec/17/copenhagen-police-tactics-revealed.

Vidal, John. 2009a. "Copenhagen Climate Summit in Disarray after 'Danish Text' Leak." *The Guardian*, December 8. http://www.guardian.co.uk/environment/2009/dec/08/copenhagen-climate-summit-disarray-danish-text.

Vidal, John. 2009b. "Rich and Poor Countries Blame Each Other for Failure of Copenhagen Deal." *The Guardian*, December 18. http://www.guardian.co.uk/environment/2009/dec/19/copenhagen-blame-game.

Vidal, John. 2012. "Doha Climate Conference Diary: Qatar's First Environmental March." *The Guardian*, December 3. http://www.guardian.co.uk/environment/blog/2012/dec/03/doha-climate-conference-diary.

Vidal, John. 2013. "One in 10 UK Adults Involved in an Environmental Group, Figures Show." *The Guardian*, November 27. http://www.theguardian.com/environment/2013/nov/27/1-in-10-uk-adults-environmental-group.

Vielkind, Jimmy. 2012a. "Cuomo: Need to Rebuild for 'New Reality' (Video Added)." *Capitol Confidential*, October 30. http://blog.timesunion.com/capitol/archives/162627/cuomo-we-need-to-plan-rebuild-for-new-reality/.

Vielkind, Jimmy. 2012b. "Cuomo: 'Climate Change Is a Reality...We Are Vulnerable.'" *Capitol Confidential*, October 31. http://blog.timesunion.com/capitol/archives/162798/cuomo-climate-change-is-a-reality-we-are-vulnerable/.

Wagner-Pacifici, Robin Erica. 1986. *The Moro Morality Play: Terrorism as Social Drama*. Chicago: University of Chicago Press.

Walker, J. Samuel. 2004. *Three Mile Island: A Nuclear Crisis in Historical Perspective*. Berkeley: University of California Press.

Walley, Christine J. 2004. *Rough Waters: Nature and Development in an East African Marine Park*. Princeton, NJ: Princeton University Press.

Walsh, Bryan. 2009. "Lessons from the Copenhagen Climate Talks." *Time*, December 21. http://content.time.com/time/specials/packages/article/0288041929071_1929070_1949054,00.html.

Warren, David. 2009. "The Skeptics Are Vindicated." *Ottawa Citizen*, November 25.

Washington Post. 2010. "A Stand for Science; Why the University of Virginia Should Push Back against Mr. Cuccinelli's Inquiry." May 13, A16.

Washington Post. 2011. "Warming to the Obvious." October 25, A15.

Washington Times. 2009a. "Editorial: Denying the Global-Cooling Cover-Up; Obama Team Puts Politics above Science on Climate." December 1. http://www.washingtontimes.com/news/2009/dec/01/denying-the-global-cooling-cover-up/.

Washington Times. 2009b. "Editorial: Universities Take Action on Climategate; Investigating Academic Fraud by Global-Warming Theocracy." December 2. http://www.washingtontimes.com/news/2009/dec/02/universities-take-action-on-climategate/.

Washington Times. 2009c. "Editorial: The Tip of the Climategate Iceberg; Misleading 'evidence' Is Central to the Global-Warming Fraud." December 11. http://www.washingtontimes.com/news/2009/dec/11/the-tip-of-the-climategate-iceberg-55941015/.

Weart, Spencer R. 2008. *The Discovery of Global Warming*. Cambridge, MA: Harvard University Press.

Weart, Spencer R. 2010. The Idea of Anthropogenic Global Climate Change in the 20th Century. *Wiley Interdisciplinary Reviews: Climate Change* 1(1):67–81.

Weber, Max. 1967. *Ancient Judaism*. New York: Free Press.

Weber, Max. (1906) 2009. "The Protestant Sects and the Spirit of Capitalism." Pp. 302–22 in *From Max Weber: Essays in Sociology*, edited and translated by H. H. Gerth and C. Wright Mills. New York: Routledge.

Weiner, Albert. 1980. "The Function of the Tragic Greek Chorus." *Theatre Journal* 32(2):205–212.

West, Brad, and Philip Smith. 1997. "Natural Disasters and National Identity: Time, Space and Mythology." *Journal of Sociology* 33(2):205–215.

White, Richard. 2012. "Bill McKibben's Emersonian Vision." *Raritan Review* 31(2):110–125.

Wilkinson, Katharine K. 2012. *Between God and Green: How Evangelicals Are Cultivating a Middle Ground on Climate Change*. Oxford: Oxford University Press.

Willis, Rebecca. 2013. "Drink Local? The Climate Change Act in the Lake District." *The Guardian*, November 28. http://www.theguardian.com/science/2013/nov/28/drink-local-the-climate-change-act-in-the-lake-district-rebecca-willis.

Wittgenstein, Ludwig. 1966. *Lectures and Conversations: On Aesthetics, Psychology and Religious Belief*. Berkeley: University of California Press.

Wohlforth, Charles. 2005. *The Whale and the Supercomputer: On the Northern Front of Climate Change*. New York: North Point Press.

World Wildlife Fund. 2010. "Media Advisory/Photo-Op: Ice Bear Sculpture in Toronto for G8/G20 Summits." http://www.marketwire.com/mw/rel_us_print .jsp?id=1281226.

Worster, Donald. 2004. *Dust Bowl: The Southern Plains in the 1930s*. 25th anniversary ed. New York: Oxford University Press.

Wuthnow, Robert. 2010. *Be Very Afraid: The Cultural Response to Terror, Pandemics, Environmental Devastation, Nuclear Annihilation, and Other Threats*. Oxford: Oxford University Press.

Wynne, Brian. 1980. "Technology, Risk and Participation: On the Social Treatment of Uncertainty." Pp. 173–208 in *Society, Technology and Risk Assessment*, edited by J. Conrad. New York: Academic Press.

Wynne, Brian. 2004. "Misunderstood Misunderstandings: Social Identities and Public Uptake of Science." Pp. 19–46 in *Misunderstanding Science? The Public Reconstruction of Science and Technology*, edited by Alan Irwin and Brian Wynne. Cambridge: Cambridge University Press.

Wynne, B. 2010. "Strange Weather, Again Climate Science as Political Art." *Theory, Culture, and Society* 27(2–3):289–305.

Yearley, Steven. 1999. "Computer Models and the Public's Understanding of Science: A Case-Study Analysis." *Social Studies of Science* 29(6):845–866.

York, Richard, and Riley E. Dunlap. 2012. "Environmental Sociology." Pp. 504–521 in *The Wiley-Blackwell Companion to Sociology*, edited by George Ritzer. Chichester: John Wiley.

YouTube. 2008. "The Girl Who Silenced the World for 5 Minutes." http://www .youtube.com/watch?v=TQmz6Rbpnuo.

YouTube. 2011. "Anjali Appadurai Mic Checks: Deep Cuts Now! Get it Done!" http://www.youtube.com/watch?v=5w7d5SVAvrw.

Yusoff, Kathryn. 2010. "Biopolitical Economies and the Political Aesthetics of Climate Change." *Theory, Culture, and Society* 27(2–3):73–99.

Zerubavel, Eviatar. 2007. *The Elephant in the Room: Silence and Denial in Everyday Life*. New York: Oxford University Press.

Ziser, Michael, and Julie Sze. 2007. "Climate Change, Environmental Aesthetics, and Global Environmental Justice Cultural Studies." *Discourse* 29(2):384–410.

Index